YORK'S GREAT RACES

Steve Carroll

YORK'S GREAT RACES

Scratching Shed Publishing Ltd

First published by Scratching Shed Publishing Ltd in 2011
Registered in England & Wales No. 6588772.
Registered office:
47 Street Lane, Leeds, West Yorkshire. LS8 1AP

www.scratchingshedpublishing.co.uk

ISBN 978-0956478795

Unless otherwise stated, photographs provided by York Racecourse
and the archives of *The Press* and *Yorkshire Evening Press*.

A catalogue record for this book is available from the British Library.

Typeset in Warnock Pro Semi Bold and Palatino

Printed and bound in the United Kingdom by
L.P.P.S.Ltd, Wellingborough, Northants, NN8 3PJ

To my granddad Bert
who fostered and encouraged my love of sport

Contents

...Before his eyes
The stately towers of York arise.
'But what,' said he, 'can all this mean?
What is yon crowded busy scene?
Ten thousand souls, I do maintain,
Are scattered over yonder plain.'
'Aye, more than that,' a man replied -
Who trotted briskly by his side,
'And if you choose, I'll be your guide:
For sure you will not pass this way,
And miss the pleasures of the day:
These are the races, to whose sport
Nobles and gentry all resort.'
Thought Syntax I'll just have a look;
'Twill give a subject to my book.'

The Tour of Doctor Syntax in Search of the Picturesque –
William Combe (1812)

ACKNOWLEDGEMENTS

THERE is no way I can give enough thanks to everyone who has helped along the way, and there have been many. But let's have a go anyway.

It was William Derby, chief executive and clerk of the course at York Racecourse, who humoured me when I came to him – in August 2008 – with an idea to chronicle the wonderful racehorses and races which have made York a track envied across the globe. He deserves special credit for putting up with the phone calls, the emails and the incessant demands for just a few more moments in the archives.

With that in mind, this book could not have been written without the help of the queen of York's library, Dede Scott Brown. She moved a holiday to allow me to spend time sweeping through old files, cuttings and textbooks. I am forever grateful, yet will never forgive myself for making her take all those trips up to the Ebor Stand loft to drag out another decrepit old racecard.

I also owe grateful thanks to the trainers – those architects of York racecourse successes – who gave up their time and permitted interviews: Ian Balding, Mark Johnston, Luca Cumani, Clive Brittain, Amanda Perrett, Jeremy Noseda, Rod Millman, John Best, Tim Easterby, Jim Bolger, James Given, Michael Bell and Robin Bastiman.

On the riding side, there is George Duffield, Freddie Tylicki, Kevin Darley and a host of other stars of the saddle who, in the melee of racecourse excitement, didn't even know they were being interviewed for a book. Without them, this becomes merely a recollection of statistics. They, the ones who masterminded those famous wins and rode those great victories, bring the colour to proceedings.

When I think about colourful, my mind immediately turns to the brilliant Tom O'Ryan, the *Racing Post*'s man in the north. Not only am I grateful for a fabulous interview but also for the hints, tips and general pointing in the right direction. If there's a man who knows more about racing, I've yet to find him. He has helped my career in so many ways, be it with a phone number or an invaluable fact, words can't express my gratitude.

Thanks are also due to Tim Richards, the former *Daily Mirror* and *Racing Post* reporter, whose memory did not fail him despite all his worries to the contrary.

Graham Orange, the voice of York Racecourse and Yorkshire racing as a whole for more than 25 years, was a great source of knowledge and information.

John Smith and John Sanderson, who with William Derby are the only other surviving clerks of the course, went out of their way to give me their time and their memories as did Nick Smith, head of communications at Ascot Racecourse, who revealed the inside story behind Royal Ascot at York in 2005. Then there's the people who did the real donkey work, and actually read the thing. They, along with you, deserve the most praise of all. Stuart Martel and Will Hayler, you are true friends who have frankly gone beyond the call of duty.

Finally, my family. Kathryn, my wife, who has put up with me bleating about this book for as long as I care to remember – it nearly scuppered the wedding – my dad, Michael, mother Berenice, my three brothers and a host of supporting cast who I am now relying on to stump up for a few copies. Their support and belief is why you have this book in your hands.

I do not claim this to be a comprehensive account. There are far worthier tomes that express Knavesmire's glorious past in grander, and weightier, prose than I could ever hope to achieve. In this chronicle of York's great races, there will be performances omitted – breathtaking displays perhaps not given the credit and prominence they deserved.

I do not claim this to be a comprehensive history. What I hope I have done is give you a sense of the passion, and the pride, that winning at York meant for those who experienced thoroughbred greatness at such close quarters. For, as the York Race Committee reminds us at every meeting, it is all about the horses.

INTRODUCTION

FLASH bulbs are forbidden at racecourses but it is difficult to play security guard when thousands of people are popping shutters at the same time.

The focus of their attention, the horse that is making people run towards the York Racecourse parade ring, isn't bothered in the slightest by the fuss. As the people cram, six or seven rows deep to catch a fleeting glimpse of his bay skin, he simply struts round the oval track.

Racehorse trainers, from the country's biggest to the handlers with barely a handful of runners, have taken advantage of the privilege being in racing's inner circle affords them. While the spectators crane their necks outside the ring, they, along with a gaggle of owners, pressmen, and 'connections', are getting up close and personal with Sea The Stars.

That York Racecourse could woo trainer John Oxx and get his 2,000 Guineas, Derby and Eclipse hero to grace the track's flagship Juddmonte International in August 2009 says everything about the way the course is viewed and revered around the world. There were bigger prizes elsewhere. Sea The Stars, who had won a raft of Group 1 races and would go on to strike gold at the Prix de l'Arc de Triomphe, hardly had anything to prove. But Oxx brought him anyway – brought the greatest racehorse since Nashwan to the old medieval city.

Walk through the doors of the main Ebor Stand at York Racecourse and its history slaps you in the mouth. That big glass cabinet to your left is not just for display – inside are the priceless relics which only come with nearly 250 years of being. Trophies, silks and programmes – all priceless mementos. There's an aura about Knavesmire. The sense and the spirit of those great performances pervade every nook and cranny.

Every day when he comes to work, William Derby is surrounded by ghosts of the past. Their images are everywhere. Like George Stubbs's painting of Gimcrack, which crowns a suite bearing the horse's name. They are in the busts and ageing turf annuals in the plush York Race Committee rooms. You can feel them when you step out onto the track, you can hear the pounding of hooves – the cries and exultations from the stands. Then there's the anticipation of what is to come.

That's one of the best things about horse racing. You treasure the times you see something special – like a Mill Reef, a Dahlia or a Sea The Stars. But the very next race, meeting or year there's the possibility you are again about to witness something absolutely wonderful.

Derby, the current chief executive and clerk of the course, is well aware of the prestigious company he keeps. Sea The Stars is merely the latest legend to forever write his name into York Racecourse lore. They have raced on Knavesmire since 1731, when the region's aristocracy swapped one piece of boggy, sodden land at Clifton Ings for another. The 'Knaves-mire' was as synonymous then with public executions as it was with the horses.

York's Races haven't always been great. In the mid 19th Century, a tarnished racecourse needed extreme measures to save it from an indifferent public and a reputation for skulduggery. But they survived and flourished. Judging racing across the globe between 2006 and 2008, only the Breeders' Cup Classic and the Prix de l'Arc de Triomphe were rated higher than the Juddmonte International, the flagship contest during York's showpiece Ebor Festival. This book is about that race. It's about the great contests that propelled York to the summit of the horse racing world. It's about great horses. It's about the stories of Mill Reef, Brigadier Gerard, Shirley Heights, Shahrastani, Motivator and many more marvellous thoroughbreds to have run on the historic turf. It's about triumph and tragedy, joy and disappointment.

These are York's Great Races.

MAY

THE FLYING DUTCHMAN v VOLTIGEUR

FROM Sheffield, from Cleveland, from Leeds, from Tadcaster, they came. Crowds of men – miners, farmers, factory hands – trekked, walked or rode their way to Knavesmire.

They slept in sideways, in hedges and on roadsides. They packed what trains were running. Floors were full; there wasn't standing room in the inns. They arrived early – thousands of them striding to the course to get a precious place on the rails. It was an enormous march. But it wasn't a Royal visit that had the masses streaming into York on May 13, 1851. It was a horse race.

Hindsight calls the contest between the two thoroughbred heroes the 'Match of the Century'. It spawned songs, poems and legend. More than 100 years after the epic race was run, the tale was still being told in the northern racing heartlands.

The history-making match race did as much to revive the prestige of York Racecourse as any Great Ebor Handicap of the era. Those who flocked, from both north and south, gave the course its largest attendance known up to that period.

So what made those people make the visit? Embark on journeys which took days? What made them trudge those many miles? The answer was Voltigeur and The Flying Dutchman.

***

VOLTIGEUR was the darling of the north. Bred at Hart, and trained at Richmond, the son of Voltaire had done something for which his owner, Thomas Dundas, Earl of Zetland, had yearned for a lifetime. He won the Derby.

Not that Zetland was at all convinced when the yearling was reportedly first brought before him in 1848. While his trainer Robert Hill had spotted potential, the Earl rejected the chance to buy the Robert Stephenson-bred animal.

There was good reason for this. While Voltigeur's offspring would become the head of a dominant sire line around the turn of the century, his sire Voltaire had not been similarly blessed. Voltaire had finished second in the St Leger, and had won the Doncaster Gold Cup, but by the time Voltigeur came around, the old man was 21 and had only one outstanding son to his credit – the St Leger, Goodwood Cup and Doncaster Cup victor Charles the Twelfth.

It was even worse with Martha Lynn, Voltigeur's dam. She had won only three races and had yet to give birth to anything of promise. Combine this with Voltigeur's awkward poise and heavy neck and it is not a surprise the youngster failed even to make his reserve price in the Doncaster sales ring.

Hill, however, didn't give in that easily. Finally persuading Zetland to bring the colt to Aske Hall on loan to the Earl's brother-in-law Robert Williamson, Voltigeur was put to the test against Yorkshire Oaks winner Ellen Middleton, Castanette and Cantab. He beat them out of sight.

The horse that couldn't even make his reserve price was now bought for £1,500, with a £500 contingency on each big race win. Once reluctant, Zetland couldn't get his money out quickly enough. Hill didn't mess about when it came to training the Earl's new great hope. The colt was galloped in two hoods in an effort to change the heaviness in that neck but, while Voltigeur was worked hard at home, he only ran once as a two-year-old. That came when he captured the Bright Stakes, at Richmond, winning by a length at 6-4.

***

ON the day of the 1850 Derby, you could get 16-1 on Voltigeur. There's no doubt his Yorkshire roots contributed to southern cynicism about the colt's chances but a difficult train journey, combined with an uncomfortable first gallop over the undulating Downs, kept the price high. It will also have made some of the colt's northern followers rich.

Job Marson was the jockey bearing Zetland's lifetime of hopes and dreams and neither he, nor Voltigeur, disappointed. It was an easy win. He was ten lengths clear of the 2,000 Guineas winner Pitsford and in a time ten seconds faster than the three minutes posted for the mile and a half contest by the 1849 winner, The Flying Dutchman.

***

THE Flying Dutchman was an irritable runner, prone to pulling hard on the reins in protest. But he was also an amazing sight in full flow, moving at such speed that he was rarely challenged by horses coming alongside him.

He was owned by Archibald William Montgomery, the thirteenth Earl of Eglinton, and trained at Middleham by John Fobert. Bathsheba had won the Ayr plate when Eglinton was only 19 and he enjoyed a prodigious career as an owner. Blue Bonnet had won him a St Leger in 1842 and he'd had a near miss in the 1847 Derby with Van Tromp. It was Van Tromp's dam, Barbelle, who bred The Flying Dutchman with Eglinton having agreed to pay her owner, Colonel Henry Vansittart, 1,000 guineas for every foal she produced.

The Flying Dutchman, the first under the arrangement, came along in 1846 – a brown colt by Bay Middleton, who had won the Derby in 1836. The Dutchman was sent to Fobert, at Middleham's Spigot Lodge stables, and was often unaccompanied when galloping. When jockey Charles Marlow first got on board, the biographer The Druid reported the rider returned to Fobert exclaiming he 'had never been on such a one before'. Turf experts reckoned his two-year-old season, which brought victories at Newmarket's July Stakes, a £1,400 sweep in Liverpool, the Champagne Stakes and the Two-Year-Old Stakes in an undefeated five-race campaign, had never even seen him extended.

The Flying Dutchman went straight to the Derby in 1849 and, held on awful ground following days of heavy rain, the quick-footed runner was thought likely to struggle in the sticky conditions. Even with the undoubted promise of that opening season, it was at Epsom where The Flying Dutchman displayed the grit and heart which would see him hailed by all racing fans. With half a mile left, he led by a length but was challenged and passed by Hotspur, an outsider who revelled in the heavy going. Almost a length behind, with the finish fast approaching, it seemed the unbeaten record was to come to an end. Marlow struck his mount twice with his whip, in what would be the only time the horse was ever hit, and The Flying Dutchman surged forward under the command. Hotspur was defeated by a short neck.

Next, the St Leger came just as easily, with 2,000 Guineas victor Nunnykirk seen off by two lengths. It was part of a procession for an imperious champion. There were walk-overs, forfeits with owners paying up rather than having to subject their horse to a pasting. There were massive victories – like the eight lengths in Newmarket's Belvoir Stakes.

The following season, 1850, he came to Doncaster having destroyed his rivals in the Emperor of Russia's Plate and put ten lengths on the field in a Goodwood sweep. But, on the Town Moor at the Doncaster Cup, a younger rival was about to teach him a lesson.

***

AS Voltigeur turned into the home straight, unable to shake off the Irish colt, Lord Zetland's dreams of a euphoric homecoming were not going to plan at all.

After his Derby day dreams came true, both the Earl and trainer Robert Hill were determined to show off their fabulous colt to a welcoming audience. The St Leger may no longer be the fashionable route for an Epsom winner in today's world of multi-million pound stud fees but, in the mid 19th Century, it was a de rigueur route for a thoroughbred favourite. Hill was planning something a little more spectacular. Yes, the colt would run in the St Leger. But he would also run in the Doncaster Cup just two days later – with the Scarbrough Handicap in between for good measure.

It was a Herculean task and as the St Leger reached its climax it was appearing too hard for Zetland's unbeaten star. Only eight horses went to post with the 13-8 favourite but, as his rivals stepped aside into supporting parts, 20-1 shot Russborough stubbornly held on. Gaining ground with every stride, Russborough thundered past the judge's chair neck and neck with the Derby champion. They could not be split. It was a dead-heat, although those training Russborough, owned by the Earl of Milltown, were convinced their horse had won by a head. So, a couple of hours later with Voltigeur stalking round the stables, the pair went at it again.

With Zetland's charge the 4-6 favourite, the betting public believed there would be no fluke this time from the Irish raider. There wasn't. Russborough went ahead early and still kept his lead into the straight but, when Job Marson gave Voltigeur a reminder, he swept alongside and won, easily in the end, by a length.

A walk-over in the Scarbrough Stakes now set the scene for a clash of the titans in the Doncaster Cup. The unbeaten The Flying Dutchman against the similarly perfect Voltigeur – head-to-head. No one expected the younger Voltigeur to prevail – particularly given his exertions two days earlier in the St Leger. But the horse, with Nat Flatman riding, somehow found exceptional reserves.

There were excuses for the older champion. The first was the weight. The Flying Dutchman gave his rival 19 pounds. Then there was the tough gallop the Dutchman's trainer John Fobert had given his horse over the Doncaster course just the day before. How about that the horse wasn't fully wound up to run, or that the Dutchman refused to eat before the race? Consider the claim that the jockey, Marlow, was drunk and, even if he wasn't, still refused to ride to orders. Allegedly told to wait until six furlongs from the post to let The Flying Dutchman really get into his stride, as they passed the stands for the first time, Marlow had the horse making the running. He couldn't keep up the intense pace.

As the pair approached the Red House corner, Voltigeur sat a couple of lengths behind his older foe and reined him in. Marlow tried to push the button but found, to his horror, The Flying Dutchman had nothing left to give. Voltigeur came home for a half length success, and an upset which stunned the crowd and the turf world.

***

ALMOST from the second Voltigeur crossed the line in front, a rematch looked inevitable. Partly this was down to demand. The race quickly became the talk of the town and the ale houses.

The clamour for a repeat – from the Voltigeur supporters who wanted another famous victory and The Flying Dutchman fans eager to turn the tables – was powerful. It might also have been down to simple economics. Prior to the Doncaster upset, The Flying Dutchman had been sold, or leased, to the Rawcliffe Stud Company. When the horse lost, a rematch became paramount to try and salvage his reputation for a firm which was planning to rely on the animal for the next few years to come.

And so Eglinton and Zetland agreed to a sequel and what would become one of the most famous match races in racehorse history.

They would hold their confrontation at York on the old course, over two miles and for £1,000. It would be staged on May 13, 1851. The date was of some significance for those in charge at Knavesmire. It signalled the return of the Spring meeting for the first time since 1843 and the match race was the main event. The handicapping was handed over to Captain, soon to be Admiral, Rous. Four years later, he would become the Jockey Club's first official handicapper. Voltigeur versus The Flying Dutchman was his first notable engagement in the field. He took his time, and gave the older horse eight stone, eight and a half pounds. Voltigeur would carry eight stone. Flatman would renew his acquaintance with the Doncaster hero while Marlow, having laid off the alcohol this time, would retain his ride on The Flying Dutchman.

The contest was third on the card and Voltigeur and The Flying Dutchman emerged onto the course to a captivated audience. Voltigeur went off fast from the start. Setting a quick pace in tricky ground, the four-year-old was soon three lengths clear and charging. But this time, The Flying Dutchman was the one who was sitting, waiting for his time to strike. He was a shadow to the younger horse. As they rounded the last turn, Marlow urged his mount into action. The crowd roared them on as they passed the stands side-by-side but, around 100 yards from home, it was Voltigeur who was tiring first. The Flying Dutchman surged through with that impressive winning stride and succeeded by a length in a cauldron of noise. Revenge was sweet for Eglinton.

The very next day, he announced The Flying Dutchman's retirement – the five-year-old having just that Doncaster loss to Voltigeur on a 16-race resume. It wasn't quite so cosy for Voltigeur. Hill entered him in the Ainsty Hunt Cup the day following the match race and, giving away 37 pounds to a filly named Nancy, he lost again – but only by a length and to a classy horse who would win a Great Yorkshire Stakes and the Great Ebor Handicap that year.

In the biggest irony, Voltigeur returned to York the following year, as a five-year-old, and would win: The Flying Dutchman Handicap. And while Eglinton's Dutchman won the battle, you could argue that it was Zetland's Voltigeur who won the war. For his is the name remembered every year – in the Great Voltigeur Stakes held in August during the Ebor Festival. He is also immortalised in the current York Racecourse logo. Not bad for an unlucky loser.

THE DANTE STAKES

IT was a mark of the man but also one of the age in which he lived. No shouting, no hyped headlines. If Lord Halifax had high hopes for Shirley Heights there was no song and dance, no declaration of intent. He kept his counsel. He kept his dreams to himself.

The north had not had a Derby winner of any kind – trained or owned – since 1945. Since Dante. Now the race which bore that horse's name, remembering his fantastic feats at the end of war, was about to give praise to a new hero in 1978. Lord Halifax had paid 12,000 Guineas for Hardiemma at the December sales nearly five years previously, and she had been bought with one purpose – to mate with Mill Reef, the 1971 Derby hero, who now earned his crust at stud. The product of their union was Shirley Heights.

Mill Reef, of whom we shall learn a lot more later, was an outstanding horse and put on one of the most devastating displays ever seen at York when winning the Gimcrack Stakes in 1970. When Hardiemma was lined up to visit him, he had been retired to The National Stud in Newmarket. Though he would later sire the future Dante, Derby, Great Voltigeur Stakes and St Leger winner Reference Point, and the 1,000 Guineas winner Fairy Footsteps, Shirley Heights was his first really great success as a stallion. But while the father was a speed machine, his son, trained at Lambourn by John Dunlop, was essentially a stayer. And after wins as a two-year-old in the Limekilns Stakes at Newmarket and the Royal Lodge Stakes at Ascot, Classic ambitions were on both his and the mind of Lord Halifax, the chairman of York Racecourse and Knavesmire's father figure. But enormous potential is frequently unfulfilled and, as the clock ticked down to the return of York races in May following the winter break, Lord Halifax, whose Garrowby Hall home was almost within touching distance of the track, was still apprehensive.

'He was a great supporter of British racing but he was a gentleman of his era,' says John Sanderson, York's clerk of the course between 1972 and 1986. 'They didn't shout or leap around about this fantastic horse. He said: "I've got a nice horse and we are rather hoping to win". We didn't see him much in the winter but one of his habits was to come down on the Monday before the May meeting and have a wander around and look at the track. I remember him saying to me: "I'm rather hopeful on Wednesday" and he was pulling my leg a bit about the track. "Make sure it's all filled in," he told me. That's all it was.'

Whitstead had put a dent in Lord Halifax's ambitions when dismissing Shirley Heights by ten lengths at Sandown's Classic trial the month before York's Dante Stakes in May, but the colt bounced back quickly, and in some style, at the Heathorn Stakes at Newmarket. So he arrived at Knavesmire right back on track, carrying Lord Halifax's high, but understated, hopes. Ante-post Derby favourite Leonardo da Vinci and 2,000 Guineas runner-up Remainder Man were in the field, along with the Irish-trained Lenygon, Persian Bold and Julio Marnier. They need not have bothered turning up. It was a procession.

Shirley Heights, a 10-1 shot, won with such aplomb, it seemed inconceivable he wouldn't be favourite on the famous Epsom Downs three weeks later. Stalking pacemaker Tarzan with Julio Marnier, Lord Halifax's colt took charge two out and put the contest out of sight within the space of a furlong. It was so easy, jockey Greville Starkey even eased him down in the last 75 yards and took a peek back at the floundering Julio Marnier, trailing a length and a half behind, and Sexton Blake.

The Derby, however, would turn out to be an even better

performance. Losing ground coming into the straight, Shirley Heights overtook ten horses – and found eight lengths on the leaders – to fire past Hawaiian Sound while bolted onto the rail in the last 50 yards. He snatched Derby glory by a head.

'It was a popular win – very popular when he won the Dante,' Sanderson remembers. 'I was also at Epsom the day Shirley Heights won the Derby. It was an amazing race when Greville Starkey weaved his way through that wall of horses. Shirley Heights was a very handy little horse.'

A winner of the Irish Derby as well, he is also, incidentally, the only Derby winner in the subsequent three decades to have been sired by an Epsom victor (Mill Reef) and to have fathered a Derby winner – Slip Anchor in 1985. His overall legacy was to begin the process of blasting the Dante Stakes back to the forefront of racing's early season calendar. With North Light, Motivator and Authorized the most recent to have scooped the Dante-Derby double, whoever wins the York May showpiece always figures strongly in the Epsom betting. But in the late 70s, things were different.

Sanderson, at Knavesmire's helm during the unfashionable decade, was fighting routine – and the superstition of trainers. 'Races go in fashions,' he says. 'The Dante wasn't always what it has become. We sometimes struggled to get the right horses in the Dante because they would go to Chester and win there instead. Once one trainer has won the Derby taking that Chester route then others start to follow. They are a bit like lemmings, trainers.'

Shirley Heights was a popular winner and began to turn the tide. But, as far as Sanderson is concerned, it would take Shahrastani, eight years later, before evolution became revolution. 'It broke a mould I was happy about. Chester and Sandown seemed to be the route to the Derby and not necessarily the Dante. It has had a golden period recently and it will probably hold on to it because racing has developed in different ways. It's a changing tableau. People now don't really talk about those Chester races in the same glowing terms that they did 20 to 25 years ago.'

***

FOR a horse who never set foot on the Knavesmire track, Dante has quite a fan club at York. Visit the racecourse and you can step inside the Dante Suite, the lavish room on the second floor of the Ebor Stand, with its own terrace and starry view of the Winning Post.

Dante was the last northern trained victor of the Derby, winning the race at Newmarket just after the end of war in Europe in 1945. Jockey Willie Nevett guided him home ahead of Midas – adding to his wins as a juvenile in the Coventry and Middle Park Stakes. Trained by Matt Peacock at Middleham and owned and bred by Sir Eric Ohlson, his career was both brilliant and brief. After taking the Derby the St Leger, which was to be held at York that year, seemed at his mercy. But an eye injury, which had held up his early season work and saw him lose by a neck to Court Martial in the 2,000 Guineas, meant Dante was going slowly blind. He would not make the St Leger. In fact, he would never race again.

His legacy is remembered in York's trial for the Epsom spectacle. Held around three weeks before the Derby, it is the main attraction of the racecourse's three-day May Festival. A curtain raiser at a time of hope and promise. For former clerk of the course John Smith, however, it was a period which 'used to frighten me to death'.

'We had not been racing for seven months and then you have the May meeting and all the expectation,' says the man in charge of York from 1987 to 2002. 'It is fresh ground, fresh horses and it sets the form lines for the rest of the season. It is proved time and time again. You see all these horses that have been talked about in the winter, and those that haven't even been mentioned because they are yet to run. Suddenly they come out at York in the spring and it is something very special.'

The idea of then clerk of the course, Major Leslie Petch, who also delivered the Magnet Cup among a host of other improvements during his two decade stint in charge on Knavesmire, Bald Eagle was the first Dante winner, in 1958, trained by Cecil Boyd-Rochfort. Petch was an innovator. In 16 years as clerk of the course he helped to establish many of the races which now form the bedrock of the modern York Racecourse programme. The Dante Stakes along with, later, the Benson & Hedges Gold Cup (now the Juddmonte International) are his two finest creations.

'He was a hard task master and a great impresario,' remembers Sanderson of Petch, who was his uncle. 'He was a man of great attention to detail. He taught me a lot in that regard and when he wanted something doing you had to do it. He used to lecture all the staff and he put up a notice in his office which said "Do It Now!" This was because Churchill had a notice in his office which said "Action This Day" and "Do It Now" was one of his great sayings. You would agree to do something and it would be "When are you going to do it? Do It Now!" If he didn't like something you got told off. But then it was over. He was quite a strict disciplinarian. He worked hard himself and he expected people to deliver. But he was fair and I learned an awful lot from him.'

From the start, the fate of his Dante Stakes would depend on how many challengers it produced for the Derby the following month. So it was in 1960, with St Paddy, that the Dante Stakes bequeathed its first real contender. Owned and bred by Sir Victor Sassoon, he had some famous relatives. He was sired by Aureole, the King George VI and Queen Elizabeth Stakes winner, and his grandsire was the legendary Hyperion, the 1933 Derby and St Leger victor who was the leading sire in Britain six times before his death in 1960. He was trained by Noel Murless and would become synonymous with Lester Piggott. But, like his father, it did not take a lot to set St Paddy off. Highly strung, and easily spooked, Piggott would remark that something as simple as a bird flying up on the gallops could be enough to see St Paddy bolt. It should, therefore, not have surprised either Piggott, or Murless, when St Paddy showed his worst side on his racecourse debut at York in August 1959.

Coming out on to the track from the paddock, he was on his way immediately – and it took the jockey nearly half a mile before he could bring him under control. His chance was gone, but he still ran, Piggott observing that here was a chance to still teach St Paddy something about life on the racecourse. He finished in the middle of the pack. With a crossed noseband employed on his next start – the Royal Lodge Stakes at Ascot – to help the jockey handle this uncontrollable monster, winning proved to be somewhat more straightforward. He triumphed by five lengths. Problem solved.

Murless took the same route with St Paddy as he had travelled with

Crepello, who started his three-year-old campaign by winning the 2,000 Guineas and then the Derby in 1957. But Murless was not expecting a Newmarket victory from St Paddy. The object was to get the horse on the road to glory, to get him fit for bigger battles ahead. He didn't win, finishing sixth, but would look a completely different animal in the Dante Stakes. Piggott won the race without even having to take St Paddy off the bridle. Settled near the head of the field early on, he cruised into second spot at the three furlong marker, breezed to the front past Ancient Lights and won easing up by three lengths.

Again the noseband, which St Paddy wore on his way down to the start, had done the trick. It was equipment which had to be surrendered before the race. Even in 1960, the crossed noseband was considered too severe to be used in the heat of race battle. With the rest of the Dante field strung out in vain pursuit of St Paddy, and the horse now in tip-top physical condition, Murless was able to take him to Epsom with some confidence. He was not the Derby favourite, however. That honour went to the French horse Angers. St Paddy was the joint third-favourite at 7-1. It was a remarkably undramatic race for horse and jockey. As at York, Piggott kept him up with the pace from early on and, after sending him to the front at the two furlong marker, was able to keep him in front – three lengths ahead of Alcaeus – without resorting to any real urging or the whip. This, Piggott believed, was the only way St Paddy could really run at his best. He was the jockey's third Derby winner.

Beaten in the Gordon Stakes at Goodwood on his next outing in late July, his first since the Derby, St Paddy returned to York for the Great Voltigeur Stakes in peak fitness after his run on the Sussex Downs. When trained to the minute, there was very little to stop him among that year's Classic generation. Given the stop-start progress of the horse – that win one, lose one nature depending on whether he was stripped to fitness – critics wondered aloud whether the Derby had actually been very good that year. St Paddy gave his answer in the Voltigeur.

Despite his Goodwood set-back, Murless's colt was the 4-11 favourite – nearly the shortest price in the ten year history of the race (only Acropolis, the winner in 1955, had been shorter at 2-7). He was made to work for it though – despite the field only containing four

27

runners. Oak Ridge, who had been beaten by a dozen lengths by St Paddy in the Dante and by the same distance in the Derby, went to the front with Piggott's mount tracking a couple of lengths behind. Oak Ridge tried to steal a march turning into the straight but, crucially, St Paddy was still on the bit and he had soon forced his way into the lead.

The race was not yet won. Another challenger, Apostle, a four-time victor that season, drew up alongside. For a moment, travelling slightly the better, it seemed Apostle might actually topple St Paddy but the classy colt was still pulling and he gradually drew away inside the final furlong. The distance was three quarters of a length with Oak Ridge back in third.

Surprisingly, Piggott had never won the St Leger before he took St Paddy to Doncaster the following month – but one mile and six furlongs later and it was a statistic consigned to history as the pair won easily. They were three length victors over Die Hard and eased down once again at the post. Just as good as a four-year-old, the Jockey Club Stakes, the Hardwicke Stakes and the Eclipse would be claimed in 1961 before, at the end of the season, St Paddy was retired to stud at Beech House in Newmarket. As a stallion, he would be most notable for siring Jupiter Island, who won the Ebor Handicap at York in 1983 – again ridden by Piggott – and later the Japan Cup for trainer Clive Brittain. He died, aged 27, in 1984.

***

RHEINGOLD had a love-hate affair with York. He played his part in the greatest drama the track has ever seen – when Brigadier Gerard's unbeaten record was smashed by Roberto in the inaugural Benson & Hedges Gold Cup in 1972. But he would suffer Knavesmire misery when flopping as the odds-on favourite in the rich York race the following year. That summed up the career of the Barry Hills-trained colt, who could be as baffling as he was brilliant.

He was arguably more successful in France, where he would win the Grand Prix de Saint-Cloud in both 1972 and 1973 with the second of those successes followed by his biggest achievement, the Prix de l'Arc de Triomphe. He would also be the horse that helped rocket Hills, then a fledgling 35-year-old trainer at Lambourn, towards the top of his profession. That lay ahead. Despite his later York toil, it was at the track and the Dante Stakes of 1972 where the son of Faberge II would really announce his arrival on the racing scene.

Bred in Ireland, in County Tipperary, Rheingold had shown promise in his two-year-old season – finishing second in both the Champagne and Dewhurst Stakes after scoring on his debut at Newcastle in August 1971. He cost just 3,000 guineas as a yearling and was owned by the classical violist Henry Zeisel who, it is said, on the night before the Derby, sold shares in the horse to a syndicate which included Robert Sangster on the proviso the horse remain in his colours.

Rheingold had already run twice as a three-year-old before the Dante – an easy victory in a bog-standard race at Redcar and a slightly below par fourth place finish at Epsom in the Blue Riband Trial Stakes. They were both over around eight furlongs, however, and when Hills stepped up the colt to a mile and a quarter at York there was instant improvement. The race came down to a head-to-head between Rheingold and Moulton, trained by Harry Wragg. Losing ground at the start, Ernie Johnson, on board Rheingold, manoeuvred his mount into a challenging position with a quarter of a mile left and then dived through a gap on the rails to hit the front. Moulton immediately came to challenge, giving Rheingold a hefty bump in the process, but it was not enough. Rheingold dug deep, quickened effectively, and came through to win by half a length with Coup de Feu the best of the chasers in third.

Moulton would have his revenge over his Dante conqueror, becoming the shock winner of the Benson & Hedges Gold Cup in 1973. By then Rheingold knew all about that race. After failing by a nostril in a titanic battle with Roberto in the Derby three weeks after his Dante win, he had to play a supporting role in the inaugural running of York's new international contest in August.

After Moulton stunned him a year later, Rheingold repaired the damage by winning the Prix de l'Arc de Triomphe at Longchamp. Retired with a race record of nine wins from 17 contests, he stood as a stallion in Ireland before being sold in 1980 to Japan. He died in 1990, at the age of 21, with two-time Ascot Gold Cup winner Gildoran among the best of his progeny.

***

SHAHRASTANI is the horse who really put the Dante Stakes back on the racing map. The first since Shirley Heights, eight years earlier, to win both at York and at Epsom, the Aga Khan-owned colt arrived at a perfect time for York Racecourse. The money madness of the 80s was in full swing and Shahrastani caught a mood among the racing public which propelled Knavesmire's mile and a quarter trial right back up to the top of the early season racing calendar. Never again after this win, and Reference Point's the following year, would the supremacy of the Dante Stakes as the leading Epsom trial be in doubt.

Shahrastani was sired by Nijinsky, the Triple Crown-winning horse of 1970, and was trained by Sir Michael Stoute at Newmarket. Like so many of the top contests in his career, Stoute was to find the Dante Stakes to be very profitable indeed. Shahrastani would be his first of five winners.

The distinctive colt with the white blaze down his face began his three-year-old season still a maiden after finishing runner-up at Newbury in his only outing as a juvenile in 1985. Indeed, one of the outstanding things about Stoute's star was his mature performances both at York and Epsom – despite his relative inexperience. The Dante was only his third ever race and followed an impressive victory in Sandown's Classic Trial the month before.

Prominently positioned midway down the straight, Walter Swinburn, Stoute's stable jockey, pushed Shahrastani into the lead past Dancing Zeta only to watch Nomrood range onto his hindquarters on the rail. Nomrood had been blocked half a furlong earlier when looking for running room but now he was only half a length behind as the pair passed the furlong marker. Try as he might, though, the challenger looked a step behind. Shahrastani always had more fuel in the tank. Shahrastani was considered, by some experts, to have made hard work of it but it is a verdict that looks harsh in hindsight. Swinburn only had to resort to his whip twice, despite Nomrood's persistent attentions, and he rode past the line using hands and heels a length and a half the superior. Perhaps those concerns were partly why he was sent off at 11-2 in the Derby, a price which would turn out to be a bargain.

Dancing Brave, who had won the 2,000 Guineas, had never raced beyond a mile while only four of the 17-strong field had won over the Classic distance of a mile and a half. On that knowledge, the Dante winner had to be well in the mix and Swinburn stepped up to give Shahrastani a corker of a ride. In a slowly run race which didn't pick up any sort of pace until the runners were past the halfway mark, he was in the ideal spot coming round Tattenham Corner. He attacked soon after the runners came into the straight, looking to catch Dancing Brave off guard. With a furlong and a half to go, Shahrastani had the Blue Riband in his hands. But the Guineas winner was moving fast – making a concerted effort to get back on terms. It was too late, the gap was too great. Swinburn had timed his assault perfectly. He had half a length over Dancing Brave at the line.

There was shock and surprise at Dancing Brave's defeat. His jockey, Greville Starkey, who had won the Derby on Shirley Heights eight years earlier, is arguably best remembered for this loss and was pilloried, perhaps unjustly, for losing the race.

'I know everyone remembers Dancing Brave getting beaten but I think Greville was a top rider – there wasn't much doubt about it,' says Tim Richards, the distinguished former racing reporter for the *Mirror* and the *Racing Post*. 'He made mistakes but they all make mistakes. He rode all those good horses and it's a shame he's remembered for Dancing Brave. He (Starkey) was a great trickster, he loved pulling fast ones on people and he was a great joker. He was quite a character, although quite shy at the same time.' Richards also feels the subsequent fuss over Dancing Brave was quite harsh on the Derby winner. 'One of Stoute's longest serving lads, Jimmy Scott, who has travelled with top horses all over the world for him always thought Shahrastani was a very good horse,' he adds. 'He thought he was much maligned – partly by us, the press – because he appeared a lucky winner of the Derby.'

The beaten horse would have his compensations. Shahrastani, on the other hand, would take the Irish Derby in superb fashion but would never win again. Fourth in both Ascot's King George VI and Queen Elizabeth Stakes and the Arc at Longchamp, each of which was won in brilliant fashion by Dancing Brave, Shahrastani was retired to stud in Kentucky.

Perhaps the Arc winner's ultimate revenge came here. For unlike Dancing Brave, who has been successful as a stallion, his rival has not enjoyed the same kind of record. Now standing in Leicestershire, the best among his rather average offspring include the multiple Listed race victor Dariyoun and the 1993 Gordon Stakes winner St Mawes – although he is the damsire of Alamshar, the 2003 Irish Derby and King George VI and Queen Elizabeth Stakes winner. For former clerk of the course John Sanderson, however, Shahrastani did much more than just take the York-Epsom double. He 'broke a mould'.

'He was a good horse,' he says. 'We were very pleased he had come to run. If you look back before Shahrastani, they haven't necessarily covered themselves in glory after the Dante. As I said, we went through a period of time when it wasn't the fashionable route. Shahrastani was a good horse, though, and won well and went on to great things. It broke that mould. The Dante delivered a Derby winner.'

**

JUST like its counterpart for fillies, the Musidora Stakes, the leading trainer throughout Dante Stakes history is one Henry Richard Amherst Cecil. The Warren Place handler, ten times champion trainer and winner of 34 Classics, has won the race on seven occasions – beginning with Approval in 1970.

But of those victories, which also include Lyphard's Wish in 1979, Hello Gorgeous a year later and Tenby, the last, in 1993, only one managed to achieve the double of Dante and Derby. The horse was Reference Point. The year was 1987. Shirley Heights was the first great son of Mill Reef but Reference Point, his second Derby winner, was even better – pinpointed early on by racing experts Timeform as the one to watch at Epsom following the end of his two-year-old campaign.

'Few if any of Reference Point's contemporaries could be said to be better bred for a Derby,' they wrote in their *Racehorses of 1986*. 'He looks the part too – a strong, compact, attractive colt of considerable presence and considerable scope. His second season should be something to savour.' They would not be wrong.

It would be a year all the more impressive because the horse had

Left: An early photograph of Voltigeur - picture courtesy of York Racing Museum

Below: The Great Match - Voltigeur and the Flying Dutchman, with Admiral Rous, Lords Zetland and Eglinton, as painted by Harry Hall, 1851

Above: Before the 1945 St Leger - picture courtesy of York Racing Museum

Right: Brown Jack is led in following his Ebor victory in 1931 - picture courtesy of York Racing Museum

Above: Geoff Lewis takes the plaudits in the winner's enclosure after Mill Reef's brilliant 1970 Gimcrack victory

Left: The racecard for the first Benson and Hedges Gold Cup in 1972

Benson and Hedges Gold Cup Day.

York.
Tuesday August 15th 1972.
Programme Price 10p.

UNDER THE RULES OF RACING.

Above: Brigadier Gerard pictured in full flow in 1972

Above: Lester Piggott, on board Escorial, the winner of the Musidora Stakes in 1974

Above: Jockey Johnny Seagrave and Music Boy ahead of their Gimcrack Stakes victory in 1975

Right: Shirley Heights romps to victory
in the 1978 Dante Stakes

Right: Lord Halifax,
chairman of York Racecourse, receives the
trophy from Miss World Mari Stavin,
following Shirley Heights' Dante Stakes win

Above: Jockey Jonjo O'Neill receives congratulations after Sea Pigeon's 1979 Ebor Handicap success

Above: Troy, left, strides to victory in the 1979 Benson & Hedges Gold Cup

Above: Jockey Willie Carson on the turf after Silken Knot broke both legs in the 1981 Yorkshire Oaks

Above: Ardross (left) wins the Yorkshire Cup, 1982

Right: Jupiter Island gives Lester Piggott his final Ebor Handicap win in 1983

Above: Commanche Run, right, gets to the finish line first in the 1985 Benson & Hedges Gold Cup

Above: Chaumiere defends his John Smith's Magnet Cup title in 1986

Right: Shahrastani, ridden by
Walter Swinburn, is ridden to
victory in the Dante Stakes of 1986

Above: Steve Cauthen wins the International Stakes on Triptych in 1987

been bedevilled by sinus problems. His first campaign had comprised three runs. Third on his debut at Sandown, when the 11-10 favourite, Reference Point lost his maiden back at the same track when winning the Dorking Stakes by a crushing eight lengths. But it was his Group 1 victory in the William Hill Futurity Stakes at Doncaster, now the Racing Post Trophy, which was the real eye-catcher. Sent off the 4-1 second favourite, he was a seven length winner having made all the running – a result Timeform described as 'utterly convincing'. It was the widest winning margin for 20 years.

The irony was that Reference Point had not even been Cecil's first string horse in the race. Suhailie would never enjoy that mantle again. So with racing fans and pundits alike champing at the bit, his return to the track in 1987 was much anticipated. It came at York.

Cecil may have harboured Triple Crown ambitions before the start of the year but any thoughts he might have had of achieving the treble of 2,000 Guineas, Derby and St Leger were scotched when Reference Point had an operation to clear his infected sinuses. That had robbed him of a month's work and there were natural doubts about whether he would have the fitness to win the Dante after all that had happened. Those worries increased when Cecil himself estimated the colt's fitness to be around '80 per cent', but he shouldn't have been too concerned. Reference Point still had enough in his locker to deal with the Dante challengers.

If there were any worries, they had not put off the public either. Reference Point, with Cecil's stable jockey Steve Cauthen in the saddle, was sent off the 13-8 favourite. He had to be ridden a little firmer than usual and Cauthen was forced to get to work. This was no seven length triumph. At the finish a hard-chasing Ascot Knight, from the stable of Cecil's Newmarket rival Michael Stoute, was only a length back. He'd had some problems with the home turn, as well, and changed his action several times down his passage of the York straight. How would he deal with Epsom's notoriously undulating surface – a track either loved or hated by those who took on the challenge? But, considering Reference Point's lay-off and subsequent lack of race fitness, the Dante win was still a highly satisfactory result. That he had led throughout the contest, and resisted a firm challenge, only added to the positives.

Cecil certainly thought so, believing his colt was improving all the time and would be in peak condition three weeks later in the Derby. He was the favourite once more, this time a 6-4 chance, in a field which featured the unbeaten French horse Sadjiyd among the 19 runners. On board again, Cauthen always led, but for a few strides at the start, and, after swinging round Tattenham Corner, Reference Point held off the attentions of Most Welcome, who had almost come alongside in the final quarter of a mile, to win by a length and a half.

Having had so much time off in the early part of the season, Cecil now campaigned his Derby winner vigorously. He was beaten by Mtoto in the Eclipse Stakes three weeks after his Epsom exertions and, in a spectacular display of front running, destroyed a field including Tryptich, who would shortly win the International Stakes at York, in the King George VI and Queen Elizabeth Stakes. Reference Point would go to York as well, but would not compete over a mile and a quarter.

Missing the Guineas had ruined the dream of a Classic treble but Cecil showed his determination to take the St Leger by running him in the Great Voltigeur Stakes. The race had been established in 1950 as a stepping stone to Doncaster's Town Moor and a host of horses had successfully staged Leger assaults following the York trial, including the likes of St Paddy and Bustino. Perhaps the most notable other winner had been Vincent O'Brien's Alleged in 1977, who subsequently won back-to-back Prix de l'Arc de Triomphes.

Reference Point was the shortest priced runner in the race's history – sent off at a staggering 1-14. With opposition from only two horses, Colchis and Dry Dock, it was little more than a gallop and Cauthen still had a tight hold of the reins as Reference Point cantered home with lengths to spare. Cecil, praying for softer ground to help his colt, got what he wanted but the surface was perhaps too soft even for a horse which liked a little give.

'At York, you know the northern people love to see a quick horse,' Cecil said. 'Reference Point won the Voltigeur but the ground was so soft he slipped and pulled a muscle. It took everything I had to get him back for the Leger.' But that he did. At 4-11 he duly collected – Mountain Kingdom despatched by a length and a half.

'He won over a mile and a half at Epsom and these days they tend to come back to a mile and a quarter,' says John Smith, the former York clerk of the course who was in his first season in the job when Reference Point ruled supreme. 'In those days, he was going up – to one mile six furlongs. That was a big difference really.'

Unfortunately, his career did not end gloriously, a foot problem hindering him on firm ground in the Arc. He finished eighth of 11 to Trempolino. His life would also be tragically cut short. 'He retired to the Clifton Stud and I was coming back from Market Rasen on Boxing Day (1991) when I heard on the six o'clock news he had been killed,' remembers Smith. 'He got killed in the paddocks. I was shattered.' He was just seven.

***

FLAWED but fast, Erhaab only won four races in a career cruelly ended by injury. But two of those were most important – York and Epsom.

Erhaab was blessed with a blistering turn of foot and that was to give Willie Carson, approaching the end of his long glittering career, the last of his 17 Classic victories in the Derby of 1994. The Dante, by contrast, was not a race in which the jockey had shone. In fact, prior to Erhaab, Carson had won it only once – on the instantly forgotten Hobnob in 1975. Compare that with the race's leading rider, Pat Eddery, who won the Group 2 on six occasions.

Trained by John Dunlop, Erhaab had a busy juvenile career. Running on six occasions, he was unusually busy for a Classic prospect. But then, before the Dante, he probably hadn't been one. The closest Erhaab got to Group honours as a two-year-old was third place in the Horris Hill Stakes at Newbury. His record read: won two, lost four. Those two wins hadn't been in major contests either although the second, a seven length destruction of four rivals at Leicester, suggested he had talent.

After opening his Classic year as a runner-up in a Listed race at Newmarket, he travelled to York a month later as the 11-2 third favourite. At the top of the market was formidable opposition in the shape of the 2,000 Guineas winner Mister Baileys. Trained locally at Middleham by Mark Johnston, the colt was the sentimental choice for punters and went off the 7-4 favourite.

To begin with, he looked the part as well. Initially too keen, his jockey Jason Weaver had settled the Guineas winner well and Mister Baileys was travelling strongly turning for home. Still on the bit with three furlongs left, and shaken up to challenge at two, Johnston was convinced that nothing could beat him. He was wrong. When maximum effort was needed, Mister Baileys gave out. His legs could no longer hold off his pressing challengers. It seemed the mile of Newmarket was his limit. He finished third.

Ian Balding's Weigh Anchor, who had led from the off, now went for glory but he was quickly headed by the Erhaab express. Bursting clear from the centre of the pack, the horse took three and a half lengths out of the Kingsclere runner in the space of a furlong. It was an impressive sight. Carson was elated. On dismounting, he wasn't just confident. He was positively arrogant about Erhaab's Epsom credentials. 'My horse is going to get a mile and a half, he acts on firm ground and he is one of the few horses I've seen this season with a turn of foot, and that is all important at Epsom,' he said. 'I don't visualise any problems with the course and he's got all the credentials to be a Derby winner. Take the price.'

That price was 7-2 favourite, from a morning 20-1 – odds not so much shaved as hacked to bits with a scimitar. 'I wasn't amazed with the result because he's always been a nice horse and he's been longing for decent ground,' Dunlop said in the winner's enclosure. 'He's a very strongly built horse but he's not awkward and I can't think that Epsom will worry him at all. He knows what he's doing.'

To Epsom then and a finish which will live long in the memory for those lucky enough to have been at the track to see it. Part of a massive field of 25, and the last time the race would be held on its traditional Wednesday before switching to a Saturday, it was the Dante challengers who again locked horns. Mister Baileys, despite the stamina concerns, lined up along with Weigh Anchor and King's Theatre, who had finished fourth at York. Johnston's colt tried to run the others into the ground and had six lengths on the rest at Tattenham Corner before, once again, running out of gas. That seemed to leave the way clear for King's Theatre and Colonel Collins, who swept past Mister Baileys at the furlong post. Erhaab, eighth coming into the straight and some ten lengths adrift of the leader with two furlongs left to travel, got to work as the field flattened out and was on the heels of the two leading rivals with 200 yards left. He did not let up the pace, surging past the pair up the hill and winning by a length and a quarter in the most comprehensive fashion. It would be his last hurrah. Appearing twice more, in the Eclipse and the King George VI and Queen Elizabeth Stakes, Erhaab disappointed in both races before a vet's examination revealed damage to the ligaments behind both his knees. His career was over.

Sakhee, meanwhile, six years later, would not scoop Dunlop another Derby. Racing under the Godolphin colours, the horse had been harvested by Saeed bin Suroor when picking up his biggest achievements – the Juddmonte International and the Prix de l'Arc de Triomphe as a four-year-old. But he did give Dunlop a third Dante Stakes victory – emulating Shirley Heights and, of course, Erhaab.

Having won two of his three starts in his first season, Sakhee opened up his campaign in 2000 with victory in the Classic Trial at Sandown before lining up in a small field of five at York. Ridden by Richard Hills, Sakhee – 5-2 joint favourite with, ironically, Godolphin's Best Of The Bests – hung right and had to be driven out in the final furlong but still won by a length and a quarter from Pawn Broker. Sinndar was subsequently a length too good at Epsom but it was in 2001, under the direction of bin Suroor, where Sakhee's star really rose. He won the Juddmonte by seven lengths and the Arc by six.

Retired to Shadwell Stud after four seasons on the track, he has since sired the highly successful Sakhee's Secret, who won four successive Group 1 races in 2007.

***

HE has saddled racehorse winners all over the world – in America, Dubai and Europe. There have been Classic victories, Breeders' Cup triumphs and glory in the biggest money contests. But John Gosden has only won the Dante Stakes once. And Benny The Dip's York success was to also hand the Newmarket trainer his only Derby as well.

Gosden learned his trade from the best. Assistant trainer to conveyor belt-winning trainers Noel Murless and Vincent O'Brien, he set up in America and won the first Breeders' Cup Mile in 1984 with

Royal Heroine. On returning to England in 1988, he won his first Classic eight years later when Shantou won the St Leger at Doncaster.

Benny The Dip had already won twice on the track by then and, within nine months, would give Gosden another huge victory. Named after a pickpocket in a short story by Damon Runyon, he was owned by septuagenarian Landon Knight – an American who contracted polio at the age of nine and had been confined to a wheelchair ever since. York arrived with his charge having not won since beating Desert Story in the Royal Lodge Stakes at Ascot in his juvenile season. Third in the Racing Post Trophy and second on his reappearance as a three-year-old in Sandown's Classic Trial, he was still considered to be the leading light of a nine runner Dante field and was sent off the 100-30 favourite. He had been restricted at Sandown by a mucus problem and there were concerns before the race as to whether he had completely recovered.

Gosden would later reveal that Benny The Dip got upset when coming across the track during his pre-race preparations – leading the trainer to tell jockey Olivier Peslier to let the horse 'use himself'. With that in mind, Peslier just steered the ship. Benny The Dip broke smartly from the stalls, led immediately, and was never caught. It was a fabulous post-to-post performance. Quickening with a quarter of a mile to travel, he ran on impressively and gave the impression there would be more to come when stepped up to 12 furlongs at Epsom.

Desert Story, being beaten by Benny The Dip for the third time in his short life, was again the bridesmaid. He had found little under Mick Kinane and was two and a half lengths in arrears in settling for second. 'Peslier is a top jockey and he rode a great race,' said Gosden afterwards. 'The horse went nicely.' Understated, perhaps, but the trainer meant business with Epsom just three weeks away.

It would turn out to be a thrilling Derby. With Willie Ryan in the saddle, Benny The Dip won by the narrowest of margins. A short head. The battle was expected with the hot-favourite Entrepreneur but it was another who asked the sternest of questions. Making a bid for glory with fully half a mile to go, the 11-1 shot Benny The Dip had to withstand a storming fight back from Pat Eddery on Silver Patriarch, who found a rocket gear in the final furlong. Benny The Dip had just enough in reserve. The two horses flashing past the post together, Gosden endured several nervous minutes before learning the joyous result.

For Gosden, who had so often been the Derby's nearly man having had four placed finishers in seven previous runners, there was joy and a dedication of the race to his father Towser. Silver Patriarch's compensation would arrive later in the St Leger but that was not Benny The Dip's destination. He was to take on his elders, back at the scene of his Dante triumph, in York's Juddmonte International. There, he would be bested by a mighty horse.

It was not Bosra Sham, Henry Cecil's odds-on multiple Group 1 winner, who flopped and finished last. It was Singspiel. He was about to bring the curtain down on a wonderful career, which had included Group 1 wins in the Japan Cup and the Dubai World Cup, in the best possible style. Benny The Dip employed usual front running tactics but as soon as Frankie Dettori and Singspiel took him on, three furlongs out, the destiny of the race was never in doubt. Gosden's hero would finish third. Even Desert King got the better of him on this day.

To put Singspiel's win into context, Dettori instantly labelled him 'the best horse I've ever ridden' – considering him better than both Lammtarra and Halling, the latter of which had won the Juddmonte International twice. 'For all round performance and guts he has to be the best in the world,' he said.

Singspiel's story finished right there and Benny The Dip also had just one more run, a down the field display in the Champion Stakes at Newmarket, before he was sent to stud. Unfortunately, his life ended tragically at the age of ten. Initially standing in America and then at Cheveley Park, he was moved to Ireland in 2003 but – just two weeks after his arrival at the Rathbarry Stud – he was put down after fracturing a knee in the paddocks.

***

MOON BALLAD didn't win a Derby. After his Dante win in 2002, he was still considered to be Godolphin's second string when he moved on to Epsom – where he did not succeed on the undulating track. In fact, he only won one other race in England. But he still merits inclusion in a history of York's greatest race runners, if only because he won the world's richest contest in 2003.

Foaled in Ireland in 1999, Moon Ballad's sire was Singspiel   the winner of the International Stakes two years previously. It was a case of like father like son for these two. Moon Ballad, who cost 350,000 guineas as a yearling, would follow his dad in winning the Dubai World Cup. That he would prove to have a liking for artificial surfaces should not be too much of a surprise.

After starting his career in a Newmarket maiden, the Godolphin colt, trained by Saeed bin Suroor, began his three-year-old season racing at Nad Al Sheba in owner Sheikh Mohammed's home country of Dubai. Winning his opening excursion, Moon Ballad followed up by finishing fourth in the UAE Derby before returning to England with York and then the Derby in mind. With Jamie Spencer up, the pair were placed in the Listed Newmarket Stakes before going to the Dante. It was a race they dominated from start to finish, and in a record time to boot. The 13-2 chance led from the moment the stalls opened and pulled away impressively from a field which had included the fancied favourite Sir George Turner, trained by Mark Johnston, and Sir Michael Stoute's Right Approach. Moon Ballad was a length and a quarter better than runner-up Bollin Eric, who would go on to win the St Leger for locally-based trainer Tim Easterby four months later.

But, even following this win, the Derby ante-post market was not set alight by the performance. Indeed, he was not Godolphin's number one contender for the Derby. 'Moon Ballad has speed as you saw there and, although there is a question, I think he should stay a mile and a half,' said stable racing manager Simon Crisford. 'But at the moment Naheef would be our leading hope for Epsom.'

It was not to be at Epsom for Moon Ballad, or Naheef, but there was no disgrace as the former finished third to the superb High Chaparral and Hawk Wing. He proved his quality that season regardless, winning Group 3 honours in the Select Stakes at Goodwood in September before finding only Storming Home too good in the Champion Stakes at Newmarket the following month.

Kept in training, Frankie Dettori steered the four-year-old to victory in the Sheikh Maktoum bin Rashid al Maktoum Challenge Round II back at Nad Al Sheba before the pair took their chances in the six million dollar Dubai World Cup. Part of a field of 11, including Marcus Tregoning's Juddmonte International winner Nayef, the 11-4 second favourite was in command throughout most of the mile and a quarter distance. Dettori pushed him out to a five length win over the American-trained Harlan's Holiday – and a first prize of £2.25 million. It's hard to top an achievement like that and Moon Ballad could not.

Back in England, he was only ninth at Royal Ascot in the Prince of Wales's Stakes and fifth in the Sussex Stakes at Glorious Goodwood. After High Chaparral reminded him who was really the boss in the Irish Champion Stakes – where he could only finish fifth – Godolphin sent him to Belmont Park in America for the Jockey Club Gold Cup. Hall of fame rider Jerry Bailey was unable to get a different tune out of Moon Ballad, though, and the pair were last of the five runners. Retired following that disappointing display in New York, he stood for Darley Stud in Japan, where he was ranked in the top ten leading first and second crop sires' list, until being transferred to Ireland at the end of 2009.

***

NORTH LIGHT began a quite golden period for the Dante Stakes – one which would spawn three Derby winners in four years. The 2004 race would also prove a reliable indicator of the talent of that year's Classic generation. The runner-up, Godolphin's Rule Of Law, would go on to St Leger victory at Doncaster that September and North Light met Rule Of Law in both the Dante and the Derby. The two races were oddly similar.

Trained by Sir Michael Stoute, who had already tasted Dante success twice, North Light would provide more Classic joy for the Newmarket handler. He'd won the Derby the year before with Kris Kin and his association with stable jockey Kieren Fallon was at its zenith. The Dante was hailed a champion effort for the rider, who had to hold off a surging Rule Of Law in the final furlong.

Sheikh Mohammed was at York that day to take a look at Rule Of Law on his first ride for the Godolphin stable but Fallon kicked North Light to the front from five furlongs out and got away from rival rider Frankie Dettori. Rule Of Law ate up the ground as the line approached but Fallon battled gamely and kept his principal rival half a length at bay. Let The Lion Roar, the 3-1 favourite saddled by John Dunlop, was third.

It was virtually an identical story at Epsom. North Light kicked on and went two lengths clear of the field with two furlongs to travel. Rule Of Law, once again last during the early stages, flew down the straight with mighty speed and, as at York, too late to really affect the result. Staying on well, he snatched second spot at the post from... Let The Lion Roar. The Dante 1-2-3 was also the Derby's.

North Light failed to win again after Epsom – continuing a Derby trend which, beginning with Kris Kin, would not be broken until three years later when Authorized won the Juddmonte International. Runner up to Grey Swallow in the Irish Derby and fifth in the Arc he remained in training as a four-year-old but ran just once, finishing second in the Brigadier Gerard Stakes at Sandown. Now a stallion in Kentucky, he is the only champion sired by Danehill at stud in America.

***

PAYING £6,000 apiece to join, the well-heeled members of the Royal Ascot Racing Club included Sir Clement Freud and the TV talent show king Simon Cowell in their ranks. They were used to celebrity. But, in the horse racing world at least, the Montjeu colt they bought was about to become just as big a star as the glitterati who paid the bills.

Motivator was the thoroughbred fairytale. Not just for the owners, who numbered 230, but for the trainer Michael Bell. Based in Newmarket at Fitzroy House, Motivator was the colt Bell dreamed of training. A licensed trainer for 16 years, he had enjoyed Group race success before Motivator came along, but it had been limited. That was about to change. Motivator would bring Bell his first English Classic success.

He ran only twice as a two-year-old, but that was all that was needed. After doling out a six length thumping in a Newmarket maiden, Motivator then claimed the influential Racing Post Trophy at Doncaster in equally impressive fashion to alert anyone watching that he was a special horse in the making. They didn't need much persuading. Or much telling. In the run up to the Dante Stakes in 2005, the first appearance of Motivator's three-year-old career, there was no excuse for not knowing the colt inside and out.

Sensing a great story in the making, with the Rocky-like trainer trying to prove himself in the big time, the *Racing Post*'s Brough Scott chronicled the story with a brilliant column as Bell sought to take Motivator and his eclectic bunch of owners to the summit at Epsom. That brought pressure and expectation. It made the wait for York in May an anxious and nervy time for Bell.

'Obviously he was a very high profile horse and it was being chronicled in the *Racing Post* every week by Brough Scott and we were under a bit of pressure,' he says. 'He was an unbeaten Group 1 winner and a short-priced favourite for the race. It was very much phase one of the plan to try to win the Derby and his season depended on a good result in the Dante. I was more nervous going into the Dante then I was later at Epsom because I'd seen what he had done in the Dante by then and knew it would take a serious horse to beat him in the Derby. But we needed to see that evidence and it was the first time Johnny Murtagh had ridden him as well in a race.'

Following North Light's Dante/Derby double 12 months previously, the York race was now indisputably the leading indicator of where Epsom glory would lie. Even more so when Motivator skipped the 2,000 Guineas at Newmarket to open his season on Knavesmire. But now there was a change of jockey to consider. Kieren Fallon had ridden the horse in his first two victories but he had been snapped up as Aidan O'Brien's stable jockey at Ballydoyle and Murtagh, an impeccable rider and twice a Derby winner, had stepped into the breach.

On the face of it, it looked a stylish victory at York and one which immediately installed him as the one to watch the following month. The even money favourite beat The Geezer by a length and a half after tracking the leaders and quickening to the front at the furlong marker – staying on comfortably for victory. Nothing had really threatened his win, with the Ballydoyle pair Falstaff and Albert Hall trailing back in third and fifth. Clive Brittain's Kandidate, bred at nearby Dunnington and later the winner of Listed and Group races at Sandown, Kempton and Nad al Sheba, was fourth.

To illustrate the quality of the field, even Proclamation – last of the six runners – was a top class horse who went on to win the Jersey Stakes at Royal Ascot at York the following month. Naturally, there was delight in the winner's enclosure.

'It was a funny race,' said Murtagh. 'There wasn't much pace but when I asked him to quicken he did it very well. I think he'll come round Tattenham Corner come Derby day. He was only having his third run and I expect a lot more improvement – he has what it takes. Good horses adapt and to win the Derby he has to overcome it all. I think he has a great chance.'

Bell was similarly positive. 'It's been an agonising six months since the Racing Post Trophy,' he added. 'We made the decision to come to the Dante and it is now looking a sound decision. I can't tell you the part the team at home have played. He is quite highly-strung but today he was very calm in the preliminaries. We kept everything low key before the race and he behaved immaculately before, during and after the race. I am absolutely delighted. His whole day has been very smooth and it will take a good one to beat him at Epsom.'

There were still some minor concerns. In the final furlong, Motivator had hung badly to his right and, as Brough Scott would soon reveal, the colt's work rider Shane Featherstonehough didn't buy Murtagh's explanation that he was moving across to better ground and that Motivator was a bit green. Bell, however, never doubted that he was the real deal.

'Watching that I thought 'This wins the Derby' after he won the Dante,' he says. 'I was very happy with it. He never had a smack. It was his first time going a mile and a quarter, the first time Johnny had ridden him. At York, from a horse's point of view, I always think that stand can catch their eye a bit. It's a massive, daunting sight and if they're a little bit green in front they see that stand and hear the noise of the crowd. If a short-priced favourite goes clear, the noise is huge and it's a great atmosphere. 'Horses aren't stupid and, if you are out in front and it was only the third run of his life, they are entitled to be a bit green and show a few signs of inexperience. I thought he was very impressive. Obviously Brough, when he was writing his stories, is having to use artistic licence. I was very satisfied with Motivator. It was crucial (to put in an impressive performance). Had he trailed in third, the Derby dream would have been over. We hoped we had a serious Derby horse on our hands and we drove home from York with the short-priced favourite.'

There was, indeed, no cause for alarm. Starting the 3-1 favourite at

Epsom, Motivator's performance was absolutely scintillating. Murtagh almost missed the race, only able to mount the colt in the 226th Derby thanks to a reprieve from a ban. His third win, after Sinndar in 2000 and High Chaparral two years later, was – in his own words – the easiest of the three. In contrast, it was only Bell's third Derby runner. Five lengths was the gap over the unfortunately named Walk In The Park after Motivator, who handled concerns about how he might take to the undulating Epsom Downs and the tight Tattenham Corner with some ease, bolted clear with two furlongs left to travel. The victory sparked some of the most memorable scenes ever seen in the Epsom winner's enclosure as it seemed nearly all the Royal Ascot Racing Club's members – bedecked in top hats and tails – crowded in to celebrate the victory.

'We've had some good ones but I don't think there are many Derby winners who would have beaten him that day,' says Bell looking back at Motivator's Epsom heroics. 'It was an exceptional performance and we probably never really had him at that level after that. A very talented horse.'

There were no nerves during the race either. 'It wasn't during the race it was in the weeks, in the days and on race day,' Bell adds. 'As soon as the stalls opened, the nerves had gone and you are just concentrating on the race. It is no time for nerves then. Then, I hadn't won a Derby. I hadn't won a really high profile race in England so it was probably vital to my career that he came along just at the right time.'

Epsom was indeed the zenith of Motivator's career on the track. Starting a heavily backed favourite next time out in the Eclipse at Sandown, the colt was beaten by Oratorio. Fast ground was said to have been a factor in that defeat but Oratorio beat Motivator again in the Irish Champion Stakes at Leopardstown. After finishing fifth in the Arc at Longchamp in October, an appearance at the Breeders' Cup was pencilled in but, when the horse went lame in the run-up, he was retired to The Royal Studs in 2006.

***

ANOTHER son of Montjeu was to do even better than Motivator two years after he had scorched the York track.

Authorized wouldn't just win the Dante Stakes, he would give

Frankie Dettori the race he craved – a Derby. He would also lend a new lease of life to trainer Peter Chapple-Hyam. After the likes of Dr Devious and Rodrigo de Triano had taken him to the top of the profession in the early 90s, he had slipped towards relative obscurity. Authorized would be a redeemer.

The horse was foaled in 2004, bred by a partnership which included the Irish jockey Mick Kinane. Chapple-Hyam paid 400,000 guineas for him at the Newmarket sales in October 2005 for Kuwaiti racing partners Saleh al Homaizi and Imad al Sagar. Authorized began quietly, finishing only third in his opening foray on a racecourse at Newbury, but the experts felt there was always more to come – noting that he was bred to make a better three-year-old. He did not take that long to show his star potential.

Returning to Newbury for the Racing Post Trophy, the horse – ridden for the first time by Frankie Dettori – was a length and a quarter victor from Charlie Farnsbarns. At 25-1 he had sprung a big surprise over the odds-on favourite Eagle Mountain but the victory wasn't enough to send the layers into a tizzy over his Classic prospects just yet. But at York, and Authorized's first outing as a three-year-old in the Dante Stakes, the secret was well and truly out on Chapple-Hyam's colt.

That hype wasn't only about the horse, who was sent off the 10-11 favourite in the Epsom trial, but about the jockey as well. Dettori had won almost every important race on the calendar, and had at least a brace of all of the other Classics – but the Derby was yet to be added to his CV of achievements in the saddle. Fourteen times the Italian had competed at Epsom. Fourteen times he failed to scoop the Blue Riband contest. He had never finished better than third. Dettori felt he would not get a better chance than with Authorized and, in the Dante, the colt showed him why. He could even afford to be tardy out of the stalls, quickly tracking the leaders and then moving impressively on the bridle. Challenging at two furlongs, and moving to the lead with half that distance travelled, Authorized cruised to the line. Raincoat was his nearest rival, four lengths adrift, with Al Shemali third – a result and performance which pushed him to Derby favouritism. For Chapple-Hyam, Authorized's win and the manner of the performance, confirmed that this was the best horse he had trained.

'He has just so much class,' he said, reporting that he continued to be in tip-top shape following his Knavesmire romp. 'It was a great day and we hope there are more to come with him. He seems fine after his race – good as gold. There are no problems at all with him.'

Dettori, however, had not cleared space on the mantelpiece for the Derby trophy just yet. For one thing, there was a conflict of interest to overcome. 'If Godolphin have a runner then I will ride for Godolphin because that is my stable,' the Italian insisted after taking the Dante plaudits. But Godolphin chief Sheikh Mohammed, realising his yard were lacking a true Epsom contender, released Dettori from his stable commitments. The Italian would get his chance to grab Derby glory. Simon Crisford, Godolphin's racing manager, stressed it had been a 'sporting decision'. 'At the moment we don't have a strong contender and after talking to Sheikh Mohammed he was very aware of that situation and he thought it was the sporting and right thing to let him ride the favourite,' he said.

Authorized was the clear favourite on Derby day, following his stand-out warm up at York, and he justified the tag emphatically. Faster than Motivator the previous year and the quickest Derby winner since Slip Anchor in 1985, Authorized won by five lengths and finally scratched Dettori's nagging itch. But, as we will see later, the colt was to return to York later that year to post an achievement every bit as good as that triumphant Epsom day.

***

FAILURE in the Dante Stakes had always been the death knell for a promising colt's chances at Epsom. In all previous runnings of the race, one statistic stood firm. If you competed in the Dante but didn't win it, you could not win at Epsom. Workforce, therefore, is unique.

In 2010, Sir Michael Stoute's three-year-old did what had never been done before and, in the process, added a new dimension to York's Classic trial. He would win at Epsom without winning on Knavesmire.

The gallops rumour mill had been awash with stories of the brilliance of the son of King's Best before he had ever appeared on a racecourse. That hype had not dimmed even though Workforce had only run, and won, once before taking on the Dante contenders at York.

That victory had come in a maiden at Goodwood, over seven furlongs the previous September, and it had been an impressive six length display. Interest in Stoute's newest contender continued to peak when the runner-up, Oasis Dancer, went on to win a valuable sales race at Newmarket. Stoute, in public anyway, was still only cautiously optimistic ahead of Workforce's reappearance on Knavesmire. 'He is not spectacular at home but he has been giving us more encouragement of late,' he said the Saturday before the Dante.

On paper, Workforce had impressive opposition to overcome as well. There was Chabal, the Godolphin colt, who was narrowly at the head of the Dante betting market. He had impressed with a comfortable victory in Sandown's Classic Trial ahead of Azmeel, who had gone on to take the Dee Stakes. There was also the Aidan O'Brien-trained Cape Blanco. The Ballydoyle trainer was developing just as strong a liking for Dante glory as Stoute having won the race three times before – including 12 months previously with Black Bear Island.

Cape Blanco was taking an unbeaten record of three victories into the race, with two of those being Group wins. 'He has lots of speed but is lazy in his races,' said O'Brien in the pre-race build-up. 'All his wins last season were over seven furlongs and he made all in two of his races.' The trip, however, did not pose a problem and neither did a cut the colt picked up when cantering at home. 'We think he should get a mile and a quarter and maybe further.' That should have been a hint. But, at 2-1, there were plenty of people at York who felt Workforce was the one to watch in a select field of five.

Circumvent, a French Group 3 winner trained by Paul Cole and ridden by local hero Paul Hanagan, became the pacemaker as the stalls opened and was tracked by both Coordinated Cut, trained by Michael Bell, and Cape Blanco, ridden by Ballydoyle stable jockey Johnny Murtagh. Workforce was held up with Chabal, and Frankie Dettori, bringing up the rear. It was Bell's colt which moved first. Coordinated Cut ranged up on Circumvent as the runners turned into the straight but Murtagh moved Cape Blanco ominously into position and then pushed his mount out to challenge at the two furlong marker. Workforce, by contrast, was hanging left with jockey Ryan Moore trying to rally. The horse faltered decisively when the bit went through his mouth. Despite reeling in the tiring Coordinated Cut in the last 100 yards following a concerted rally, Workforce was never seriously threatening the leader. Cape Blanco, if anything, stretched away. It was a decisive win – three and a quarter lengths.

Murtagh was delighted. 'I really like this horse,' he said in the parade ring. 'They went a good gallop, it was a fast-run race and a very good trial. He's a bit lazy off the bridle but that was good.'

There were concerns for Cape Blanco in a mad post-race half hour which was almost as dramatic as the contest itself. He appeared to be lame at the finish and, despite any worries being brushed off by the Ballydoyle empire, he immediately drifted in the Derby betting market. In the meantime, O'Brien was also falling foul of the authorities. It transpired that Cape Blanco had banged the same heel he'd knocked in his pre-race canter the previous week. Due to be examined by the racecourse vet, O'Brien halted a request for his now valuable colt to be trotted up for an inspection. When his groom Pat Keating failed to meet the Stewards, O'Brien was referred to the British Horseracing Authority and was later charged with rule breaches.

'It's the most insane thing I've ever heard,' O'Brien had angrily railed on Dante day. 'Why would you want to trot him again on a bruised heel and cause him more pain?' O'Brien would later be fined £10,400 by the British Horseracing Authority over the incident after he was found to have acted in a manner 'prejudicial to the proper conduct of horseracing in Great Britain'.

But for Workforce there were bigger questions and concerns. He had failed to win. Would he even go to Epsom at all now? Lord Teddy Grimthorpe, racing manager to the horse's owner Prince Khalid Abdullah, wasn't sure in the immediate aftermath. 'He's a big, once-raced baby,' he said. 'I wouldn't want to say he would go to the Derby or not, he wouldn't be ruled out. He hung a little coming into the straight and the bit slipped out of his mouth slightly. The ground was definitely as quick as he would want it. We'd let Sir Michael decide if he's good enough for Epsom.' Stoute didn't take much convincing.

A good workout at Lingfield a couple of weeks after his York exertions booked his place and Workforce went to Epsom as the 6-1 joint third favourite. He produced a spectacular performance there, smashing the track record and obliterating a field which included the 9-4 favourite Jan Vermeer by seven lengths. That capped the best of weekends for jockey Ryan Moore, who had won the Oaks the previous day on Snow Fairy.

Although Workforce flopped subsequently in the King George VI and Queen Elizabeth Stakes at Ascot – a race lit up by a phenomenal display by Stoute's other runner Harbinger – the colt would bring the Newmarket trainer Longchamp glory when winning the Prix de l'Arc de Triomphe in Paris. While Workforce was excelling at Epsom, Cape Blanco swerved the Derby finishing mid-division instead at Chantilly in the Prix du Jockey Club. But big race success was only three weeks away. O'Brien's colt won the Irish Derby at the Curragh and would achieve another Group 1 success in the Irish Champion Stakes.

***

IT remains to be seen if Workforce's Dante Stakes win in 2010 will have any discernible effect on the race in subsequent years. Horses who did not stand out in the contest were invariably scratched from Epsom plans – the quick three week turnaround usually considered too short a period of time to re-find form.

Workforce, of course, hardly failed in the Dante. He was runner-up and performed creditably, if not spectacularly, at York. In the end, it proved a good workout on the way to Derby glory. But lifting a half-century old tradition – that Dante losers could not win the Derby – may persuade some trainers of beaten horses of the merits of taking the Epsom route after all.

What Stoute's horse did there, and subsequently at the Arc, has only added to the prestige of the race. It has now evolved into the richest, and most important, of all the contests that lead on the road to Epsom. With the likes of North Light, Authorized and Motivator among just the very recent winners who went on to take the Blue Riband, the fact that a horse like Workforce did not taste York victory but could still go on to such great things speaks volumes for the depth of talent it attracts. And while Derby winners and contenders continue to flow from its participants, its pre-eminent status should not be in doubt. If anything the game has changed.

While former clerk of the course John Sanderson railed earlier about how Chester's May meeting interfered with York plans in the distant past, if anything the choice now – thanks to talents like Sea The Stars – can often be between the 2,000 Guineas or the Dante as a pathway to Epsom. Given that Classic comparison, it is incredible that York's spring highlight continues to only hold Group 2 status. Surely it will be elevated into the highest echelons of British racing in the not too distant future.

THE MUSIDORA STAKES

THEY are a bunch of romantics at York Racecourse. Gimcrack, Dante and Musidora – none of them have won on Knavesmire and the latter two never set foot on the famous turf – but all are immortalised in sporting history by the York Race Committee's decision to name important contests in their memory.

Musidora, so called after Jeanne Roques, a French silent movie star, was the winner of both the 1,000 Guineas and the Epsom Oaks in 1949, and was trained in Malton by Captain Charles Elsey. On the famous Downs, she was ridden by Australian jockey Edgar Britt and beat the French horse Coronation V, who would go on to win the Prix de l'Arc de Triomphe at Longchamp. Nothing special as a broodmare, she would doubtless today be merely a name in the record books had the chiefs at York decided not to brand their new trial for the Oaks as her legacy.

Now a Group 3 contest, and an important early affair in the calendar of Classic contenders, this mile and a quarter race for three-year-old fillies was established in 1961. Ambergris, trained by Harry Wragg and ridden by Lester Piggott, was the first victor – a 4-9 odds-on shot justifying her market price. While favourites had an appalling record in the early years of races like the Benson & Hedges Gold Cup, in the Musidora Stakes, if the money was down, it paid to take notice. None of the first five winners were a bigger price than 5-4 and, of them, Noblesse in 1963 was the best. She began a three year spell where the Musidora Stakes was dominated by the jockey Garnet Bougoure.

Ela Marita, 12 months later, and Arctic Melody in 1965, would bring him a hat-trick in the race but what set Noblesse apart was that she was the first filly to win both the Musidora and the Oaks at Epsom. Paddy Prendergast, training on the Curragh, had a reputation for brilliance with juvenile horses. Bought as a yearling for 4,200 Guineas, Noblesse was hardly the belle of the ball. Those racing experts at Timeform, the men and women who know all about conformation, described her as 'no beauty to look at'. But she proved that you didn't have to look pretty to do the business where it counted – on the track. She was the champion two-year-old, following a five length winning debut at Ascot, and then went on to claim the Timeform Gold Cup at Doncaster without even coming off the bridle. It was a win which made history. No other filly has ever won the race, which is now known as the Racing Post Trophy.

Classic hopes were immediately raised and, as 1962 came to a close, Noblesse was the early favourite for both the 1,000 Guineas and the Oaks. She wouldn't get to the former – Prendergast unable to get her up to speed following a cold spring – and so she reappeared at York for the Musidora. Noblesse was brilliant that day, smashing her rivals by six lengths after moving away inside the final two furlongs. It is hard to believe, but she was even better at Epsom. Starting as the 4-11 favourite, Noblesse destroyed the field to win the Classic – victorious by ten lengths after Bougoure asked her to go on and win at the furlong marker. It is still one of the finest displays ever seen in the race.

Hampered by injury, she would run just once more. At the Prix de l'Arc de Triomphe, short of fitness and preparation, she would finish third and was retired to stud afterwards. There, she continued to exert her influence on the Musidora Stakes. The fabulous filly was also a good broodmare. She produced Where You Lead, who won the race in 1973, and of the five foals she bore before her death the previous year, all won on the racetrack. Her memory lives on in the Noblesse Stakes at Cork.

Arctic Melody's win two years later, incidentally, was tainted by controversy. It was believed the dope gangs had struck at York. It is hard to overstate the effect the nobblers, who drugged horses and fixed races, had on racing in the first couple of decades following the end of the Second World War. The fear was both real and psychological. A poor performance could be all that was needed to start the tongues wagging. Was it 'got at'? So when Night Off, the 1,000 Guineas winner and the Oaks favourite, trailed home last of the five runners in the Musidora of 1965, there were immediate allegations of skulduggery.

'I have never seen a horse more distressed than she was and owner Major L B Holliday said she must have been either doped or poisoned,' wrote Ivanhoe in the *Yorkshire Evening Press*. 'With a little over two furlongs to go, just when we were expecting to see Night Off and her main rival Arctic Melody come from the rear of the field and fight it out, Night Off dropped away beaten. In a second she was out of the race, going slower and slower.'

Who knows if it was a trick of the mind. But the poor performance of the favourite, Look Sharp, the previous day only heightened the hysteria. Ivanhoe reported that security arrangements were 'about as fool-proof as could be' but the doubts inevitably cast a shadow over Arctic Melody's win.

***

ESCORIAL was the one that nearly got Ian Balding stuck in the Tower of London. Twice.

'She was a very difficult filly I trained for The Queen,' he remembers. 'She came up for the Musidora in May 1974 and The Queen was there.' She had made an impromptu visit, flying into the nearby Rufforth airfield from Heathrow, but can't have been delighted with what she saw on her arrival. 'I was in the Royal box with The Queen and I had a lad leading Escorial and the travelling head lad going across with her,' Balding adds. 'They get half way across Knavesmire and Escorial rears up, the boy comes off and she gets loose. She gallops down to the bottom end of the track, down by the six furlong marker, and an old Yorkshire trainer caught her and brought her back.'

With Escorial's chances having seemingly disappeared thanks to this runaway gallop, Balding wanted to be anywhere but in the presence of the horse's Royal owner. But Escorial then proceeded to pull a metaphorical rabbit out of the hat, and save his skin. With Lester Piggott in charge, and starting at 4-5 despite her pre-race mischief, she put in a dominating display – a champagne performance as the *Yorkshire Evening Press* reported – and beat Lauretta, piloted by Pat Eddery. In doing so, she headed to the summit of the Oaks market at 7-2.

'She won the race very easily,' adds Balding. 'It was quite remarkable. She was a bloody good filly and she had won the fillies' race at Ascot the previous season. She was high class.' But Balding could not avoid another disagreement with Her Majesty a month later at Epsom. 'She didn't run terribly well in the Oaks. I can remember The Queen saying to me 'I thought you said it would be all right'. I got out of the box as quick as I could.'

***

BIREME, in 1980, was the first filly since Noblesse 17 earlier years to win the Musidora and then also claim the Oaks at Epsom the following month.

She was trained by the dynamic duo, the wonderfully successful partnership of jockey Willie Carson and trainer Dick Hern. By Grundy, the 1975 English and Irish Derby winner, Bireme was a late starter and was only seen on the course twice in her first season – winning on her debut in a 30-runner cavalry charge at Newmarket in October before following up with a third place at the same track later that month. She would only run twice in 1980 too, but what a double of contests they turned out to be. The Musidora was the first of them.

A tough race to win at the best of times, Bireme's task seemed even harder considering it was her first race of the season. Against a field of battle-hardened veterans in comparison, including Our Home – who finished second in the 1,000 Guineas – and the Lingfield Oaks Trial winner Gift Wrapped, it is perhaps not surprising there was not a massive clamour for Hern's horse in the betting market. Going off at 5-1, and with her fitness in question, her rivals, who also included the Princess Elizabeth Stakes winner Bay Street, looked to test her stamina from the outset. They sent her to the front. But Bireme did not shirk the task, or the responsibility, of leading the field. Both Our Home and Gift Wrapped came after her. As they made their way down the straight, Carson was asking Bireme for everything she had from fully two furlongs from home. It seemed the effort would come to nought when, heading into the final couple hundred of yards, the surging Gift Wrapped actually got herself in front and into a half length lead. But Bireme was brave and refused to let go of victory. When others may have downed tools, she pulled herself up once again and ground down the 1,000 Guineas runner on her way to winning by a length.

It was now on to the Oaks where Bireme started joint second favourite, valued at 9-2 with the Lupe Stakes winner Vielle, behind the 1,000 Guineas victor Quick As Lightning. The latter was trying a distance of more than a mile for the first time and it would prove too big a task. Bireme, on the other hand, up against some familiar rivals including Gift Wrapped, would once again show she had plenty of guts and determination, this time on a Classic stage, finishing two lengths ahead of Vielle after wearing down The Dancer inside the final quarter mile.

Hern and Carson, who also won the Derby with Henbit, now became the first stable to hold both Epsom Classics at the same time since Crepello and Carrozza won in 1957 for Noel Murless. For Bireme, her Epsom Oaks triumph was the final chapter in a too brief racing career. She was retired to stud shortly after the race following injuries picked up when getting loose on a road close to Hern's West Ilsley stables. Bireme died in 2002.

***

CONDESSA, as we will see later, was to play her part in one of the most dramatic races ever seen at York – the 1981 Yorkshire Oaks – but, three months earlier, Jim Bolger's super filly paved the way for future glories with an impressive display in the Musidora Stakes. She would turn out to be something of a bargain.

'It all started because I used to live in Ballymore and the man who built that house for us rang me seven or eight years later,' Bolger remembers. 'He said he was retiring from building and wanted to buy a racehorse. I said "Flat or jumps" and he said "I will leave that to you". 'He gave me £20,000 to go to the sales and I got Condessa for £12,000. I wasn't able to get a second one so I had to give him £8,000 back.'

Bolger, it seemed, was determined to give his owner value for money. Condessa was a busy girl in her two-year-old season. She ran eight times, winning twice, both times at Gowran Park, and won a handicap at Clonmel over a mile and a half to open her three-year-old campaign before travelling to England, just four days before York, for the Lingfield Oaks trial.

'She was very talented,' Bolger adds. 'She was basically a mile and a half filly but we brought her back to a mile and a quarter for the Musidora. She was in a very competitive handicap over a mile and a half in Ireland and we went to Lingfield for the Oaks trial and she was third there. I said to the owner "We might as well get value for the trip" and so we went to York as well three or four days later. I thought she'd give a good account but she was up against the 1,000 Guineas winner. Henry Cecil ran Fairy Footsteps.'

Bolger was optimistic. No one else was. Surely she would have to find more than a couple of minor handicap wins to compete with a Musidora crowd? With the Guineas heroine in the line up, Condessa went off at 16-1 and stunned her highly rated rivals. The early pace was fast, on soft ground, and Condessa initially struggled to cope with the speed of the contest. When the five runners came into the straight, Bolger's underdog was last of all. But at the three furlong marker she began to hunt down the others. With 200 yards to travel she was well clear and, at the post, she was four lengths up on Madam Gay, who had been fifth in the Guineas at Newmarket. The winner of that race, Fairy Footsteps, was back in the rear view mirror and made to look like she didn't relish the distance. For Bolger, it was a landmark success.

'As someone just starting out it was great to beat the 1,000 Guineas winner and to beat Henry Cecil and I have great memories of that still. Condessa had class and stamina. She wasn't easy to train and she wasn't easy to ride out either. She certainly knew how to hang left and hang right.'

It seemed, at first, as if the bookmakers may have been right all along. Condessa's Musidora might have been a fluke. Following York,

Bolger took her to Royal Ascot where she was desperately disappointing – finishing eighth of nine runners in the Ribblesdale Stakes. A runners-up spot in the Irish Oaks eased concerns, but fourth in the Blandford Stakes – three days before a scheduled appearance at Knavesmire – had only served to reinforce doubts. But by the end of the week, both Condessa and the Yorkshire Oaks would be firmly in the headlines.

***

ONE name stands out above all others. One man has made the Musidora Stakes his own. Henry Cecil. The master of Warren Place has won the race an astonishing nine times and written the names of some of racing's greatest fillies into its history book.

In the late 1980s and early 90s there was virtually no one to touch him in York's Oaks trial. At his height, he won it seven times in 12 years. But his influence over the race continues right up to the present day. Aviate, his Musidora winner in 2010, proved Cecil's ability with fillies had not diminished.

The first came with Fatah Flare in 1985 but his domination of the contest peaked with the performances of three wonderful fillies in the late 1980s. They were Indian Skimmer, Diminuendo and Snow Bride. All three were ridden by the brilliant American rider Steve Cauthen, who was Cecil's stable jockey, and owned by the Dubai royal Sheikh Mohammed who was yet to establish his formidable Godolphin operation in the United Arab Emirates and at Newmarket. Indian Skimmer came along during former York clerk of the course John Smith's first season at the helm on Knavesmire in 1987.

'The horses that came that year were astonishing,' he says. 'The dream was having Indian Skimmer to start off with. Henry Cecil was at the height of his training prowess and I thought she was a lovely filly.'

She certainly was. Bred at the Ashford Stud in Kentucky, the grey with the distinctive white blaze down her face was sired by the influential Storm Bird, who also produced a raft of big race winners after being retired as Britain and Ireland's champion two-year-old. Indian Skimmer, named after a rare bird found in southern Asia, would start the season in the lowest of company but by the end of the campaign would be a Classic champion. Her reintroduction came at Wolverhampton, in a graduation race worth a pittance, and won by ten lengths, before she announced herself at Newmarket in the Pretty Polly Stakes. It was a contest she won without even leaving the bridle. Victory there meant that when she came to York and the Musidora next, the bookmakers were ready for her.

You would have had to put two pounds on to get a pound back – such was the confidence behind Cecil's fabulous filly – that and the fact that only two dared to take her on at Knavesmire. She would not disappoint her backers. Her two opponents were Bourbon Girl, owned by Khalid Abdullah and trained by Barry Hills. She was the ante-post second favourite for the Oaks when she started her campaign in the Musidora. The other was Mountain Memory. As is often the case in small field contests, the race turned out to be something of a sprint. Well down the straight, Indian Skimmer – furthest away from the rail – swept past her two rivals on the outside and left them trailing in her wake. The distinctive grey won at a canter. Four lengths was the official distance over Bourbon Girl, who would go on the following month to finish second at Epsom in the Oaks, but Indian Skimmer had plenty in hand.

In the York aftermath, Cecil moved his filly on to French targets. First came the Prix Saint-Alary at Longchamp where she won by two and a half lengths with the rest of the field well strung out behind her. It was one thing to do that but quite another to achieve an even wider margin victory in the Prix de Diane at Chantilly – the French equivalent of the Oaks. The world was at her feet and, after five races and five victories, it was still only midway through the season. But, with summer yet to hit its height, she was struck down with an injury. A back problem ended her progress and left racing fans wondering whether she would return to fight another day. Cecil, however, had no doubt. Bringing her back into action the following year, she eased her way into the campaign and returned to the track, almost a year after she had last been seen on it, in the Brigadier Gerard Stakes at Sandown at the end of May. Cecil, who would later say Indian Skimmer was one of the best he had ever trained, watched as she finished third.

Maybe it was early rustiness, maybe she was not at her best, but it would be September before she got off the mark. Fourth in the Eclipse, she was second in the International Stakes at York behind Shady Heights. She actually finished third but Persian Heights, who beat Shady Heights, was judged by the Stewards to have interfered with Indian Skimmer as he moved past and they subsequently promoted her and dropped him to third. On ground that was thought to be too firm, her performance in the International buoyed the spirits. From that point, she would now prove almost unstoppable.

Revenge was gained over Shady Heights in the Phoenix Champion Stakes before the grey then beat Infamy in the Sun Chariot Stakes. But at the Champion Stakes at Newmarket she routed the colts before finishing third to Great Communicator in the Breeders' Cup Turf at Churchill Downs. Retired from racing at the end of the following season – a year which brought victories at the Prix d'Ispahan at Longchamp and the Gordon Richard Stakes at Sandown – Indian Skimmer went to stud.

***

SHE was small, just 15 hands in height. But she caught Sheikh Mohammed's eye. At the Kentucky July Yearling Sales in 1986 at Fasig-Tipton, he personally picked out this daughter of Diesis and forked out $125,000. He called her Diminuendo. In 1988, she was arguably the most popular horse of the year.

We shall see later how she totally dominated the track during that Flat season but, even before she arrived at York for the Musidora Stakes early on in May, she had already marked herself out as a very special talent. Making her debut the previous June, Diminuendo started as she meant to go on when dominating a maiden at Leicester. Looking green, she could even afford to miss the break, and still win easily by ten lengths.

If that effortless victory was merely an indicator of how good she could be, Diminuendo proved herself at headquarters when taking both the Ewar Stud Farm Stakes and, more importantly, the Cherry Hinton Stakes at Newmarket. The latter proved to be the more taxing, as she came up against the Queen Mary Stakes winner Princess Athena. But as the race reached its climax, she cut through the field and won by a length and a half – beating the two-year-old track record in the process.

Her trainer Henry Cecil, conscious of a pedigree which suggested middle-distance trips were her future, stepped Diminuendo up to a mile for her final start of her juvenile season at Ascot in the Fillies' Mile. It was victory once more as she came through with a terrific late burst to win by two lengths. Four outings, four victories. But Diminuendo started the following season in defeat. Twice to be precise. Both came at Newmarket in the Nell Gwyn Stakes and the 1,000 Guineas where she finished second and third respectively. It was hardly a disgrace but it revealed one crucial fact. A mile was no longer enough. Diminuendo required further, and she was to get it at York in the Musidora Stakes.

She took on five rivals and, despite trying a longer distance for the first time, the punters had taken the hint that further would suit her – sending her off the 8-13 favourite. Their money was never in danger. The race did not begin until four furlongs from home, when Diminuendo just cruised to the head of the field. From there, her jockey Steve Cauthen could sit perfectly still in the saddle. In front and speeding away in the space of half a furlong, she was four lengths clear of Asl at the finish. The rest were strung out miles behind.

It was a win which immediately propelled her to the front of Oaks favouritism and she was to put up a breathtaking performance at Epsom.

Snow Bride, meanwhile, also came out of the Kentucky conveyor belt and gave Cecil and Cauthen their third Yorkshire Oaks win on the bounce the following year. She would also win the Oaks but that was a result which would come in the Stewards' room rather than on the track. Snow Bride was given the race after the Epsom winner, Aliysa, tested positive for a banned substance following the contest. In the Musidora, however, there was nothing to stop her.

In a six runner field which included the even money favourite, Pilot, trained by Dick Hern, it was very straightforward for the comparative 4-1 outsider. Cauthen had Snow Bride in front early on, got after her at the three furlong marker, and ran on in the final furlong to win by a length and a half. Pilot, ridden by Willie Carson, tried to hang on to her and challenged as the final furlong drew near. But she quickly tired, edging left, as Snow Bride poured it on all the way to the line.

After Epsom, Snow Bride went on to the Prix Vermeille, finishing fourth, before ending her career, and moving on to stud, with a win in the Princess Royal Stakes at Ascot. Her main contribution in the barn was Lammtarra, the treble Group 1 winning colt who was the Derby, King George VI and Queen Elizabeth Stakes and Arc winner in 1995. She died, aged 23, in 2009.

***

HAVING made his name on the northern circuit with Jimmy FitzGerald and Lynda Ramsden among others, Kieren Fallon was cashing in during 1997. Appointed stable jockey to Henry Cecil at the start of the campaign, the big winners, the best horses, were finally his to command. By the end of the year, he would be Champion Jockey for the first time and his fledgling partnership with Warren Place maestro Cecil paid immediate dividends at York thanks to Reams Of Verse in the Musidora Stakes.

The chestnut was sheer poetry in motion. Foaled in 1994, Reams Of Verse was actually beaten in her first start on the track – a maiden at Newmarket. But at the same course the following month she got off the mark, following up at Doncaster in September with the Group 3 May Hill Stakes and the Fillies' Mile at Ascot a couple of weeks later.

Her three-year-old campaign began at Newmarket and the 1,000 Guineas but she could only finish sixth, the suggestion being that she needed further. So Reams Of Verse came to York for the Musidora and would become the best backed horse of the May Festival. Cecil had given punters a clue that he was serious about the three-year-old. She was his only runner of the day, and they piled in accordingly.

It was calculated that bookies paid out more than £80,000 in major bets alone as Reams Of Verse put on a sensational display. Fallon was up for the first time yet he knew exactly what to do with the 11-10 favourite. Held up early on, in a field of ten which included a Godolphin filly, Entice, who had won her first three races, Fallon sent her ahead half way up the home straight and she bolted clear. Running on strongly is how the race record officially described her winning run to the line. It didn't even begin to do Reams Of Verse justice. Vagabond Chanteuse, who came in second, had been utterly obliterated. She trailed in 11 lengths behind. Reams Of Verse was hardly easing up at the line, travelling as brilliantly at the end as she had when Fallon shook the reins to see what she had in the tank. Half the field had only just finished as Fallon was already steering his victor towards the winner's enclosure.

Cecil's seventh Musidora win since 1985, the filly was immediately installed as the even money favourite for the Oaks. It would be the third time the trainer would complete the Musidora-Oaks double. She did not get the best of passages around Epsom's undulating circuit, being bumped and hampered at the two furlong marker, but the 5-6 favourite was still a length and a half too good for the 33-1 outsider Gazelle Royale I. Her Musidora win might have been brilliant but Reams Of Verse's memories of York would not end fondly, however.

Cecil brought her back that August for the Yorkshire Oaks, for her next run, where she was again the darling of the backers. This time, in a field of eight, she was the 4-7 favourite but there were early signs her return to Knavesmire was not destined to have a happy ending. Fallon took her down to the start early after she messed about in the parade ring and the blistering turn of speed which had characterised her earlier brilliant victories was absent on this occasion. Sent to challenge at the three furlong marker, Reams Of Verse was soon being hard ridden by the soon to be champion Fallon. The game was up before she even reached the final furlong – horse and jockey having to settle for fourth place, more than four lengths behind the winner, My Emma.

Maybe the spark had gone at Epsom. For she did not markedly improve in her final outing on the track – the Sun Chariot Stakes at Newmarket – although, finishing third, she was behind the equally exceptional One So Wonderful, who would win the Juddmonte International at York the following year.

***

KALYPSO KATIE was the Oaks victory that got away for Newmarket trainer Jeremy Noseda. But the Musidora in 2000 was still an important early Group winner for the then fledgling trainer, who had cut his teeth working for John Dunlop, as an assistant to John Gosden and then at Godolphin before setting up on his own at Newmarket in the late 1990s.

'It was a good result that day,' he remembers. 'She came into season the day before the race and I can remember being very anxious but she still won.' The Musidora was only Kalypso Katie's second race, after she had been bought in the spring in a private deal by Michael Tabor. It was slowly run to boot, on fast ground Noseda was sure also would not suit his filly. Mick Kinane was up and it needed all of his experience to get her home in front as the race developed into something of a charge. Prominent and always in touch, the 100-30 chance had to chase 14-1 outsider Lady Upstage, trained by Barry Hills, who put in a game front-running display. She ran on to lead inside the final furlong but, as Lady Upstage tired, was bumped as the line approached. It was a narrow margin of victory. Kalypso Katie won by a head, with the favourite High Walden, another Henry Cecil contender, back in third. Noseda had admitted he had virtually 'given up the ghost' before the Musidora. Now, potentially, he had a top class filly on his hands. But while the Musidora was her day, the Oaks was not – Kalypso Katie having to settle for second behind Love Divine, who won by two lengths.

'She always stands to this day as disappointing because that Musidora was just a prep race for the Oaks (at Epsom) and she came second to Love Divine in the Oaks,' Noseda adds. 'Coincidentally, she's the dam of Sixties Icon (who won the St Leger at York in 2006). It was great day at York, we looked forward to the Oaks and, sadly, she was runner-up. She bled in that race and I always look back and think if she hadn't have run into that sort of problem she could have won that day as well.'

Kalypso Katie ran once more in Europe for Newmarket-based Noseda, finishing fifth in the Irish Oaks, before Tabor switched her to America where she finished up her career and became a successful broodmare. Three years later, Cassis would give Noseda a second Musidora, but the 16-1 outsider was merely a bonus for the trainer. After a maiden win at Lingfield, the Knavesmire victory would be her only other win in 12 starts.

'We came and rolled the dice a little bit,' he explains. 'She had never run further than seven furlongs at the time and I thought she would get the trip but we came not really expecting a lot. They are always fun days, when they win and you are not expecting it to happen really. Any Group race is tough to win and then there is the number of horses

Left: Steve Cauthen rides Reference Point to an easy victory in the Great Voltigeur Stakes in 1987

Right: Snow Bride surges to the Musidora Stakes crown in 1989

Above: Quick Ransom, with Dean McKeown in the saddle, prevails in a tight finish to the 1992 Ebor Handicap

Right: Mr Confusion, ridden by 17-year-old apprentice Ollie Pears, gets home in the 1992 John Smith's Magnet Cup

Below: Rodrigo de Triano takes the glory one more time for Lester Piggott in the International Stakes of 1992

Above: Lochsong bolts clear of Paris House (grey, right) to win the Nunthorpe Stakes in 1993

Below: Hasten to Add (grey horse) succeeds in the Ebor Handicap of 1994

Above: Classic Cliché and Walter Swinburn, left in blue, head Mick Kinane and Annus Mirabilis in the 1995 Dante Stakes. The horse would become a York legend

Above: Coastal Bluff, who dead-heated the Nunthorpe Stakes of 1997, in action

Above: One So Wonderful, right, wins a titanic Juddmonte International from Faithful Son, centre, and Chester House in 1998

Above: Islington, with Kieren Fallon on board, is an easy winner of the Yorkshire Oaks in 2002

Above: Falbrav dominates the
International Stakes of 2003

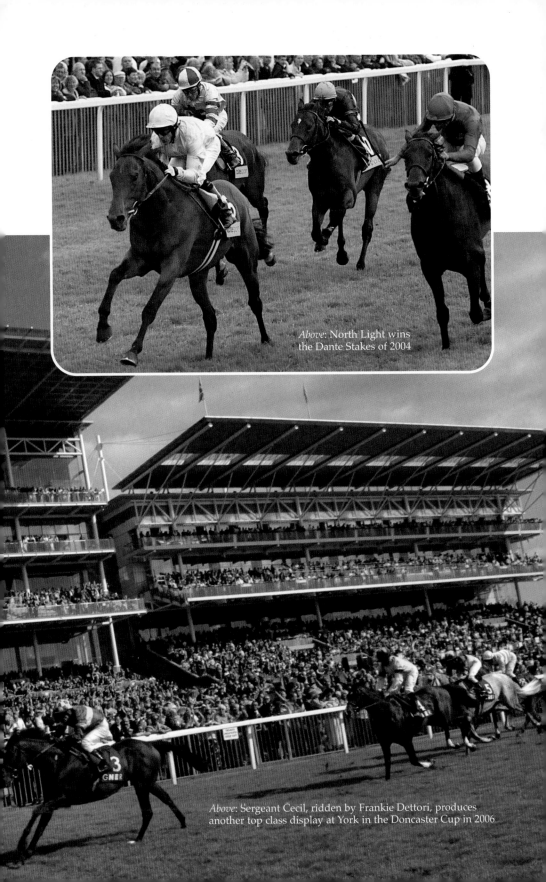

Above: North Light wins the Dante Stakes of 2004

Above: Sergeant Cecil, ridden by Frankie Dettori, produces another top class display at York in the Doncaster Cup in 2006

Above: Jockey Jamie Spencer, left, can't hide his surprise as he, and Glistening, are pipped by Mudawin in the 2006 Ebor Handicap. Picture courtesy of Louise Pollard

Above: Frankie Dettori points the way as Sixties Icon wins the 2006 St Leger Stakes

that we train that are good enough even to compete in those Group races, let alone win them. Those horses that can compete are the smallest minority of the horse population.'

***

ISLINGTON would win greater glories in time for Sir Michael Stoute and Kieren Fallon but it was at York, and the Musidora Stakes of 2002, where her journey would really begin. The daughter of the super-stallion Sadler's Wells and Hellenic, the Yorkshire Oaks winner of 1990, Islington would prove to be one of the world's best. She also loved York, never losing on the track, but it was a racing CV that began slowly.

Her first two outings as a two-year-old the previous year, both maidens at Newmarket, had been nothing special and neither had they got her off the mark. But she opened her account in style at Newbury on her first start the following spring before making her way to York. It had not been a devastating performance at Newbury by any means, a one and a half length win in a maiden, but Stoute saw something in Islington.

'I like her,' he said before his filly came to York. 'She was in a good position at Newbury in a slowly-run race, and she ran on well to win. The Musidora represents a big test for her, but she is a lovely, quality filly who has a little spark about her. By that, I mean she is alert, alive, and on the ball.' She also had a jockey on board with a point to prove.

Fallon had been roundly criticised 12 months earlier when he had failed to win on the race favourite Flight Of Fancy, only finishing fourth to Time Away when it looked like she was running on strongest at the line. He was determined there would be no repeat. Not that it all went completely to plan. Fallon found himself in front three furlongs from the finish after flashing past Half Glance. He had wanted to wait a little longer on the filly who, remember, was only having her fourth ever race. The jockey need not have really worried. Islington found the extra gear Fallon was looking for and moved sweetly away from Alexander Three D and Fraulein. She also stayed on well, holding firm as Spinnette, ridden by Jamie Spencer, launched a late bid for glory. It was as comfortable a victory as a length can be.

'I had to go way too soon and she found a good turn of foot to get me out of jail,' said Fallon. 'But I would have been happier with cover for longer. She hasn't got the brilliance of a Reams Of Verse, but she's a different type. She stays well, goes on any ground and you can ride her anywhere. She's a nosey sort of filly, keeps looking at things and she will have learned a lot from today.'

Epsom was immediately on the agenda, with a raft of bookies making her the favourite after the York win, but Stoute wasn't so sure. 'The 1,000 Guineas was a wonderful trial, better than this, and won by a filly who will be perfectly suited by the step up to a mile and a half,' he said following Islington's win. He was talking of Kazzia and his words would turn out to be eerily prophetic. On testing ground, Godolphin's stamina-packed Kazzia would win the Oaks, with Islington finishing only eighth. But Stoute's filly would have the chance to get her revenge later that season, and York would again be the venue.

***

'THE Musidora Stakes is a very prestigious race,' says Jim Bolger, who first won it in 1981 with Condessa but did so spectacularly again in 2008 with Lush Lashes. 'It merits Group 2 status at least but it's still a Group 3. York is the place to be at that time in May and that Musidora in 2008 was the realisation of promise with more to come. It wasn't the same as winning it the first time but it was still pretty exciting.'

Like Condessa, Lush Lashes was a brilliant filly. 'A few months before she'd won the fillies' Million and she had run previously on bad ground at the Curragh,' recalls Bolger. 'We went to the Guineas and she ran a very good race so we were fairly confident (going to the Musidora) even though it was the first time she had run over a mile and a quarter.'

Going off the 2-1 favourite at York, much of the pre-race talk had still focused on John Gosden's Dar Re Mi. Seven of the eight runners had also been entered at Epsom for the Oaks but it was Lush Lashes who would mercilessly crush her opposition. Following a frantic start which stretched the field, it had still looked anyone's race with a couple of furlongs left to travel. Four fillies were in a line on the track.

But when Lush Lashes, piloted by Kevin Manning, who rode her in all but one of her races, pushed the accelerator she simply stormed away from Cape Amber and Dar Re Mi to take the honours, and the lion's share of a £60,000 prize fund, by five lengths. It was a consummate performance and one which immediately installed her as the Oaks favourite.

'She did it very easily and Kevin was very happy with her. I am delighted she held up the Classic form as well,' said Bolger's travelling head groom Ger Flynn in the post-race aftermath. 'She's a very athletic filly and there's no question of her suitability for Epsom, so we'll just have to see how she is.'

There had been murmurs over whether Lush Lashes would even go to the famous Downs at all – with the Irish Oaks a tempting alternative target for the Irish trainer. In the end, they plumped for Epsom and probably wished they hadn't as Lush Lashes finished only fifth behind Look Here. The Musidora was the only time Bolger's filly would appear at York. After bouncing back to form when winning the Coronation Stakes, and losing by a head to Halfway To Heaven in the Nassau at Glorious Goodwood, Lush Lashes was primed for a huge challenge in the Yorkshire Oaks in August. She would win the race as well, beating old foe Dar Re Mi by a length and a quarter as the evens favourite. But not at York.

The race was held at Newmarket, a hastily rearranged encounter after the Ebor Festival on Knavesmire had been washed out by torrential rain. It was also her highpoint. At the time of writing, Bolger continues to run Lash Lashes, having bought her himself, but her best days seem squarely behind her. After Newmarket, she won her next start in a Group 1 at Leopardstown, but despite continuing to run in the highest company she has not been in the winner's enclosure since.

***

SARISKA was one of the easier Musidora winners in 2009 – and what a winner she turned out to be. When Michael Bell saddled Motivator to Dante, and subsequently, Derby glory, he thought he had been given the horse of a lifetime. But Sariska would become the apple of his eye, and at York she displayed her potential in sensational style.

'I was pretty confident because she had been training well,' says Bell. 'We knew the way she ran in the Fred Darling at Newbury (when finishing fourth on her first appearance as a three-year-old) she was going to appreciate the step up in trip but, again, the form at that time of year – it's a very exciting time because form is evolving. All these fillies have shown potential and are all potential Epsom horses but most bubbles burst by definition. How many actually get there? It is full of expectation and disappointments. So you go to those Classic trials, and it's basically a whole load of bubbles bursting and a few surviving.'

There was never any question that the Sariska bubble would burst on Musidora day, however. From the moment jockey Jamie Spencer led the three-year-old to the front of the field at the two furlong pole the race was over. Comprehensive is an over-used word in sport but there was no other way to describe it. At three and a three quarter lengths, Sariska swept past Star Ruby. She hadn't even been the favourite. That honour had gone to Enticement, owned by The Queen. The punters piled in and the Royal horse went off the 7-4 favourite but could only finish third. Now Bell, who had bypassed the 1,000 Guineas to take Sariska to Knavesmire, had a superstar on his hands. And he knew it.

'I love the filly,' the Newmarket handler cooed with the one and a quarter mile contest confined to the record books. 'She has always been the apple of my eye and she will take a bit of beating hopefully.' The odds compilers thought the same as they immediately slashed the odds on Sariska. From 9-1, she became the 4-1 favourite to win the Oaks at Epsom.

There, she was brilliant again in victory – heading the talented Midday at the line before moving to the Curragh and sweeping to the Irish Oaks. So Sariska returned to York that August looking for an Oaks treble by adding the Yorkshire version to Epsom and Irish wins. But, as we shall see later, the best laid plans do not always come to pass.

***

LIKE its equivalent for colts in the Dante Stakes, the Musidora Stakes represents promise and hope. With a season of big Flat races still ahead, a notable performance in a race like the Musidora can set the tone for the rest of the year. For the new Classic generation who put themselves in the shop window when racing as two-year-olds, it can often be the first real test. Have they improved or have they been overhauled by their rivals? Those that win are riding on the crest of a wave to Epsom just over three weeks later.

While this chapter has focused mainly on those May York winners that went on to Oaks glory, they are by no means the only brilliant horses to have tasted Musidora success. In The Groove, who won the race in 1990, would land both the Irish 1,000 Guineas and the Juddmonte International – among other big race successes – while Pure Grain, five years later, claimed both the Irish Oaks and the Yorkshire Oaks following the stepping stone of Knavesmire in the springtime. The point is the Musidora produces champions. It is a race deserving of its Classic pedigree.

THE YORKSHIRE CUP

IT felt like a real clash of the titans. An unstoppable force against an immovable object. A race which revealed why the Yorkshire Cup can focus the thoroughbred world round a mile and six furlongs of the Knavesmire track.

Stayers always capture the imagination. Perhaps it is because their careers are not just a flash in the pan. A Derby winner is fleeting. He arrives, he wins, he almost invariably goes off to stud. Stayers endure. We learn their characters, their foibles, their strengths and weaknesses. We get to know them. In the same way that top class National Hunt horses, by their very longevity, bury their way into the psyche of the racing public so those thoroughbreds who compete over the longer Flat distances do the same. Zindabad and Persian Punch were two such animals.

'I see Zindabad in the same group as Bandari and Gateman – that is, fractionally short of top class,' says his trainer Mark Johnston, the man behind the never ending factory of winners at Middleham's Kingsley House. 'That prolongs their career in many ways. They are worth more to race than going to stud. He was a great horse.'

Persian Punch was already a legend. David Elsworth's cult hero had bagged a host of big Group race triumphs including two Lonsdale

Cups at York, the Goodwood Cup, the Jockey Club Cup and the Prix Lucien Barriere at Deauville. He had won the Cartier Award the previous year as the country's top stayer – an award he would win again in 2003. But it was about more than just victories with his horse.

Persian Punch had the rare distinction of being a legend in his own lifetime. He had his own website. He had his own fan club and, by the time he came to York to compete in the Yorkshire Cup of 2002, he was undoubtedly the most popular Flat horse in training. Attitude was the key. Persian Punch never shirked a fight. When the pressure was on, when it looked like – this time – he had to be beaten, the horse somehow found a way to win. He was a phenomenally difficult horse to pass. With an iron will, nothing could bend the horse who got the nod in an astonishing seven photo finishes.

Zindabad was hardly lacking in ability either. A 'great stamp of a horse,' according to Johnston, Zindabad had arrived at Middleham after starting his career with Ben Hanbury. Hanbury had won a Group race with him, the Winter Hill Stakes at Windsor in 1999, and after winning a handicap at Newmarket on his first start for his new handler in May 2001, he also picked up Listed race success at Leicester. A Group 3 at Newbury, the John Porter Stakes, had been won – by a neck – the following year and Johnston brought his horse to York as the favourite for the Yorkshire Cup.

In the race's 70th contest, it would turn out to be the May Festival's best of the week. The field was select. Seven horses who had won a total of 51 races between them. Zindabad's only question mark was the distance. 'I was assessing whether we needed to change his trip,' says Johnston on the decision to take his charge over a mile and three quarters for the first time. Nevertheless, despite Persian Punch's fearsome record, and indomitable character, Zindabad was sent off the 2-1 favourite. His rival was narrowly behind at 5-2.

Yorkshire connections had to have been at play. Trained in the county, the horse was also ridden by another adopted Yorkshireman, Sheriff Hutton-based Kevin Darley. Both trainer and jockey knew Persian Punch would lead from the front, trying to grind his rivals into the York turf. As it turned out, Zindabad tracked the leaders early on. But there had been no instructions from Johnston to keep the horse close to the main danger. Leading rides, and horses being kept up with

71

the pace, are a feature of the way the Scot's runners routinely take on the competition.

But Johnston explains: 'I have never given the instructions for a jockey to lead. I think it is ludicrous that we are told by the British Horseracing Authority we are supposed to give instructions telling jockeys where to be in the field. How can you tell a jockey where to be in the field when you don't know how fast the others are going to go? I do tell them I don't want any extreme restraint. I want the horse to be able to bowl along in a style where it is comfortable – no pushing or pulling. That just happens to be up front.'

Darley can count himself fortunate that Zindabad chose to be just a step or two behind Persian Punch in the early stages. For when the two drew clear, after Persian Punch had been shaken up with fully three quarters of a mile still to travel, the jockey found out what it entailed to beat the hardy warrior. Darley launched his effort into the straight and it took Zindabad half the length of York's long home run just to get on level terms with his rival. This time, on this rare occasion, Persian Punch could not keep the legs moving. But as Zindabad moved past, and Elsworth's hero faded into a fourth place finish, one more challenge still awaited. Boreas, the mount of Jamie Spencer and a York Lonsdale Cup winner for trainer Luca Cumani later that year, made a late bid to rob Johnston of the prize. Zindabad, showing some of the dogged resistance of the champion he had just bested, kept on to his task and came through to win by a length and a half.

In the parade ring afterwards, Johnston was well aware of what his horse had just achieved. 'There aren't many much tougher than Persian Punch and sticking close behind him today there was always the risk of playing into the hands of horses coming from behind,' he said. 'But as it turned out the battle between the two of them had put paid to all the others.'

Amazingly, despite their popularity and their stout will, neither Zindabad nor Persian Punch ever won a Group 1 race. Only Mr Dinos, who beat him in the Ascot Gold Cup, denied Persian Punch the Stayers Triple Crown the following year – the Goodwood and Doncaster Cups collected in a phenomenal year given the horse was now ten. His life would end tragically, however. Collapsing at the end of the Sagaro Stakes at Ascot in April 2004, Persian Punch died at the age of 11. A life-size bronze at Newmarket, where he celebrated five wins, marks his achievements.

Zindabad won just once more. But what a win. At Royal Ascot, Johnston's favourite hunting ground, he dropped back to a mile and a half and won the Group 2 Hardwicke Stakes. Fourth in the Yorkshire Cup the following year in a bid to defend his title, he was third to Bollin Eric – a St Leger winner – in the Lonsdale Stakes at that year's Ebor Festival. His final race, the Doncaster Cup, would see him finish fourth – 12 and a half lengths behind Persian Punch. But, for one day at York, it was Zindabad who had been the king.

***

NOW the first of the major stayers' cup events of the Flat season, the Yorkshire Cup, run on the final day of the May meeting, is an intriguing clash of the generations for those horses blessed with more stamina than speed. Established stars take on emerging talent each year at York, with the race providing form-lines as to who might go on to dominate the other top-class staying tests at Royal Ascot (the Gold Cup), the Goodwood Cup, back at York in the Lonsdale Cup in August, and finally the Doncaster Cup during the St Leger meeting.

The Yorkshire Cup is a revival race – recreating a contest which had originally seen members of the York Union Hunt Club come together in 1835 and give a Gold Cup for horses to compete over two miles. Won that year by Finesse, ridden by a Captain Williams and trained by Captain W.C. Smith, the Gold Cup was a much sought after trophy for a while, but faded out of favour long before the York Union Hunt Club ceased to exist in 1856.

The modern version had been talked about for some time prior to the decision to bring it back in 1926, one of the main aims being to persuade trainers to run their horses over longer distances. Like its predecessor, it was to be run over two miles, and replaced the Rockingham Handicap. The sweetener for handlers would be a prize purse of £1,000. As it turned out, those with an interest in watching history repeat itself would have to wait a further 12 months.

That year's spring meeting at York was cancelled because of the General Strike so it wasn't until 1927 that the race was given its rebirth.

The new incarnation was won by the gelding Templestowe, a 3-1 joint-favourite owned by Colonel Hugh Stobart, who was a steward at York and lived at nearby Middlethorpe Hall. The other fancied horse, Glommen, ridden by Fred Winter, was unplaced.

Supporters of the new race only needed to wait another year for the first thrilling finish when Royal Pom, St Mary's Kirk and Finglass were all separated by only heads. But these early runners were not particularly distinguished. Indeed, perhaps the most well-known was the 1930 victor The Bastard who remains in the memory only for his mischievous name rather than his achievements in the race. His moniker amused punters no end. The name, ironically, did actually come about as a result of his ancestry. The Bastard was out of Swynford, with Swynford being by John O'Gaunt. It recalled the 14th Century affair between the commoner Katherine Swynford and John of Gaunt, the son of Edward III. Their union, which produced four illegitimate children, laid the way for the coming of the House of Tudor. Swynford's great-granddaughter was Margaret Beaufort – mother of Henry VII. The Bastard was exported to Australia where his name was considered a little too coarse for taste even for the Aussies. He was renamed The Buzzard.

The Yorkshire Cup's leading trainer, meanwhile, struck his opening blow the following year. His name has remained at the summit for 46 years. Cecil Boyd-Rochfort won the contest for the first time with The Scout II in 1931 and would claim it another six times, ending with Apprentice in 1965. We will be hearing a lot of its leading rider who, with eight victories, is Lester Piggott.

***

PIGGOTT rode Pandofell, whose Yorkshire Cup win of 1961 pales compared to the challenges the horse overcame that year to be a success. He was famously the victim of the doping gangs that were the scourge of racing during the 1950s and 1960s.

The 'nobblers' were killing the image of the sport. Pinturoschio, the Derby favourite in 1961, was got at twice – once before the Dante Stakes at York and again before the Epsom Classic, after which he never ran again. Pandofell wasn't quite so unfortunate but, after winning the Yorkshire Cup and the Ascot Gold Cup the following month, he was found bleeding and confused in his box just hours before he was due to run as a hot favourite in the Sunninghill Park Stakes at Ascot. Pandofell's story had a happy ending. He recovered to win the Doncaster Cup. Many others, however, never recaptured their form.

Piggott also rode Aunt Edith, whose victory in 1966 was notable for two things. The first was that she would become the first filly to win the King George VI and Queen Elizabeth Stakes at Ascot. The second was that the year of England's World Cup win at Wembley was also the first time the Yorkshire Cup was run at its present length. After Apprentice's victory 12 months earlier, two furlongs were shaved off the contest to make it a mile and three quarters.

***

WHILE you couldn't be so cruel as to call them one-hit wonders, the 1970s were marked by a series of horses whose career highlight was undoubtedly the Yorkshire Cup.

The likes of Alto Volante, around the start of the decade, and Pragmatic, at the end, were symptomatic of the way big stayers' events were being won, and perhaps perceived, in the racing world. Timeform's *Racehorses of 1978*, when recounting Smuggler's success in the Yorkshire Cup that year, tells the story of how Lord Porchester, then chairman of the Jockey Club Flat race Pattern committee no less, was asked whether his five-year-old would move on to the Ascot Gold Cup – the doyen of staying events. According to Timeform, he replied the horse had not even been entered. 'It even devalues a horse to enter him,' he added.

The point he was making, albeit in a particularly pompous way, was that to admit your horse was a stayer was to almost kill his prospects at stud. What breeders wanted, what owners wanted – and little has really changed in this respect – was a Derby winner. They wanted a machine over a mile and a half, not a mile and three quarters. Two furlongs might not seem too much but it meant pounds and pence in the competitive bloodstock world.

Timeform considered that British staying was in decline and they even feared for the 'extinction' of the top-class stayer unless 'action is taken to restore the standard of long-distance races to a proper level'. What they meant was more Pattern races and better prize pots. When you look at the kind of horse that was winning the Yorkshire Cup back in the 70s, compared with animals like Kayf Tara and Sergeant Cecil in the modern era, you have to think they had a very good point.

Alto Volante, in 1971, was barely seen again, while Knockroe, the 1972 victor, was notable more for being a quirky animal who seemed to hate having other horses around him. He would be kept well back off the pace and then brought through wide in the straight in a bid to sweep home to victory. He had such a turn of foot that Lester Piggott, who rode him in the Yorkshire Cup, didn't even feel the need to get a move on until two and a half furlongs from home – where he then swept forward with such speed that he had the lead and could even afford to slow down a furlong from home. Good, he won the Cumberland Lodge Stakes and the Jockey Club Stakes, he was hardly top class.

Knockroe was part and parcel of a rather ordinary bunch. Bruni, in 1976 however, was among the better ones. He was a St Leger winner, having trounced the field at Doncaster, and he was an impressive Yorkshire Cup victor. But he was still indicative of the stayers' snub. Trained by Ryan Price, Bruni would also largely neglect the 'Cup' route, his Findon-based handler preferring to test him against top middle-distance horses. They were the races where the money was. At York, however, the now four-year-old was masterful. Naturally, Lester Piggott was the man for the job. The grey horse won effortlessly.

Despite giving weight to all of his rivals, horses like Mr Bigmore and Sea Anchor – who would prove to be very good in their own right – were treated with disdain. At the finish, Piggott could stay absolutely still in the saddle – no urging, no whip, no driving – and still win by half a dozen lengths as his two major rivals frantically tried to make any sort of impression.

Bruni went on to win the Cumberland Lodge Stakes at Ascot in similar fashion and would surely have taken some of the major Cup prizes had he actually run in any of them. But rather than try the stayers' events at Ascot, Goodwood and York in the Lonsdale, he instead took on the Hardwicke Stakes, the King George VI and Queen

Elizabeth Stakes and the Prix de l'Arc de Triomphe. Despite performing well, he won none of them – developing, by the time it came to Longchamp in October, an aversion to leaving the starting stalls that threatened to prove insurmountable.

The Arc was his last contest in Europe. He was subsequently sent to America to race and his 'what if' career adequately sums up the fortunes of the Yorkshire Cup in the days of disco. But Bruni's victory also had one other effect, it began to forge a lasting link between the Yorkshire Cup and the St Leger.

Moon Madness had been a St Leger victor before winning the Yorkshire Cup in 1988 while Moonax would also achieve this notable double – winning on Town Moor for Barry Hills before the Sheikh Mohammed-owned horse moved to Godolphin to win on Knavesmire the following year. That was the start of a particularly sharp trend for those who followed the fortunes of the Crown Prince of Dubai.

In the last decade and a half, five winners have come from the UAE-based stable, including Mamool and Classic Cliché. Moonax, Marienbard and Kayf Tara we will see more of shortly.

***

ARDROSS, in some 80 renewals of the Yorkshire Cup, is the only horse to have won the race twice – in 1981 and 1982. He won a staggering 13 Pattern races and 14 of his 24 starts – triumphs which also included the Ascot Gold Cup (twice) and the Doncaster Cup.

Ardross was initially trained by Paddy Prendergast but, on his death, went to Newmarket and Henry Cecil. Foaled in 1976, the colt, bred by Prendergast for his American owner Elisabeth Ireland Poe, ran only three times as a three-year-old, winning the second of those over a mile and a half. He was sired by Run The Gauntlet, a top class horse who had won the Washington International as a three-year-old.

While Ardross had not shown the same level of ability at the same age, he would step up considerably the following year. Winning twice in seven runs, his season culminated with victory in the Jockey Club Cup at Newmarket. Were it not for Le Moss, he would have captured considerably more silverware that year as well. Trained by Henry Cecil who, as we have already seen would soon add Ardross to his stable, the pair would enthral spectators in a battle of wills throughout the 1980 campaign. Fighting it out in the major cup races – the Ascot Gold Cup, the Goodwood Cup and the Doncaster Cup, a total distance of around a length separated the two super stayers. But Le Moss won them all. Ardross stayed in training, Le Moss did not – retiring at the climax of a quite glorious year.

With Prendergast's death following in the close season, Ardross went to Cecil after being bought by Charles AB St George, and was about to feel the benefit of the man who had campaigned his nemesis Le Moss so successfully. Cecil mapped out a similar schedule. It was the Cup races that were to focus his attention. So Ardross's first race for his new trainer, in 1981, would be at York and the Yorkshire Cup.

That meant quite a late start for the horse but, on Knavesmire, up against horses who'd had the benefit of a run – usually an important factor in early season contests – Ardross shrugged off any worries that he would not be able to perform at his very best. There is a photograph of the race which shows just how comfortable it was. At the extreme left of the frame is Ardross, Piggott tightly holding the reins and guiding the horse to the line. The whip is in his hand but he is not using it. He doesn't need to. At the other end of the shot is the nearest challenger, Nicholas Bill, some three lengths adrift.

What made the display perhaps more impressive was not just that Ardross might have needed the run. It was that at the business end of the race, when his challengers might have expected to exploit a perceived lack of fitness, Piggott's mount found a turn of foot which actually took him further ahead. It was the start of a golden time for the five-year-old. The Gold Cup at Ascot was soon added and, at 2-9 on, he became the shortest priced favourite to win the Goodwood Cup since Tiberius in 1935. He beat Castle Keep in the Geoffrey Freer Stakes at Newbury but was beaten by Gold River in the Prix de l'Arc de Triomphe. But Ardross was not going to end the season on a low.

Taking revenge over Gold River, he returned to Longchamp and landed the Prix Royal-Oak, writing another record in the book in the process – the first older horse to win that race. The conditions had been changed to make it an open-aged event two years previously. Cecil made the decision to keep him in training and campaign him, in similar fashion, as a six-year-old. That meant a return to Knavesmire and the aim of becoming the first horse to win the Yorkshire Cup twice. This time he enjoyed a prep race, winning the Jockey Club Stakes at Newmarket by a narrow margin in April. But Ardross was now a marked man at York. His achievements the year before meant he had to give weight to all of his rivals, making his mission ever more difficult.

Age may also have made the horse a little harder to get into gear. Once he got moving, he still flew, still had the turn of pace. But Piggott was finding that it was taking a longer to get Ardross fully wound up. And sometimes, even when he did, the horse began to wonder if the race was over and could idle. Cecil, however, had a slightly different view.

'Cecil said after the Yorkshire Cup that both the horse and jockey had been lazy,' reported the *Yorkshire Evening Press* the following day, 'but once Ardross had hit the front a furlong out, the race was over.' If a picture told a story the first time, it revealed a quite different one the second. This time Piggott is hard at work, his whip extended and is driving Ardross to the finish – a length the verdict over Little Wolf. Given that, Piggott may have felt a bit hard done by at the 'lazy' jibe. Ardross was the middle leg of a York treble for him that day. A trio which had also included Simply Great winning the Dante.

It completed a memorable week for the legendary jockey – he had also notched up a hat-trick on the Wednesday. And it had also given him his third consecutive win in the Yorkshire Cup, Ardross's two triumphs adding to the victory of Noble Saint in 1980. Ardross, not that he needed to prove it, had once again shown his stamina and class. But he was not just a top class stayer, however. He could mix it up over the middle distances as well.

In the final race of his career, he lost by just a head to Akiyda in the Arc at Longchamp. It may have been a defeat, but the performance still enhanced what had been a marvellous career. It followed a season which had seen Ardross smash a host of French challengers in the Gold Cup at Ascot and give Piggott his 4,000th British winner in the Geoffrey Freer back at Newbury as well as winning the Doncaster Cup.

'He was a hell of a horse, a hell of a stayer who almost won the Arc,' says former *Daily Mirror* racing writer Tim Richards. 'I think he should have won the Arc. He was a stayer with a turn of foot. He won Gold

Cups and, just getting beaten in that Arc, he had to have an unusual amount of speed. He wasn't iconic but he was a well loved horse. He was going for a few years and had some cracking races in top contests. I think he had something to do with rejuvenating the staying discipline.'

Ardross died at the age of 18 of a heart attack at stud in Bedfordshire. The best of his progeny included the Champion Hurdle winner Alderbrook.

***

THE 80s marched on in a haze of eye-liner, shoulder pads and, inevitably given the excess of the era, a crashing financial depression. On the York track, Line Slinger was a hugely popular winner in 1983, providing North Yorkshire jockey Edward Hide with a 33-1 surprise victor when confounding expectations to virtually make all for Malton's Bill Elsey.

Dick Hern picked up the last of his four wins in the contest the following year as Band followed Buoy (1974), Riboson (1975) and Smuggler (1978) to Yorkshire Cup glory. Eastern Mystic, originally bought by Luca Cumani for 4,000 guineas for his wife to ride in Ladies' races, exceeded expectations when winning in 1986, while one of the better victors of the era was Moon Madness, who took the prize in 1988 for Pat Eddery and John Dunlop.

It crowned the final season on the track for the then five-year-old, who had won the St Leger two years previously. The 6-5 favourite was held up before coming through in the straight and winning by a length and a half from Lake Erie. Moon Madness didn't win again that year, but added to his reputation with an impressive performance in the Coronation Cup at Epsom, where he was a close third to Triptych and Infamy, and a podium spot in the Hardwicke Stakes at Royal Ascot.

***

MOONAX, who won the Yorkshire Cup in 1995, was the longest priced winner of the St Leger for more than 70 years. Double Trigger, later to become a legendary stayer, was among his victims that day as the

Barry Hills-trained horse sprang a 40-1 surprise in September 1994 on Town Moor.

Sired by the Benson & Hedges Gold Cup winner, Caerleon, who was himself a son of Nijinsky, the Godolphin-trained Moonax had impeccable breeding. His three-year-old season, capped by the St Leger, also brought the Prix Royal-Oak at Longchamp – making him the first horse ever to complete that notable double. York, which kicked off his four-year-old season, proved to be the only other highpoint of his career.

Sent off an 11-4 favourite, Moonax had a brief tussle with Parthian Springs with about three furlongs left to travel. But once the market leader asserted with 200 yards left there was no doubting the winner. Now it was only a matter of distance, the tale of the tape at the end registering a length and a quarter victory. It might sound surprising given his Classic season form of the previous year but, once the Yorkshire Cup was out of the way, Moonax won just once more – and a conditions race at Haydock is surely not the type of contest worthy of a St Leger victor.

That doesn't quite tell the whole story, however. Moonax was a horse capable of both brilliance and mediocrity. Regardless of his Yorkshire Cup success, he is perhaps more famous for biting Always Earnest – turning his head to grab a mouthful a few yards from the post – in the Prix du Cadran at Longchamp in September 1995. Sue Montgomery, the racing writer for the *Independent*, labelled him 'perhaps the world's naughtiest horse' when, in the same race the following year, he tried to lunge back into the stable yard a furlong from home before again finishing second.

Moonax was succeeded by another Godolphin winner, and a higher class of horse altogether, in Classic Cliché. Having started out with Henry Cecil before moving to Dubai in the winter of his juvenile year, Saeed bin Suroor's prodigy actually won the Dante Stakes in his three-year-old year but it was Town Moor, and not Epsom, which was his aim. There, at the world's oldest Classic race, Frankie Dettori secured his 1,000th winner on the 100-30 favourite – beating Minds Music, ironically trained by Cecil, by three and a half lengths.

Spending the winter in the warmth of Dubai, Godolphin set their targets on Knavesmire, and the Yorkshire Cup, for their newest staying hope. Strategic Choice, the 13-8 favourite, was the victim, mowed down by a length and a half as the Dubai camp kept their stranglehold on York's early season long-distance prize. It was remarkably straightforward. Tracking the leaders, Classic Cliché's rider, Mick Kinane, wound up the pace with half a mile to travel, led with two furlongs left, and stayed on strongly to the finish. Strategic Choice didn't get close.

Victory in the Gold Cup at Ascot came next, before Classic Cliché settled for runners-up spot in the King George VI and Queen Elizabeth Stakes, followed by a disappointing display in the Arc and another winter of rest in the Middle East. It was back to York in 1996, but that triumph of 12 months previously could not be reproduced. Sent off the hot even money favourite, Classic Cliché was travelling so badly by the end of the race that Sheikh Mohammed actually closed down the Godolphin operation for several weeks afterwards amid fears the horse's poor performance was indicative of a wider problem in the yard. As Celeric produced another impressive York performance, Classic Cliché finished tailed off at the back of the field – some 20 lengths behind the winner. It was a sad farewell to Knavesmire.

His career would end on a relative high, with successive seconds in the Gold Cup, to Celeric again, and to Double Trigger in the Goodwood Cup along with a win at Deauville before he was retired at the end of the 1997 season. Celeric's win, meanwhile, had come in one of the Yorkshire Cup's most thrilling finishes. He had an interesting quirk for a stayer. Rather than grind his rivals down with a monotonous gallop, Celeric could sweep to the front with a prodigious turn of speed. It was a move which could devastate a tired field and it was part of what made him one of the most popular horses in training. With the horse invariably held up for a late run, it also meant the final furlong or two were always prime-time viewing for the racing fan. There was anticipation.

You didn't expect to see Celeric until very late on and when you did he'd be cutting down his rivals. York was also his own personal playground. Six times the horse, trained for most of those victories by David Morley before moving to John Dunlop on his death in 1998, would succeed on Knavesmire. As you would expect, for former clerk of the course John Smith, Celeric provides very special memories. But not in the Yorkshire Cup.

'With the benefit of hindsight it was an incredible race,' he remembers. 'Celeric won a number of races here and went on to win a Gold Cup at Ascot. He was a good horse and provided many fine spectacles. If you go back to 1995, it was the Batley's Cash & Carry Handicap in September over a mile and three quarters. There was nothing special about the handicap but the horse that won was Celeric – and he beat Istabraq by a head. That was a fantastic race. It was just a humble handicap and to have two horses like that, who went on to what they achieved, was something special.' Istabraq, of course, would win the Champion Hurdle three years in a row between 1998 and 2000.

When Celeric competed in the Yorkshire Cup in 1997, he had already won four times at the track and had taken a Lonsdale Stakes at the Ebor Festival the previous August. He had the best jockeys for partners – Willie Carson, Frankie Dettori and Richard Hills among those to have had the leg up. Pat Eddery was his pilot that May on Knavesmire – solidifying an association which would see him ride Celeric throughout much of the rest of his career.

As Classic Cliché led, toiled and was eased with his trainer none the wiser, Celeric took a familiar route. Held up, Eddery squeezed through in the final furlong in pursuit of Mons, who had tracked the leaders and now found himself in front. The two went toe-to-toe down that last 150 yards of the home straight and Celeric showed he didn't just have pace but a heart of granite as well. It was Mons who broke first, wandering with the tiredness and ceding the initiative. But he too had a gritty resolve also and, with rider Jason Weaver urging, rallied fast as the ground ran out. The pair flashed past the post together. The verdict was a mere short head in Celeric's favour.

After winning the Gold Cup at Ascot, Classic Cliché again a victim, Celeric did not win for nearly two years before breaking his duck back in Berkshire in the Sagaro Stakes. But he had another big result in him, one last big pay day, and it came – as you would expect – at his favourite track. With John Dunlop guiding the path of the now seven-year-old, Celeric won a second Lonsdale Stakes when seeing off Arctic Owl by a length. He actually soldiered on for another season but, when he finished seventh of eight in the 2000 Yorkshire Cup, the game was virtually up. The champion stayer had won 13 races in a long, active career and, with six of them having come on Knavesmire, he'll be forever etched into the York annals of great horses.

***

HE was a force to be reckoned with. Over extreme trips, the longer the better, Kayf Tara was a durable performer and a fierce galloper. With eight Pattern race victories, he has won the most of any Godolphin horse and he met and beat the best.

Double Trigger, arguably one of the best stayers of the late 20th Century, was just one of his notable scalps. He was named the top European stayer three years in a row from 1998. But for injury, which cruelly robbed him of the chance to compete in the Melbourne Cup, and which finished his career before he was to compete over a middle distance in the King George VI and Queen Elizabeth Stakes at Ascot, he would surely have been elevated into the highest class. As it was, he won two Gold Cups at the Berkshire track, two Irish St Legers, a Goodwood Cup and, of course, the Yorkshire Cup.

Foaled in 1994, he was a son of Sadler's Wells, the 2,000 Guineas winner of 1984 who, as a stallion, has underpinned the mighty Coolmore breeding operation and has proved himself to be the most influential European stallion of the modern era. Originally trained by Sir Michael Stoute, Kayf Tara, like so many of the stayers we have seen, was not introduced to the racecourse until his three-year-old season. He lost his maiden tag over a mile and a quarter at Ascot and, that winter, was transferred to Godolphin. A winner at Haydock on his first appearance for new trainer Saeed bin Suroor in May 1998, he was third, two lengths behind Persian Punch, in the Henry II Stakes at Sandown before beating Double Trigger by a neck in the Ascot Gold Cup.

Mark Johnston's formidable horse got revenge at Glorious Goodwood but, despite then losing in France, Kayf Tara was on an upward curve – beating Silver Patriarch to take the Irish St Leger. York punters had to be patient to get their chance to see racing's newest staying star.

Godolphin dodged the Yorkshire Cup in 1999 – the horse was not ready when the May meeting came around – and it was not until 12 months later that Kayf Tara finally graced Knavesmire. By then, he had added four more Group races to his racing record, the Prix Vicomtesse Viger at Longchamp, the Goodwood Cup, the Prix Kergorlay and another Irish St Leger by a crushing eight lengths – while also finishing third in his bid to defend the Gold Cup at Ascot.

The Melbourne Cup had been the next target but, while in Australia preparing for the race, the five-year-old was ruled out after damaging a ligament in his near-fore. So northern racing fans will have been ever more grateful when, having made a complete recovery, Kayf Tara finally made a visit to York in May 2000. For the warm favourite, a 15-8 shot, it would be a winning appearance. But it looked anything but straightforward.

Persian Punch was among seven rivals but, on slippery ground officially classed as firm, David Elsworth's horse stumbled at the start and never really got going – eased up with fully two furlongs still left to travel. There was Celeric as well. But the 9-2 shot could not feature either – the ground being jockey Pat Eddery's excuse when he could only finish seventh, having never got close to the front of the field. With his regular partner Frankie Dettori in the saddle, Kayf Tara had no need to blame the racing surface. Tracking the leading Kahtan and Sinon at first, Dettori waited before taking his mount into the lead over two furlongs out and pushing him to the finishing line. They had four lengths over Barry Hills' Rainbow Ways at the post, and Churlish Charm was a further length and three quarters behind. The rest were strung out, beaten, down the York straight. Any fears that Kayf Tara had not recovered from his Melbourne problems had been eradicated.

Dettori was so delighted, he pulled out his trademark flying dismount in the winner's enclosure. A move which, at that time, was reserved for Group 1 winners only. He rated the winner to be 'as good as ever'. Godolphin racing manager Simon Crisford added: 'The injury he sustained in Australia was severe, but he's a special horse with a great will to win.' The victory took Kayf Tara's career earnings through the half-million pound barrier. And there was one last glory day for the Godolphin performer.

Back at Ascot in the Gold Cup, Kayf Tara beat Fry Cry by a head and survived a 15-minute Stewards' inquiry before finally being awarded the spoils. No one knew it then but it was the final act. A recurrence of his injury was to bring his career to an end. Retired in July 2000, Godolphin's top stayer naturally proved popular at stud. Standing at Overbury Stud, in Worcestershire, Kayf Tara continues to be in demand. His offspring have included Kayf Aramis, Carruthers, Mad Max and Kornati Kid. He is currently one of Britain's leading National Hunt stallions.

***

RAIN has been the scourge of York Racecourse in recent years. Torrential downpours forced the cancellation of the entire Ebor Festival in 2008. But without precious precipitation, Marienbard may not have written his name into Yorkshire Cup folklore in 2001.

The Godolphin horse was something of a late developer, despite his excellent breeding. Out of the mare Marienbad, his sire was Caerleon – the French champion three-year-old and the winner of York's Juddmonte International in 1983. Trained by Saeed bin Suroor, he was not seen out on the track until he was a three-year-old in 2000 but he quickly made up for lost time, winning at Leicester and Windsor before taking a Listed race at Haydock. Runner-up in the Great Voltigeur Stakes to Air Marshall, Marienbard was sixth in the St Leger and second in his final start of the season in the Perpetual Stakes at Newbury.

It was a solid first year, but it hardly gave much of an inkling of what was to come. The Yorkshire Cup, the first start of his four-year-old campaign, would prove to be the breakthrough. Had it not rained on the day, however, Marienbard might well have been pulled out of the mile and three quarter contest. As it was, he provided a notable success for the Godolphin operation and began his ascent to superstar status. The Dubai training empire needed it as well.

'Struggling' is always a relative term when it comes to Sheikh Mohammed's racing operation but, on the morning of the Yorkshire Cup in mid May, Godolphin had yet to win a race in Britain since returning from wintering in Dubai. Marienbard, ridden at York by stable jockey Frankie Dettori, was the 5-1 second favourite for the Knavesmire staying showpiece. It was Sir Michael Stoute's Dalampour, the Queen's Vase winner at Royal Ascot the previous year, who was sent off the short priced 11-8 market leader. It didn't work out for Stoute's charge but the touch of rain, which softened the firm York track ever so slightly, appeared to make all the difference for

Marienbard. Held up by Dettori in the early stages as the John Dunlop-trained 25-1 outsider Samsaam led the way, it was a classic waiting ride from the charismatic Italian rider. He may have been shaken up with half a mile left to travel but not until two furlongs from home was Marienbard seriously asked a question. Samsaam belied his big odds, keeping on well to the line. But Dettori's mount headed the long-time leader a furlong from the finish and squeezed home to a length victory. Breakthrough for Godolphin and breakthrough for Marienbard – his first big race success. 'This is a horse with a good future', said Godolphin racing manager Simon Crisford in the aftermath.

It was thought that future would lie in big cup races, with Royal Ascot's Gold Cup at the top of the list. But Marienbard, frustratingly, would draw a blank for the rest of the campaign – bin Suroor having to settle for placed finishes in the Prix Lucien Barriere and the Irish St Leger. It was as a five-year-old that the talent the horse showed at York that day fully blossomed. In the final three races of his career, Marienbard scooped a hat-trick and what a trio it was. Three consecutive Group 1 races. The Deutschland-Preis and the Grosser Preis von Baden in Germany were topped off by one of the world's top contests – the Prix de l'Arc de Triomphe.

With a three-quarter length win over Sulamani and High Chaparral, Marienbard was instantly catapulted into the status of stand-out horse. Stud duty in Japan awaited Marienbard after his Arc farewell. He may have started slowly, but what a way to finish.

***

MILLENARY lived up to his name when winning the St Leger at the turn of the century. But who could have thought he would still be winning races at York half a decade later?

Until Sergeant Cecil took his crown, Millenary had the distinction of being the Yorkshire Cup's oldest winner. Where four and five-year-olds have dominated, having won 25 of the renewals since 1979, Millenary did it at seven. Despite his advanced years, he oozed class in the Yorkshire Cup of 2004.

Richard Quinn's mount was a 9-2 shot on his Knavesmire debut – nearly five years after he first hit the racecourse. He'd already well and truly made his mark everywhere else. Seven Pattern races, including the Jockey Club Stakes and, of course, the Leger, had been collected prior to his assault on the Yorkshire Cup. A son of the champion sire Rainbow Quest, the Great Voltigeur Stakes winner of 1984 and the Arc winner the following year, Millenary was noted for being a good mover. He travelled easily enough throughout the race with jockey Richard Quinn later saying the ride was 'smooth all the way'.

Millenary was in a field which included the Prix Royal-Oak and Henry II winner Mr Dinos, but the Ascot Gold Cup winner of 2003 was made to look pedestrian. Dutch Gold and Jelani disputed the early pace with Millenary content to be settled in the pack in a watchful role. His rider switched him to challenge the pair with just over a furlong to go and the response was immediate. Millenary quickly pulled clear without having to be asked a serious question. 'He is a class horse and he showed that today,' said Quinn, basking in the glory of a three length cushion over Alcazar. Mr Dinos was fourth. 'He wanted to get on with it and when I asked him it was immediate. He's always been class and he has won plenty of Group races. He's got speed and he stays.'

Like so many others, Millenary tried and failed to defend the Yorkshire Cup. A year later and now an eight-year-old, some feared he'd had his fill of racing. Not only had he been reluctant to come out of the stalls, he trailed in last of the nine runners – some 22 lengths behind the winner Franklins Gardens – having hung badly right in the home straight. But the good times weren't quite over.

Millenary, a 12-1 chance, stunned the Gold Cup runner-up Distinction (the 8-11 favourite) in a superb piece of race riding from Quinn to win the Lonsdale Cup during York's Ebor Festival in August. And, having dead-heated in the Doncaster Cup with Kasthari the year before, Quinn's waiting ride tactics paid dividends again when Millenary prevailed over the excellent Sergeant Cecil on Town Moor the following month. He was retired to stand as a jumps stallion.

***

IT was like a rock star coming back for one last triumphant gig. Sergeant Cecil crops up frequently in this book. The horse is a Knavesmire legend.

In 2007, on his favourite track, Devon trainer Rod Millman's old stager had one more big day left in him. At the scene of his Ebor win, his Lonsdale, his Doncaster Cup, he produced yet another excellent display – this time in the Yorkshire Cup. At eight, he is the oldest horse to have won it. Millman says: 'We got the horse back (following the winter break) and we got him really 100 per cent fit first time out. You have got to be careful with older horses but we had him spot on for the Yorkshire Cup. He put up a hell of a performance. Geordieland, on his day, is a very good horse and we were giving him weight with a Group 1 penalty.'

He was willed on from the start by an adoring public. Jockey Jimmy Fortune dropped the Sergeant to the rear at the beginning of the contest but, despite a good gallop set by Orcadian, Millman's charge was always handily placed. Geordieland, who had been making headway from three out and led coming to the final furlong while still held on the bit by his rider Tom Queally, looked to have displayed a winning turn of foot. But Fortune drove Sergeant Cecil on. He hit the front, resisting Geordieland's best efforts, and was driven out to win by three quarters of a length. The stands erupted into huge cheers. Partly, no doubt, this was because a lot of them had just won on the 100-30 favourite. But that wasn't the only reason. The York public had taken Cecil to their hearts. His best came in front of their eyes and being suckers for a resilient horse, he was a hero.

'This is his best track,' Millman said in the winner's enclosure. 'He can come down either side and everything suits him. He's proved it time and time again. We're very lucky to have him.' But he wasn't racing with Millman for much longer. You could not have told by looking at him in the unsaddling enclosure afterwards, but that final effort had taken a little extra out of the old man. He never won again.

'He's the oldest horse to win the Yorkshire Cup and that was Cecil's swansong,' explains Millman. 'He was never really the same horse again after that. He was very fit for the race and, by then, he was public property. We were just the custodians. He was eight and they can't go on forever. He probably should not have run the next year but he was tough – a real professional. He never shirked anything in his life and he was a real hard racehorse.'

Last in the Gold Cup at Royal Ascot on his reappearance after the

Yorkshire Cup, he had no better luck in either the King George VI and Queen Elizabeth Diamond Stakes or back on familiar ground in the Lonsdale Cup at York. Millman gave it one more go the following season but, when he was last in the Goodwood Cup, 32 lengths behind Yeats, the trainer knew the fire had gone out. But, as we shall see, the horse had already left an indelible mark on everyone who had seen him on Knavesmire.

***

A YEAR after Sergeant Cecil had dashed his dreams, Geordieland finally shed his bridesmaid's tag. Maddening and unfortunate in equal measure, Jamie Osborne's grey horse had been leaving both trainer and punters tearing their hair out. In two years, and ten runs, the undeniably talented Geordieland had been a perennial runner-up. Was he merely unlucky or, as his critics liked to suggest, a 'professional loser'?

Racing is full of villains who somehow snatch defeat from the jaws of almost certain victory. And in seven starts in 2007, Geordieland had finished second five times. True, he had been slugging it out with the best. Yeats had been a length and a half too good in the Ascot Gold Cup and Septimus had beaten him in the Doncaster Cup.

The horse hadn't always been an unlucky loser. Geordieland's career began in France where he had won Listed races and the Group 2 Grand Prix de Chantilly in 2005 before being bought by Osborne the following year. But that win had been his last and, at 13-2 come race time at York, it seemed the punters were no longer prepared to back Geordieland with their wallets. Osborne kept the faith. Redemption was about to come calling, and not only for the horse either.

His jockey had been through the mill as well. Shane Kelly had been back in racing just 16 days when he climbed aboard Geordieland in the Yorkshire Cup. Tainted by allegations he had passed information for reward, and forced away from the sport by a year-long ban, Kelly also had something to prove. He also needed nerve. Geordieland had to be produced with precision timing or the horse with the irritating habit of being second might repeat the trick once more.

Aidan O'Brien's Honolulu, runner-up in the Ebor the previous year, was the punters' choice but it was Royal And Regal who threatened to deny Osborne yet again. In a relentless display of front running, the Michael Jarvis-trained horse looked to have the race sewn up with a furlong still to travel. Geordieland, held up by Kelly during the early stages, was making headway but still had four lengths to find on the leader and was squeezed for room with a furlong to go. But, as the line drew near, Royal And Regal started to edge. Geordieland, always the victim, now went for the kill. Kelly got him there on the line. This time, there was no chance he was being caught. Geordieland won by a head.

'It's just a huge relief – for him to finally win one of these is just fantastic,' said Osborne afterwards. 'He's the most talented horse we have, so it's been hugely frustrating. We thought of buying him a bridesmaid's dress but we can cancel that now.' Geordieland continues to thrill and frustrate despite finally finding a streak of ruthlessness at York.

Second again, albeit to the breathtaking Yeats once more in the Gold Cup the following month, a win came in the Henry II Stakes at Sandown in May 2009 after a Stewards' inquiry. The Gold Cup, however, has continued to elude him. He finished third to, guess who, in his third successive appearance in Royal Ascot's crown jewel and it is determination to succeed in this contest which seems to be the reason behind Osborne's continued campaigning of the grey. At the time of writing, the now ten-year-old horse may already have been out on the track in 2011.

'I know it's unusual to run a ten-year-old in the race, but he doesn't have any miles on the clock,' the trainer has stated. Time will tell whether it proves a wise move.

***

ASK had all the answers in 2009. The Sir Michael Stoute-trained horse came to York a heavy favourite and, although he hadn't won for more than a year before the Yorkshire Cup, Ryan Moore's mount had still been in reasonable form – witnessed by a sixth place finish behind Zarkava in the Arc the previous October. And Ask had the pedigree.

Three Group 3 wins – the Ormonde Stakes, the Cumberland Lodge Stakes and the Gordon Richards Stakes – showed him to be a solid performer at Pattern level. He'd also had two near misses at York. Beaten a short-head by Trick Or Treat in the Melrose Stakes in August 2006, Ask came back a fortnight later and was fourth behind Sixties Icon when Knavesmire held the St Leger during Doncaster's redevelopment. So it was a sense of third time lucky for Ask in the Yorkshire Cup. He was the punters' darling. A 2-1 favourite, a significant portion of the crowd was cheering Ask and Moore on as the £140,000 contest got under way. Neither disappointed. In a field which included the rising young challenger Fiulin, and a former winner in Percussionist – the 2006 champion – Ask was contemptuous of the opposition.

'Travelling comfortably, when the gap opened he took full advantage and streaked clear of his seven rivals,' reported York's newspaper *The Press*. 'He was ridden to a six length victory over Blue Bajan, a 33-1 shot, and Veracity.' Moore had pounced at exactly the right time. Having held up his mount at the back of the field in the early stages, the jockey saw his chance halfway up the straight and stormed through a gap which opened up. It was a perfect move, carrying Ask into a healthy lead while taking the wind out of the sails of the rest of the field. Moore's horse hung left in the final furlong, visibly tiring under Moore's clever move, but, with six lengths in hand, he could afford to be breathing deeply at the finish line.

His delighted owner, Patrick Fahey, reported: 'He (Moore) said he might have gone a bit too early but it was a lovely opening and he thought he would put it to bed – but he was getting tired.' Fahey initially suggested the Irish St Leger would be Ask's prime motivation for the rest of the year. But the horse was seen out much sooner than that – dropping back in trip for Epsom's Coronation Cup.

While many of the thoroughbreds described were tailor made for longer distances, despite the lure and the prestige that winning at a mile and a half and a mile and a quarter offered, Ask seemed more than comfortable whatever the race journey. Youmzain was beaten a nose on the famous Downs before Stoute's charge showed his versatility once again when winning the Prix Royal-Oak at Longchamp over two miles.

***

THE closing feature race of the Dante Festival in May, the Yorkshire Cup is the first act in a play which thrills throughout the season.

In the warming spring, when the eyes of racing fans turn naturally towards the opening Classics and towards the promise of youth, it is a chance to welcome back familiar faces – as long-serving staying heroes once again gather to do battle. For the defending champion, there is the knowledge that the stiffest of challenges awaits – one only Ardross has successfully overcome. For the younger generation, there is an early opportunity to shake up the established order and make a mark ahead of the crown jewel of staying prizes, the Gold Cup at Royal Ascot, a month later.

The Yorkshire Cup is marked out as a veritable who's who of the staying category, a race which appeals to both punter and purist. From 2011, the prominence of the contest as one of the top staying events was to be enhanced further as a plank in the long distance category of the new Champions' Series. The initiative, launched by Racing For Change, the body charged with reinvigorating the sport, planned to give an easy to follow narrative for the season, culminating in a big money Champions' Day at Ascot in October.

Whether the Yorkshire Cup needs any more hype, given its undoubted prominence as the Flat season's first big stayers' contest, is a moot point. While it continues to loom large on the plans of every trainer with a stayer worth his salt, no flash advertising campaign, or PR tricks, will ever be required to boost its enviable reputation.

JUNE

ROYAL ASCOT...AT YORK

AMID a grey Yorkshire sky, the tiniest speck of red suddenly lights up the distant horizon. It is June but the expectant crowd is huddled, for warmth, from the specks of rain, as the dots grow larger with every second. Up the track, the horse-drawn Landaus march in military fashion along the Knavesmire straight, flanked impressively by immaculate soldiers in rouge. This signals the moment for which York has waited two years.

At the head of the procession, beaming brightly, and dressed in pink, comes The Queen. It means Royal Ascot at York has finally arrived.

***

'IT was one of the biggest one-off projects that racing has ever put together,' says Ascot head of communications Nick Smith. 'It was bigger than the Breeders' Cup by a country mile – and we did it as a one-off, with no blueprint whatsoever.'

Such was the challenge in moving Royal Ascot lock, stock and barrel to another track in the summer of 2005. York's new £20 million Ebor Stand hadn't even been opened to the public when the first whispers were heard, in the early spring of 2003, that Knavesmire might host the Royal meeting. Ascot, weary of a grandstand which belonged to an era long since vanished, was considering shutting down for a £180 million redevelopment. So what becomes of their flagship meeting – five days of sumptuous Flat racing and some of Britain's biggest Group races? There were two choices. Abandon it for a year, or take it on tour. Ascot chose the latter.

The speculation grew louder, the questions intensified. Where would it go? For William Derby, York racecourse's chief executive and clerk of the course, it was a strange time. He knew all about Ascot, having been commercial director at the Berkshire track before arriving at Knavesmire to take over the reins from John Smith in 2003. Though he had been shadowing the former clerk of the course since the middle of the previous year, he'd only officially been in charge at York for a few months. Even he hadn't known exactly what was on the cards.

'In my previous role it was the early days of planning for the redevelopment and the outline early plan was to stay at Ascot,' he says. 'So it wasn't even considered while I was still there to take Royal Ascot on the road. Then Ascot said they were thinking about closing down for around 18 months and taking Royal Ascot, and their other big meetings, to other tracks. They asked if York were interested. They were talking to all the big racecourses. We talked about it as a team and as a board and submitted a tender application to stage the meeting.'

York weren't the only players to put their hats in the ring. Newbury, Newmarket and even Cheltenham wanted a piece of the action. But Knavesmire was the logical choice – even if that did mean several months of beating around the bush. At Ascot, Nick Smith reveals there was never really any doubt that York was the only track for the job.

'It was the worst kept secret in racing that it would end up at York,' he laughs. 'But in terms of ticking the right boxes, we had to effectively tender the relocation to a certain extent. I don't think it came as a huge surprise that York won. In reality, York was the only place which had the racetrack and the facilities that would be remotely capable of coping. With Newbury and Newmarket, there was no problem with the track but it would have been extremely difficult to accommodate the people we would expect (to attend Royal Ascot). It must have been quite difficult for York, knowing they had to be massive favourites and knowing it was theirs to lose. It was extremely straightforward in reality. Unless something massively unforeseen happened and Cheltenham had invested £10 million in a Flat track, it was pretty much going to go to York.'

Even so, there was still joy when the 'worst kept secret' finally came out in August 2003 – announced on the BBC by then Ascot chief executive Douglas Erskine-Crum. York had been given Royal approval, and the hard work was about to begin. But unlike the St Leger, which would be staged at York the following year because of similar renovation work to transform Doncaster, Knavesmire would not have the task of running the Royal Meeting. It was firmly Ascot's show.

'They were very much in control of the meeting and we always knew that. We were content with that approach,' Derby states. 'It was something we were obviously very excited about, something we were very proud to have won but were very daunted about all the things that had to be put in place before it. All we did was try to present York in the best light. The best way we could do that was to run our racecourse in the best way we could and to be open to what Ascot wanted to achieve, to empathise with that, and to help deliver a stage that would work for the meeting.'

They went the extra mile – even altering the shape of their track to help Ascot run the meeting as smoothly as possible. The horseshoe of Knavesmire's turf became circular as York installed a new south bend, which has remained in use ever since. The reasoning was simple enough. Royal Ascot's centrepiece race, the Gold Cup, was traditionally held over two and a half miles. For York to stage such a contest, the horseshoe had to go.

***

THAT 'Magnificent Seven' in 1996, when the entire card went his way, made Frankie Dettori 'Mr Ascot'. No jockey has been more identified with the track or the finery of the Royal Meeting. But when the five-day festival made its trip north to Knavesmire, the people's favourite wasn't there for the ride. With the meeting ten days away, Dettori picked up a six-day ban for careless riding at Haydock which ruled him out of York entirely.

The Italian was riding Royal Orissa in a six-furlong handicap when the horse edged right and bowled into Aversham, who took a crashing fall. The Stewards were unimpressed and Dettori, although philosophical about the ban, decided to get himself as far away as possible. He wrote in *The Times*, on June 4: 'It was a freak accident but I won't be appealing against the ban. I'm just relieved and pleased that no harm was done. I'd like to take the family away with me to Sardinia during Royal Ascot week and get away from it all. I couldn't sit there and watch on television. It would rip my heart out every time a Godolphin horse won. I work all year for meetings like Royal Ascot, but this year I'm not going to be a part of it.'

There was worse for the Yorkshire punters. Attraction, Middleham trainer Mark Johnston's fabulous multiple Group 1 winning filly had failed to recover from a muscle strain, robbing racegoers of the chance to see one of the best horses the county has ever produced. But they would not be missing out on The Queen. Her Majesty committed to all five days of the meeting and that meant more than simply giving the Royal Box a lick of paint. It meant staging the Royal Procession.

'It was an amazing thing to replicate it,' Ascot's Nick Smith says. 'The event felt right because it had the Royal Procession every day. 'Had we done it in a half-hearted manner it would have been a complete farce and we would have been a laughing stock. It had to be all or nothing. We said this was going to be Royal Ascot at York and it was going to be a proper, full blown, Royal Meeting. No holds barred.'

So, in the early afternoon of June 14, 2005, after two years of planning, of meetings, of traffic plans and of rehearsals, a clutch of Landaus made their way from Bishopthorpe Palace and arrived to make their way down the home straight at York Racecourse to the applause and cheers of 35,982 spectators who braved the rain, and the clouds, for the opening day of Royal Ascot at York. They were off.

***

ROYAL Ascot at York opened with the Coventry Stakes. A Group 2 dash over six furlongs to get the pulse racing. Red Clubs got things off to a fabulous start for father and son team Barry and Michael Hills with an impressive victory. Hills forged his mount to the front and around the furlong marker strode away from the 66-1 shot Pacific Pride, who had set the pace for much of the contest, and the local hope Amadeus Wolf, trained by Hambleton's Kevin Ryan.

The drama had started even before the stalls went up when Seb Sanders' mount Imperial Sword bolted down the track and had to be withdrawn. But it was Godolphin, minus Frankie Dettori, who stole the show with Shamardal on that opening day in the St James's Palace Stakes. Australian rider Kerrin McEvoy might have been the supersub, but the three-year-old colt was the star on what was his final appearance on a race track. It was a demolition job.

McEvoy took the French 2,000 Guineas and Derby winner straight to the front and Shamardal did the rest – winning by three lengths, easing down, in the Group 1 mile contest from Ad Valorem. It was Shamardal's third Group 1 success inside a month. It was also brilliant for McEvoy, who had been picked as Godolphin's number two after catching the eye on Beekeeper in the 2002 Melbourne Cup.

'It was easy as he travelled so well,' he enthused. 'I couldn't believe how far clear he was. It's a fantastic thrill to have my first Royal Ascot winner. I've picked up some lovely rides this week and the pressure is off with this under my belt. It's so competitive here that there is a surge of excitement when you win.'

Despite McEvoy's optimism, the feature race of Royal Ascot's opening day would prove to be the highlight for the mighty Dubai-based Godolphin in the week's major contests. The big races were destined for other trophy cabinets. One of those was the Queen Anne Stakes, which didn't just find a new cabinet but a new country. The brilliant Rakti, who had won six Group 1 races, appeared unstoppable but French trainer Andre Fabre knew better.

Despite his odds-on opponent, who had been superb in winning the Lockinge Stakes at Newbury the previous month, Fabre supplemented Valixir for £20,000. Ridden by Christophe Soumillon, the 4-1 chance powered past Rakti at the two furlong marker and held off his rival's late rally for a length and a half success. But it was a victory claimed in dramatic circumstances. Rakti's rider Philip Robinson claimed the temperamental colt, never the calmest on the racetrack, had been spooked on his way to the start.

'A woman, as we went out, just started clicking like mad (with her tongue) and it just set him alight,' he explained. 'You can't do that with a horse like this. It may have ruined his race, and he ran a remarkable race considering.' Robinson had been forced to ride rodeo to stay on the careering colt but, for Soumillon, Valixir was the true performer. 'He never had a real rush, but to beat Rakti – a true champion over a mile – like that he needed to be a true champion,' he cooed.

Valixir wasn't the only successful raider on the opening day. Chineur, piloted by Christophe Lemaire, made it the biggest French invasion since the Norman Conquest when scooping the King's Stand Stakes.

***

ASK Jeremy Noseda about Royal Ascot at York and he'll tell you it helped to change his career. The Newmarket handler is a self-confessed admirer of Knavesmire and Ascot so when the two linked hands the man who cut his teeth at Godolphin watching Classic Cliché win the Dante and Halling dominate the Juddmonte International was thrilled.

The moment that would change everything would come on day four in the Albany Stakes but, by then, Noseda would have already made his mark at Royal Ascot at York – thanks to Proclamation in the Jersey Stakes, the opening Group 3 contest of day two. Proclamation was no stranger to York, having been smashed by Motivator in the Dante but, having bounced back at Goodwood, Noseda was in fine fettle ahead of the Jersey – despite a terrible draw.

'It was a fabulous race,' he says. 'We'd had a bad day at York in the Dante when I totally got things wrong – thinking he would be a Derby horse – and he tailed off last behind Motivator. He pulled too hard. 'He came here for the Jersey and he got an awful draw. I think he was drawn right outside, in the field, and a lot of people said to me he couldn't win from that draw.'

They were wrong. It was a breathtaking performance. Drawn 20 he may have been but, with Johnny Murtagh in the saddle, Proclamation blistered through the seven furlongs. Having been held up early on and hampered round the final turn, once Murtagh hit the front, with a furlong remaining, there was nothing to stop Proclamation, who romped in with two and a half lengths to spare over the Henry Cecil-trained Camacho.

'I felt that he would definitely win and he did in real style,' Noseda recalls. 'It was an extremely enjoyable day. Royal Ascot is great and, winners at York, you can't beat it.' But if that was pleasing to Noseda, La Chunga's Albany Stakes victory on day four was the icing on the cake. 'I think the meeting coming to York actually sparked Sir Robert Ogden, now one of my big owners, into becoming a main owner in Flat racing. When it was transferred he rang me up at about Christmas time. He already had one horse with me and he said 'I need to have something to run at Royal Ascot at York. How are we going to go about it? We went off to Florida to the sales in Miami and we looked at a couple of fillies there. They both ended up being at Royal Ascot at York. One was fourth in the Chesham and the other filly was La Chunga, who won the Albany. It was a great result for Sir Robert with it being his local track. It was that decision, when Ascot closed and it came to York, which meant Sir Robert has become one of my main patrons on the Flat. It was great to win the race and the coincidence of everything that happened put a great new player into my set-up.'

Three and a half lengths was the verdict over 50-1 shot Vogue as Jamie Spencer held up La Chunga and smoothly cruised into the lead at two furlongs. She went clear of the field and it was a 10-1 shock as Rumplestiltskin, the 5-4 favourite for Aidan O'Brien, could only come third. But if Noseda was pleased on day two, then no one could have wiped the smile off jockey Mick Kinane's face. He rode a 208-1 treble thanks to Peerless in the Windsor Forest Stakes, Beautyandthebeast in the final Sandringham Handicap and, most notably, Irish challenger Azamour in the feature Group 1 Prince of Wales's Stakes.

Traditionally held at Ascot over a straight mile, York's version brought a bend into play – not that it made any difference to the 11-8 favourite. Trained by John Oxx and owned by the Aga Khan, Azamour added to his St James's Palace Stakes win of 2004 thanks to a strong late surge which crushed the life out of his rivals. Ace, with Kieren Fallon in charge, was second with Elvstroem, the Australian pacemaker, third. Kinane made headway down the straight and caught Ace at the furlong pole – streaking out to a length and a half success.

It could have been a tussle between Azamour and Ouija Board, the fabulous filly who was a dual Oaks and Breeders' Cup heroine. But the match-up the crowd of 39,875 yearned for never arrived. Ed Dunlop's star came home nearly 30 lengths behind Azamour after losing a shoe in the early stages of the near ten furlong showpiece.

***

'WESTERNER winning the Gold Cup was fantastic,' York chief executive William Derby says when considering his Royal Ascot at York highlight. 'I think people appreciated what the horse represented and I also think the ratings stood up and were the best they had been for a while.'

The Gold Cup is one of Ascot's jewels. At two and a half miles, it tests Flat runners to their limits of speed but, more importantly, stamina. For the French challenger Westerner, however, there has probably never been a cosier neck victory. The 7-4 favourite, trained by Elie Lellouche and ridden by a confident Olivier Peslier, never looked in danger – even when Distinction, piloted by Johnny Murtagh, struck for home with three furlongs to run. In one of the great displays of the week, Peslier didn't panic, made smooth progress, shook the reins on his mount and led at the furlong marker before picking up sweetly to the finish. It was the first time since 1977, and Sagaro's third victory, that the prize had been taken across the Channel.

'When I got my position I knew not to move,' Peslier said. 'I waited a minute. He has a good turn of foot, but the second was doing well, too, and we had a fight with him.'

Peslier might have been certain but Westerner's owner, Alec Wildenstein, had been anything but. 'He is a wonderful horse but I was too worried to watch the race at the track,' he said. 'I watched the race on television and I was concerned by the slow pace early on but he has done everything we have asked of him.'

***

IF Frankie Dettori is 'Mr Ascot', surely Middleham handler Mark Johnston can't be too far behind. Based in North Yorkshire he may be, but Johnston forged his big race reputation with his exploits in the Berkshire town. One of the most successful Royal Ascot trainers over the last two decades, he viewed the York meeting in simple terms. He had to have a winner.

'I loved it. I thought it was absolutely fantastic,' he says looking back. 'It might be a bit sad to say but the most important thing in my career about York is when they ran Royal Ascot there. At the moment, there are two leading (Flat) racecourses – Ascot and York. Up until that time it was in that order. Ascot and then York. A lot of people say Ascot has lost a lot of its charm (since the redevelopment). It wouldn't be a surprise, if you did a poll now, if York was considered to be the best track in Britain.'

He had to be patient, but finally, on the fifth race of day four, it was Johnston's turn. The horse was Melrose Avenue in the Queen's Vase. 'It was vital to get on the scoresheet because Royal Ascot wasn't going to happen at York again. That made it all the more desperate. To me, it was making sure I had a winner at Royal Ascot. It was a wonderful week. The highlight was the atmosphere. The singing afterwards, which is always great at Ascot, was fantastic and Yorkshire added its own flavour to it. I don't pretend to be an adopted Yorkshireman. I have actively hung on to my Scottish roots but I admire them and their county.'

The feeling was mutual when Melrose Avenue, ridden by locally-based jockey Kevin Darley, won the Group 3 race. The two mile contest was noted for its fast pace and it was Irish raider Helvetio who looked to be cruising under Pat Smullen with three furlongs to go, having been held up at the back of the field But it was the 4-1 shot Melrose Avenue who took control of affairs and Darley, then living at Sheriff Hutton, had a length in hand over Mr Vegas, piloted by one-time York-based apprentice Alan Munro, despite tiring as the line approached. Melrose Avenue had attacked with just under half a mile left and really asserted with a furlong remaining. It gave Johnston his third win in the race in five years, following And Beyond in 2001 and Shanty Star in 2003.

Having waited the best part of the week for his first, Johnston then quickly notched a second victory on the fabulous final Royal Ascot day. Bandari was the sort of horse some trainers dream of handling. A winner of the Great Voltigeur Stakes at York in 2002, the son of Alhaarth was third in the St Leger behind Tim Easterby's Bollin Eric. A prolific victor, Bandari would win 11 of his 33 starts, including six Group races, of which the Hardwicke Stakes was the last.

'I miss having horses like that,' Johnston laments. 'It's something we are lacking at the moment. We have none of these older horses that you know are going to win you Group races like Bandari. Through the late 90s, we seemed to have a succession of horses – probably a dozen – that we knew would win half a dozen Group races between them. We seem to lack that now. The York moment for Bandari was the Hardwicke Stakes. I remember Richard Hills rode the second (Maraahel for Sir Michael Stoute) and Bandari nicked round the inside when all the others were coming across to the middle.'

Rider Willie Supple made that brave decision to stay on the far side entering the straight. Leading from four furlongs out, it's a long way down to the winning post on Knavesmire but the six-year-old Bandari held on gamely by half a length and made Johnston's Royal Ascot at York a memory to treasure.

***

THEY stretched from the winning post to the three furlong marker – crammed tightly in the scorching Saturday sun. Eight thousand Yorkies determined to enjoy their day out at Royal Ascot. People's Saturday had caught on.

It was a simple idea. Take one YO postcode and offer them cut price tickets to Royal Ascot. 'From the start we wanted to make sure it was not just a national and international event, but a focus for the region and the city of York,' Ascot's Nick Smith says. 'As a thank you for York's hospitality, help and patience, we decided to put on Rails Enclosure tickets for people who did not want to pay a racing rate.' They responded massively.

The blistering weather helped, but there was a real party atmosphere that day, as the city gathered to wave a fond farewell to Royal Ascot. They witnessed a spectacular day's racing – capped by the Hong Kong raider Cape Of Good Hope setting a track record in the Group 1 Golden Jubilee Stakes. David Oughton's sprinter was a flying machine. Fourth in the King's Stand Stakes on the opening day of the meeting, the seven-year-old went for glory again at the event's climax.

Oughton had brought him to York in pursuit of the inaugural Global Sprint Challenge, then a six-race series run across Australia, Britain and Japan to establish the world's champion sprinter. Cape Of

Good Hope had already won the Australia Stakes at Moonee Valley in February and had been third a fortnight earlier at Flemington in the Lightning Stakes before he made his assault on York. Chineur beat him into fourth in the King's Stand Stakes, but Cape Of Good Hope reappeared on People's Saturday as the second favourite in the Golden Jubilee.

The horse had final day Ascot form, having been unlucky not to snatch the race in Berkshire 12 months earlier when beaten into third behind Fayr Jag and Crystal Castle. The slow break didn't help on Knavesmire, but the very quick ground was certainly in his favour. With a savvy Mick Kinane in the saddle, Cape Of Good Hope edged into the action and ran down Galeota, and jockey Ryan Moore, to get up by a head in a 15 runner stampede.

Not only did that clinch Kinane's leading rider title – it was his sixth win over the five York days – it also gave the Hong Kong horse an unassailable lead in the Global Sprint series, with two legs still to be run in Japan. The perfect People's Saturday and the perfect end to five fabulous days.

***

FIVE million pounds was spent on 120,000 bottles of champagne alone. An army of more than 4,000 waiters, bar tenders, chefs and managers helped shift 75,000 bottles of wine, 10,000 bottles of Pimms and 2,000 kegs of beer.

That was just the start. Two tonnes of smoked salmon, 5,000 lobsters and four tonnes of strawberries were wolfed down by hungry racegoers. Up to £50 million was pumped into York's economy. It was judged 'a moment in history' by the Duke of Devonshire, the Queen's representative at Ascot. He declared it 'one of the most significant racing events in living memory, something special – and I say that with no exaggeration.'

So what to make of Royal Ascot at York? It was a spectacular one-off, an event never to be repeated – at least not in our lifetimes.

'I don't think it has been dulled by time,' signs off Ascot's Nick Smith. 'It was just good fun. Anyone who was there, they just loved it. It was an amazing experience.'

JULY

THE JOHN SMITH'S CUP

THE year 1960 looks like a different world. One of flat caps and thick-rimmed NHS glasses. Men hobble around on stilts and crutches – far too many for comfort. The Second World War is painfully close in the memory.

The tic-tac men gesture furiously, the frantic hand signals changing the odds in seconds with the ever-watchful bookmakers. It is chalkboards rather than computer screens. It is a world which, with the hindsight of half a century's passing, looks grey. Across the York Racecourse stands, huge signs on the clocktower alternate. As prices change, as races pass, those big boards come up and down – naming jockeys, giving prices, revealing winners. Big screens are in the future. This is a job for men.

This is the world which gives birth to the first Magnet Cup. More than 50 years on, the John Smith's Cup, as it is now known, is the longest running sponsored race in the British racing calendar. It's also one of the richest heritage handicaps of its type. Sniffy types might sneer that it's only a handicap. But some of the country's best horses have run in this race over York's extended ten furlongs. Some good ones turned up for the first.

The Magnet Cup, representing a beer from the John Smith's

Brewery based at nearby Tadcaster, replaced the Black Duck Stakes and came with a lavish gold cup and a first prize of £4,125. The backers were making their first foray into racecourse sponsorship, and their money – cash now considered small compared with the £150,000 prize pot which frames the race today – brought a number of top horses to York. Blast had nearly won the Eclipse at Sandown and had won the Queen Anne Stakes, leading one newspaper to scream 'Blast can blast 'em' as its tipster nailed his colours to the mast.

Fourteen went to post with Right Of Way the favourite. He travelled to York after winning the Britannia Handicap at Royal Ascot. So this was not merely some handicappers' race. These were some seriously good horses with pedigree and form in the book.

As the stalls cracked back, Reactor went straight to the front, tracked quickly by the three-year-old filly Fougalle, trained by Rufus Beasley at Malton and ridden by local jockey Norman McIntosh. As they came into the straight, Fougalle was still there. Four furlongs, then three furlongs – locked in battle with Royal Painter. There was nothing to choose between them but, as Fougalle asserted as the line began to draw near, she faced another challenger. Billum flew fast down the outside, getting ever closer. It was a fine late rally, but too little too late. Fougalle held on by a head, at 9-1, to take the first ever Magnet Cup.

'Norman McIntosh comes in cool and unperturbed – as if he'd been on a quiet trot. Fougalle certainly is a fine three-year-old.' The promotional film which uttered these words claimed the race would be 'keenly followed in the years to come – taking a place with the Ebor Handicap and the Eclipse Stakes'. These weren't just idle boasts. In its early years, the Magnet Cup certainly had the talent to back up the promise. Proud Chieftain won in 1961 and he had run close Petite Etoile – the Yorkshire Oaks, Sussex Stakes and Champion Stakes victor – in the Coronation Cup and St Paddy, who won the treble of Dante, Derby and St Leger the previous year, in the Eclipse.

He was trained by Dick Hern, who was beginning to build the formidable yard that would make him a legend on the Flat circuit, and he did the double just 12 months later when Nortia took the prize. Hern is the contest's leading trainer. Bold Pirate (1976), Town And Country (1978), Bedtime (1983) and Straight Man the following year have set a target of six victories that has yet to be beaten. Those days are in the future. Already the Magnet Cup is a race that is far from average.

***

FARM Walk was trained by Rufus Beasley at Malton's Wold House Stables and the legendary trainer had intimate knowledge of the York handicap. He'd won the first running with Fougalle.

'Farm Walk was bought as a companion, as a yearling, for City Barker – a horse that was quite highly regarded,' remembers racing journalist Tom O'Ryan who, as a child, saw the horse up close as his father worked at Beasley's Ryedale yard. 'There were quite high hopes from the owner William Barker. When one came into training, so did the other. My father, Bobby, was head lad and he saw something in this horse. I was only a youngster at the time but dad was a great horseman. He was a former jump jockey who won a Champion Hurdle at Cheltenham. He wouldn't be beat easily (with horses). Farm Walk was very difficult to deal with – a real handful. He had a very awkward head carriage. To ride him they had to put a head collar under the bridle to restrain his head – with a rubber inner tube that went from under his chin. They did it with an inner tube because it allowed a little bit of flexibility. They used it with him for quite a while to get his head in the right place and to give the rider more control. He was a handful to ride. The moral of the story is that, having so fairly cheap beginnings, both in terms of never having any hopes for him and being difficult to break, a lot of people wouldn't have spent the time. But he turned out to be a very good horse.'

He had won the Vaux Gold Tankard the season before the 1968 Magnet Cup, and the six-year-old who had defied early expectations was now in the process of turning previously journeyman jockey Johnny Seagrave's career upside down. The son of a steelworker, Seagrave had averaged less than five winners a season from his first success in 1948, as a 15-year-old, to 1964. Patience had been a virtue. But Farm Walk would be part of a glorious second stanza. In the last 19 years of his career, before an eye injury forced him to retire in 1984, he booted home 849 winners.

'Having the association with, all of a sudden, a high powerful horse meant he had a wonderful later career in racing, unlike his career in the early years,' adds O'Ryan. 'He won a Gimcrack on Music Boy, won an Ayr Gold Cup with Roman Warrior and stacks of other top races. He was one of the top jockeys in the north in the last 15 years of his career. I did a little piece with him in later years and I said to him what horses do you remember – Music Boy, Roman Warrior? He also rode a horse called Meadowville that was second to Nijinsky in the St Leger and he said: "Farm Walk – the one who changed it for me. He was such a bastard to ride".'

The favourite had been Park Top, the four-year-old filly who the following year would win the Coronation Cup, King George VI and Queen Elizabeth Stakes and come runner-up in the Prix de l'Arc de Triomphe. On this day at York, she could finish only fifth. Lester Piggott's mount, Game All, was also heavily backed but finished towards the rear of the ten strong field. Farm Walk was almost last in the early stages as Polymint set the pace, followed by Big Hat, Straight King and Pertinancy. Polymint still bowled along in front at the halfway point but, as they entered the straight, Seagrave moved Farm Walk into a more prominent position. He sent him to the front inside the last quarter mile and the result was never in doubt, although Castle Yard – who had been third in the race the previous year – tried hard to keep with him.

He had won in great style and started the Indian summer which greeted the later years of Seagrave's career.

***

FARM Walk and My Swanee have something in common. The two horses that followed each other as Magnet Cup winners are the oldest to have won the race. Raccolto, in 1963, Farm Walk and My Swanee, in 1969, all took the title aged six-years-old. But while Raccolto has faded in the pages of history, and Farm Walk was a very good horse but no more, My Swanee was a handicapping legend.

His win would put down another marker. It was the only time Lester Piggott would win the Magnet Cup. My Swanee, a grey reflecting trainer Bill Marshall's favourite colour, was a hero of the crowd. Bought by Marshall in 1968, it was during the following year – the year of Magnet glory – that My Swanee would really crown his career.

Marshall had a knack for taking thoroughbreds that had failed elsewhere and, entrusted now into his care, turning them into winners. He also knew how to keep horses on the boil, getting the best out of them for the entirety of a season. My Swanee was the prime example, scooping six wins under ever increasing weights. Nine stone seven pounds was on his back at York and his performance got, so the *Yorkshire Evening Press* reported, 'the sort of ovation usually reserved for Ebor Handicap winners'. My Swanee only lined up against five rivals, but they were a useful lot including the favourite Sovereign Ruler, who was ridden by Pat Eddery. But the grey had Piggott.

At the start, My Swanee just tracked Sovereign Ruler, who was the early pace-setter, and the positions were still the same as the two horses, with Pally's Double for company, turned into the straight. Brian Lumley, the *Press* racing writer who had the pen name Ebor, wrote: 'Soon after passing the two furlong marker, Lester decided the time had come...and he allowed My Swanee to go into the lead. From that stage onwards, the race was virtually over. Nothing ever looked likely to trouble the top weight, and though Pally's Double improved sufficiently to deprive Sovereign Ruler of second place in the closing stages, he was no threat to the leader. Although Sovereign Ruler started at slightly shorter odds, My Swanee (5-2) was obviously the one that a large section of the crowd had been hoping to see first home in this valuable event – and a tremendous roar of encouragement rose from the enclosures once it was apparent the grey was going to win.'

Despite his weight, My Swanee had covered the ten furlongs in a time just four fifths of a second outside the track record. In the winner's enclosure, Marshall revealed a bloodstock agency had telephoned the night before the race in a bid to prise My Swanee from his grasp.

'Now it will cost them more if they are still interested,' he quipped. Piggott, a man of few words at the best of times, only said: 'He came really good.' Good enough to take a first prize of £3,775.

***

THERE have been only two back-to-back winners of the Magnet Cup. The first was Prominent. Trained by Arthur Budgett, who bred, owned and handled the 1969 and 1973 Derby winners Blakeney and Morston, the four-year-old had an amazing rise to the top of the handicapping tree.

In 1971, victories at Salisbury and Brighton were minor but the now-named John Smith's Magnet Cup certainly was not. Prominent started at 10-1 and was hugely impressive. Setting a fast pace from the start the runner-up Calpurnius, with Piggott in the saddle, was left two lengths adrift having never looked like threatening the leader. The horse then went on to beat Calpurnius again at Goodwood and swept to the Prix Foy at Longchamp that September – capping a quite phenomenal campaign.

The following year, the gelding again returned to York having used a fourth place finish to Brigadier Gerard in the Prince of Wales's Stakes at Royal Ascot as a tune up for the big Knavesmire handicap. Geoff Baxter, the winning rider a year earlier, renewed his partnership with the defending champion. It would be a race that would demand all his talent and experience. Because despite starting joint favourite at 4-1, Prominent had to withstand a stiffer challenge this time. St Ives and Colum, the punters' other choice for favouritism, both had a run at the champion and the former failed by just a short head – one of only two times in the race's history that such a narrow margin has decided the contest.

'Gallantly inching his way into the lead in the final few desperate strides, Prominent repeated his victory in the big event at York Races today, the John Smith's Magnet Cup,' wrote Ebor. 'It was a finish which had a big crowd roaring its encouragement as Edward Hide strove to keep the all the way leader St Ives in front, as Prominent battled alongside him. Prominent and Geoff Baxter were just in front inside the final furlong, but St Ives was back on terms with a dozen strides to go, and it was anybody's guess which of the two had made it for the £4,130 first prize.'

The camera showed it was Prominent. Brilliant for Baxter, but unlucky for Hide, the excellent northern jockey who was perennially titled Cock o' the North. That short head robbed him of a Knavesmire treble that day.

***

PROMINENT was brilliant, but Peleid is probably the greatest horse to have won the John Smith's Magnet Cup. Not just because he was Malton trained and kept the trophy in Yorkshire in the hands of trainer Bill Elsey. It is because of what the three-year-old, whose ability was forged and honed on the Highfield gallops, did next.

The Magnet Cup was almost simple enough. Prominent made a bold bid to win the race for a third successive year but nine stone proved too much weight to carry for the six-year-old. He made the running but, a furlong and a half from the finish, he weakened away and had to settle for a podium place. Perhaps the biggest disappointment was the performance of Warpath, who started joint favourite with Cop de Feu. He was well down the field and continued a run of poor results for favourites.

Only four obliged in the first 14 years of the contest. It was a record which wouldn't get significantly better in future years either. Peleid's victory was the third prize he had picked up during the season and talk of a bold bid at the Ebor Handicap was on the cards. The 6-1 shot, piloted by Taffy Thomas, scored by a length and a half from Happy Hunter. He continued to improve at a majestic rate. Fast forward to September and there is Peleid, lining up in the Classic St Leger just a couple of weeks after finishing a fine fourth in the Ebor.

'He won for the best of reasons,' wrote the *Sporting Life* in the Leger's aftermath before adding, somewhat obviously, 'At the vital stage of the race he ran faster than his opponents.' He won by two and a half lengths, securing a Magnet Cup and Leger double which has never been repeated – and is probably never likely to be. Peleid would be the last northern trained St Leger winner for 29 years, until Bollin Eric won for Tim Easterby in 2002.

***

BEDTIME put the bookies to sleep in 1983, but left the locals wide awake when winning the 23rd John Smith's Magnet Cup. The gelding was not only the 7-2 joint favourite, he carried the colours of Lord

Halifax – later to be York Racecourse chairman – whose mother Ruth, Countess of Halifax, was a steward on Knavesmire.

Bred by his owner, and trained by Dick Hern, Bedtime had a stellar jockey in the saddle in Willie Carson. Tracking the leaders into the straight, Bedtime came with a brilliantly timed run to lead a furlong from home and he battled on gamely to hold off Gay Lemur by half a length in what the *Evening Press* called a 'thrilling finish'. 'Gay Lemur, a winner at York's May meeting, fought back in the final 100 yards, but Carson was always in command,' they wrote.

Majestic Endeavour, the other joint favourite, had to settle for third ahead of the outsider Lion City in fourth. What made this victory all the more special for the owner, and trainer, was that it was Bedtime's first race for several weeks. A winner previously at Windsor, the three-year-old had been suffering from the coughing fit that was rife in Hern's yard at the time. Bedtime became one of the most popular geldings to race in this country winning, in all, ten races including the Brigadier Gerard Stakes, the Prix Gontaut-Biron as well as finishing second in the Japan Cup.

***

FROM one great horse to another. Prominent was the first and Chaumiere is the only other horse to defend his John Smith's Magnet Cup trophy. Timeform described the back-to-back winner of 1985 and 86 as a 'sturdy, workmanlike horse' and he had one other quality in abundance: heart.

He needed all of that first time round on Knavesmire when flashing past the post in tandem with Severn Bore as the Magnet Cup provided yet another thrilling climax. Sent off at 14-1, Chaumiere – ridden for both displays by Tony Ives – was nearer last than first in the early stages. But Ives threaded his way through the field in York's open straight and picked off rivals one by one. He never led before the line but there with him, matching stride for stride, was Severn Bore and it was to take a photograph to split them.

The judge examined the picture and punters with Chaumiere or Severn Bore on their tickets held a collective breath. It was announced. Chaumiere – by a short head. Winning trainer Robert Williams celebrated. Frankie Durr, going through a miserable season, would never win the race. Ives and Williams, on the other hand, only had to wait another 12 months. The opponents had changed but the style of victory had not. Long time leader Masked Ball was collared close home as Chaumiere, unfancied for a repeat at 11-1, again made a mockery of his odds.

'Chaumiere's wins were incredible really,' said Ives, who would also notch a hat-trick in the race on board Icona in 1989. The first one, we came from second last up the inside and to do it again was unbelievable. Icona's win was a big feat because we beat the favourite (Tosara, who finished eighth), who was thought to be a good thing. It means a lot to have ridden three winners of the John Smith's Cup. It's not an easy race to win.'

***

'I WILL always refer to it as the Knockando affair,' says John Smith, the eyebrows furrowing on the face of the former York clerk of the course as he looks back to the 1987 renewal. 'I had a lot of drama there I can tell you. Knockando was trained by Luca Cumani and was fancied. I remember that Ray Smith was my office manager. Ray had been here 15 years – a great character and ex-police sergeant who ran the office. Ray liked a little gamble, a little touch now and again. He'd heard about Knockando and he proceeded to have a little bit on it ante-post. Anyway it comes to the day of the race and I think Knockando won quite easily.'

It had indeed been an easy win. Knockando, ridden by Ray Cochrane, scored by a length from the hard to separate Brave Dancer and Wolsey. Then it started to get messy.

'About a furlong out, as he pulled out, Knockando interfered with one of the horses. There was a Stewards' inquiry,' Smith recalls. 'The first thing that happened was that the inquiry couldn't get under way straight away because they had to establish who was second. So we were waiting for the photograph. The photograph eventually comes through and we've got a dead-heat for second place. The inquiry carried on after the next race, because they hadn't got enough time to get it all settled, and we got terribly behind. Eventually, Knockando was demoted to third and, although one of the two horses wasn't involved in the interference at all, the fact it was a dead heat meant we had a dead heat for first place.'

Wolsey (4-1) and Brave Dancer, the 9-4 favourite, would share the prize. Delight for them, their trainers Henry Cecil and Guy Harwood and their jockeys Willie Ryan and Greville Starkey. Heartbreak for Cochrane and the owners of Knockando. And Ray Smith. The inquiry lasted 45 minutes. The result was so contentious that scuffles broke out in the parade ring, with one unfortunate bookie knocked unconscious and having to be taken to hospital.

There were other lessons learned as well. 'It was amazing the effect it had. One of the lessons I learned was about the effect it had on the betting turnover that day,' Smith says. 'Because no decision had been made prior to the next race, people were reluctant – the average punter – to go and commit any money not knowing whether they had won on the last one or not. So the betting turnover went down quite considerably.'

It wasn't quite finished yet for Smith. 'On the Monday, I got a phone call from one of the winning owners, a gentleman who was Greek and lived in Surrey. He owned Brave Dancer. The other winning owner was Lady Howard de Walden,' he says. 'Normally the horses ran in the Lord's name but she had one or two and this particular horse, Wolsey, had won. This chap, a Mr Zandona, rang me up and asked "Would I be able to purchase the Gold Cup that was presented to the winner?" I said: "Well I would have thought so because they win so many trophies but I must clear it." I rang her up and I explained what had happened. "Oh no," she said "My husband wins all the trophies and I would love to have it." I thought "Oh dear". But I went back to John Smith's and they made two Gold Cups so each could have one. I always refer to that as the Knockando affair.'

Move forward five years and there was yet more controversy. The Stewards were once again making the news at the John Smith's Magnet Cup. Ollie Pears was a 17-year-old apprentice about to pick up the biggest win of his career. Until they tried to take it away from him. Alleged interference was the claim as Pears, then a seven pound claimer, celebrated in the winners' enclosure after Mr Confusion had defeated Tell No Lies by a length.

It was apparent the horse, one of the most improved handicappers of the year following wins at Doncaster, Nottingham and Pontefract, had drifted left as the race reached its climax. But no one was arguing he hadn't been a clear winner – except the Stewards. Pears was given a ban for careless riding and the race was handed on a plate to the runner-up. Thankfully for Pears, it didn't end there. Four days later, there was an appeal to the Jockey Club as trainer Steve Norton tried to get the decision overturned. He succeeded. It was great news for trainer and jockey but, for those who backed his winning horse, it comes too late. Bets were settled on Tell No Lies, at 16-1, on the day of the race.

Pears said: 'We fancied the horse – I'd ridden him to win twice before – and it was a big opportunity for a 17-year-old 7lb claimer. To get a Stewards inquiry and lose the race for doing next to nothing was the worst feeling. We couldn't celebrate but we thought we had a good case and we got the race back four days later. It is a very special race to win – one of the best handicaps there is.'

***

PASTERNAK defied a traffic jam and faulty betting signals to win in front of a crowd of more than 30,000 in 1997. He was trained by Newmarket's Sir Mark Prescott, but was ridden by Yorkshire icon George Duffield. He was also the subject of an almighty plunge in the days leading up to the contest.

The colt had been unraced since winning at York the previous October, but that didn't stop the money piling on. Cut from 8-1 to 5-1 joint-favourite in the run-up, the cash kept coming for Pasternak – until minutes before the race took place at a sweltering track. Then his price moved alarmingly the other way. Prescott himself, and the horse's connections, insisted they'd had nothing to do with the midweek plunge. But whatever had taken place, now the money was moving in entirely the other direction.

From an opening show of 3-1, Pasternak drifted badly in the betting out to 13-2 as racegoers ignored the ante-post gamble and backed rivals Humourless and Komi, both owned by Sheikh Mohammed, in their droves. Concerns about the ground, and about the way the horse had been working in recent gallops, might have been behind the alarming drift and the withering confidence looked to be spot on with two furlongs left to travel. Then, Pasternak and Duffield were stuck behind a wall of horses – and it looked like there was no escape. But Duffield was an absolute master of finding a gap in the highest pressure situations. 'I was always going extremely well and it was just a question of getting the split,' he said with the prize pot in his pocket. 'It all came right a furlong out.'

Calmly waiting for a clear passage, when the chance came there was no one better placed to take advantage. Duffield smashed through the gap and gave himself a decisive advantage, coming home half a length clear of Najm Mubeen at the finish. A neck separated the runner-up from Game Ploy in third, with Star Manager forced to settle for fourth. The punters' favourites pre-race, Humourless and Komi, were both unplaced.

'The trainer might not know what he is doing but I can tell you that the jockey does,' said Prescott. 'George was brave and hoped that something would give him a lead. He's given him a great ride.'

What it gave Duffield was a first John Smith's Cup win and further crowned a golden period at York for the veteran jockey – capping a five year stint which had also brought Ebor, Yorkshire Oaks and Nunthorpe Stakes victories. Success had come late for the popular horseman, but it was thoroughly deserved. Pasternak went for a repeat 12 months later but had to settle for second – a length and a half adrift of the 6-1 shot Porto Foricos.

***

ARCALIS hadn't really been bought for the Flat. When County Durham trainer Howard Johnson purchased the horse from Lynda Ramsden for his backer Graham Wylie, he had a reputation as a reasonable handicapper. He had won five races at the likes of Leicester, Pontefract and Newmarket. But the intention was to send him over hurdles, while running in some early season Flat handicaps to see if they could land a bonus win.

The £140,000 John Smith's Cup of 2004 (Magnet was dropped from the title in 1998), boasting a £91,000 first prize, would turn out to be some bonus. There was a lot against him at York that day. There was the favourite, the Queen's gelding Promotion, who had been backed in to 7-2 on the back of a strong display to finish second in the Listed Wolferton Stakes at Royal Ascot the previous month. He had champion jockey Kieren Fallon in the saddle. Then there was the draw.

Arcalis went off at 20-1 and it was primarily because his starting stall position, 18, put many punters off. It had certainly put off racing pundit John McCririck. After the race, Wylie mocked McCririck for announcing boldly on the Morning Line that horses drawn higher than nine couldn't win the ten furlong contest. Wylie, and his wife Andrea, were there, he said, 'for a nice day out'. And this was a competitive handicap, of course. Of the 21 runners, only five started at odds of under 10-1.

Then there was the drama in the race itself. Young rider Robert Winston, based close to the York track, made steady headway on Arcalis from three furlongs out and drove his horse to challenge Promotion with just a furlong left to travel. Then he dropped his whip. He had been trying to change it from one hand to the other when it slipped from his grasp as the battle reached its height. For many jockeys, it could have been the moment the race was lost. Winston remained unperturbed.

'It probably didn't make a lot of difference,' Winston said. 'He was game without it – but I had to throw everything in.' He certainly did. It was a mammoth struggle but Arcalis wore down the Queen's horse to nick it by a head in the dying strides. He was the first winner of the John Smith's Cup to emerge from a double-figure draw since the Ollie Pears ridden Mr Confusion had won from the 14-box 12 years earlier. Over the sticks Arcalis trotted, where he proved himself again to be one hell of a horse. In 2005, he won the Supreme Novices' Hurdle at Cheltenham and, to date, has 11 career victories along with more than £350,000 in prize money.

***

RICHARD Fahey is only half way to matching Dick Hern's record of six John Smith's Cup victories. But here's a bet you can rely on – he'll be doing his level best to pass the famous trainer. The John Smith's Cup is a contest the Malton trainer just loves. 'It's a race we always try to win,' he told the author in July 2008 as he once again prepared a mob-handed assault on the contest.

For Fahey didn't just try to lift the trophy towards the end of the twenty-first century's first decade. He tried to utterly dominate it. His determination to win the race was forged in his mentality of training. Fahey, who had been a hard-working if unspectacular jockey, had only given training a go after being persuaded to by friends and he started out with the tiniest of strings at Butterwick's Manor Farm. There, any winner was welcome and that attitude has continued to prevail despite his meteoric rise up the ladder over the past 15 years.

From barely a handful of horses, by 2010 Fahey had more than 100 in his rapidly expanding Musley Bank yard. And what was better was that the winners now flowed relentlessly. The previous year, only Mark Johnston and Richard Hannon trained more than the likeable Irishman. Halfway through the next season, only the conveyor belt at Hannon's Everleigh yard was keeping Fahey from the top spot.

Fahey loved nothing more than scooping a big handicap and his love affair with the John Smith's Cup had begun in 2002 when Vintage Premium more than lived up to his name. The 20-1 shot left Fahey 'a bit overcome' after the five-year-old got the verdict in a three-way photo finish with Kirovski and the hot favourite Leadership. A Stewards' inquiry, seemingly a staple of the John Smith's Cup, meant the celebrations were put on a hold for a few minutes but the result stood. It was a vintage performance.

Vintage Premium led from the start but was actually passed by Leadership at the two furlong pole. When grit and determination was needed, Fahey's charge showed he had it in plentiful supply. Despite edging with tiredness in the final furlong, Vintage Premium gamely rallied and got back in front close home. The distances were just a head and a short head. It was a standout early ride from 21-year-old jockey Paul Hanagan, who clinched his 44th win of the season, and the biggest of his fledgling career, in the £135,000 race. Fahey was well aware of his talent. 'He's brilliant and he'll go all the way. He's got it all together,' was the tribute after the ten furlong triumph.

Britain's champion jockey in 2010, Hanagan has made Fahey look very clever indeed – the winners racking up ever since. But he is yet to win another John Smith's Cup. Five years later, however, Fahey went all-out for the prize.

Five of the 17-strong field were saddled by the Malton handler and, if winning was the best thing, next was the satisfaction of watching his runners fighting it out on York's famous track. Everyone in the yard had a different opinion, a favourite they were convinced could bring home the prize. There was Charlie Tokyo, ridden by apprentice Jamie Moriarty, Flying Clarets, with Kevin Darley in the saddle. Then there was Avoriaz, Fortunate Isle and Smart Prospect. Could anything stop Fahey?

Well there was the weather for starters. For the first time in the race's 48 year history, the contest was a furlong shorter – held over nine rather than ten following the sustained spell of rain which had forced the June meeting to be abandoned. Then Avoriaz refused to race after exiting the stalls. Luckily for Fahey, Charlie Tokyo was paying no attention to his lacklustre stablemate. Entering the straight, the horse was cruising under Moriarty and hit the front with a furlong to go. If it couldn't get any better for Fahey, it actually did. Coming up to dispute was Flying Clarets and Darley. Both his horses were going at it, straining for the line, with the lion's share of £150,000 in his grasp. It was the former who prevailed, by half a length, with Collateral Damage the best of the rest in third.

'It was a great race for me to watch,' Fahey said afterwards. 'Charlie Tokyo has always been a good work-horse. I never, at any stage, thought he was going to down tools. Moriarty gets on well with the horse and I was quite keen for Jamie to ride him because he believes in him. Everyone in the yard had their opinion about the five horses and fancied different ones, and to see two of them fighting it out is a great thrill.'

'He's got an unbelievable amount of ability, but he does have his quirks,' added Moriarty. 'He showed so much pace and travelled so well that it was just a matter of sitting and waiting.'

Fahey was already a leading player on the training scene in 2007 but, looking back, this might have been the race that really started to launch him into the stratosphere. So, 12 months later, how do you top a one-two finish? Just win it again. Flying Clarets had been the bridesmaid the year before, this time she would be the bride – thanks to a dominating display. Fahey again ran five in the race, but this time he need not have bothered. His five-year-old mare was always in command.

Vintage Premium had been a landmark win for Paul Hanagan, and Charlie Tokyo had boosted the career of Jamie Moriarty. This time it was apprentice jockey Frederik Tylicki who was about to find out what winning the John Smith's Cup could do for your career. German-born Tylicki, whose late father Andrzej was a three-time champion jockey in his own country, had joined Fahey at Musley Bank just six months previously. But as the likes of Hanagan and Robert Winston had learned, if you had the talent you would get the rides from the loyal trainer.

And Tylicki definitely had the talent. He gave the 12-1 shot a masterpiece ride – always keeping her head in front and displaying the necessary mettle when her rivals tried to close the gap in the final couple of furlongs. A length and three quarters was the gap over Eradicate as Fahey became the first trainer since Robert Williams in 1985 and 1986 with Chaumiere to train successive John Smith's Cup winners.

'She's an unbelievable mare,' said Fahey of his horse. 'I was meant to go to the sales with her at the end of the year, but I'm getting to that stage of my life where I need horses like her. She loves the track and the John Smith's Cup which, along with the Ayr Gold Cup, is a race I always try to win.'

Tylicki kept a notebook numbering all of his winners. Flying Clarets was number eight. 'Flying Clarets was a filly who was carrying a lot of weight and, at the time, I was claiming seven pounds and I was good value for that,' he told the author a year after his win. 'It went perfectly. She had a really good draw and she was a filly who liked to dictate up front. She got the trip well and it was brilliant – quite unbelievable. I was delighted it worked out for us.'

The John Smith's Cup proved the start of something amazing for Tylicki. The following season his ability in the saddle, and Fahey's patronage, would end in him beating David Probert to the champion apprentice's title. Only Sirvino, trained locally in Thirsk by David Barron, prevented Fahey picking up a hat-trick as the John Smith's Cup celebrated 50 years, its Golden Jubilee, in 2009. Albaqaa had to settle for third as the 16-1 shot romped home for the Maunby-based handler.

In 2010, Fahey again went to York in numbers, with five of the 19 runners in the field come the day for the ten furlong contest. Albaqaa was again among the contenders, along with Dream Lodge, Extraterrestrial and Porgy but it was Demolition who stable jockey Paul Hanagan chose to ride, and who held Fahey's strongest hopes. They were raised even further when the 9-1 chance seemed to travel so strongly as the race started to wind up to its climax. It was not to be. With just over a furlong left, Hanagan and Demolition had to stand aside and let two warriors fight it out.

There was a Yorkshire hope. Going stride for stride into the last 100 yards were Wigmore Hall, the mount of claimer Martin Lane and saddler Michael Bell, and Kings Gambit – trained by Tadcaster's Tom Tate and ridden by the former champion jockey Jamie Spencer. Tate was gunning for the biggest win of his career and it would have been an apt one as well. Not only would it have kept the trophy in the county, it would have been handed to a trainer based close to the John Smith's Tadcaster brewery.

Lane and Spencer went at it hammer and tongs. Kings Gambit led, was headed, and then surged back to rally close to the line. As the pair flashed past the post together, it would require a photograph to split them. The judge gave it by a short-head to Wigmore Hall and a delighted jockey Lane. Then came the controversy.

No sooner had the result of the photograph come through and the familiar bell, heralding a Stewards' inquiry, rang out. Not for the first time, the destination of the John Smith's Cup was in their hands. It was a tense ten minutes as they made their decision. From the head-on race replay, it looked bad for Lane and Wigmore Hall. Three times in the last 50 yards his mount veered and struck Kings Gambit – the final time almost knocking him sideways.

Spencer was convinced the places would be reversed and that he, and Tate, would claim the glory. He was wrong. They left the result unaltered. Lane joined the likes of Ollie Pears, Jamie Moriarty and Frederik Tylicki as claimers who have won the John Smith's Cup. It was the biggest win of his career and was all the better because his start had been tardy to say the least. As Desert Kiss set the pace, Wigmore

Hall was left towards the rear of the field. Lane didn't panic and built momentum on his mount before engaging in that fierce battle in the final stages.

'This means a lot to me,' he said. 'I've worked hard for this and it means so much. He likes to be dropped in and it was just a matter of coming through the field. I was always confident I had got up. My horse lost his action behind about 75 yards out and gave Jamie's horse a bump. If it had been a nose and not a short head it could have gone the other way.'

***

BEER and betting have occasionally made unruly bedfellows throughout racing's sometimes chequered history. But the partnership between a brewery and a racecourse has made the John Smith's Cup one of the most enduring, and competitive, handicaps of the season.

That John Smith's have the title on the longest running sponsorship of a Flat race – 52 renewals in 2011 – would mean little if the contest itself weren't able to live up to the expectations. A hefty prize fund, £150,000 in 2010, will always ensure a competitive entry list but that doesn't guarantee a triumph.

The John Smith's Cup, like the Ebor Handicap, is successful because the public have taken it to their hearts. As long as they continue to celebrate this most Yorkshire of institutions, so it will remain a 'must-see' event. Raise a glass.

AUGUST

THE INTERNATIONAL

FROM click to click of a stopwatch, it takes a horse about six and a half seconds to run half a furlong in the Juddmonte International. As the clock ticked round each of those in turn when the race wound to its exciting climax in August 2009, it seemed the impossible could happen...again.

A furlong and a half from the post, Sea The Stars – the horse of a generation – was in trouble. In front, two lengths ahead, his rival Mastercraftsman had engaged in a bold bid to steal the glory. Splitting two pacemakers, stablemates from the same Ballydoyle yard of Irish titan trainer Aidan O'Brien, jockey Johnny Murtagh had given Mastercraftsman a kick in the ribs and had grabbed the initiative.

Even for Mick Kinane, the wizened, calm veteran jockey on board Sea The Stars, Murtagh's move represented a worrying development. For despite that Guineas win, the Derby success and the Eclipse crown, this was the first real test his wonder mount had ever faced. As Kinane brought his whip to bear on the three-year-old, he was about to find out if his champion had the heart to match his brilliance.

***

YOU couldn't escape it. The chat was everywhere. The talk of Knavesmire was Sea The Stars. From the moment the Irish trainer John Oxx revealed his hero would miss the King George VI and Queen Elizabeth Stakes at Ascot, all eyes looked to York and the mile and a quarter £600,000 Juddmonte International. There he would make a bid to continue his utter domination of racing's biggest prizes that season by taking the crown jewel of York's contests. There was a brilliant buzz – an expectation which rose with each passing day during the countdown.

It was not the first time they had felt this way at York. Thirty seven years earlier, in the summer of 1972, the chatter was ceaseless for another seemingly unstoppable thoroughbred. Brigadier Gerard. Unbeaten and unblemished, the Classic-winning speed machine, owned by John Hislop, was the Flat superstar of the age. And he was set to meet his old rival, Mill Reef, at York in the brand new Benson & Hedges Gold Cup.

The two had clashed only once before, the 1971 2,000 Guineas, when the Brigadier had won in devastating fashion. But both of their reputations had grown since. Mill Reef, the magnificent 1970 Gimcrack winner at York, went on to win the Derby, the Eclipse, the King George VI and Queen Elizabeth Stakes and the Prix de l'Arc de Triomphe in 1971 while the Brigadier won just about every other mile and middle-distance contest on the racing calendar. That the two were to face off at York in the inaugural running of a new £40,000 race was happy coincidence, however. It had not been designed with either of them in mind.

'What we were trying to do was put together an invitation race, rather like the Washington Invitational,' recalls John Sanderson, York clerk of the course for 14 years from 1972. 'The Major, Leslie Petch, who was clerk of the course from 1955 to 1971, had been and it was the major international race in the world. We had been trying to get the Levy Board with us and they came to us and said 'If you want a big race there's something else we would rather you do' and so the Benson & Hedges Gold Cup was born.'

Getting the cigarette manufacturers on board – however health chiefs might complain about it now – was vital in getting the new contest off the ground. Sanderson reveals: 'They were looking for a major sponsorship opportunity in British racing. They forked out £40,000, which was a lot of money in 1972. Pattern racing was just developing then and it was felt that there was a need for a top class opportunity over a mile and a quarter. York had this extended mile and a quarter because of the Cherry Lane crossing so it, to some extent, lent itself to putting that kind of race on.'

Instantly the richest race ever held on Knavesmire, it also immediately became the richest wholly sponsored event to be held in Britain. The planned participation of Brigadier Gerard and Mill Reef also gave instant kudos to the fledgling venture. When the initial entries were announced in May, the two performers stood proud in a field of 99 which also included the 2,000 Guineas winner High Top, the French 2,000 Guineas winner Riverman, Pistol Packer, the French Oaks conqueror, and the French St Leger winner Bourbon. Mill Reef's participation became even more likely when the colt was pulled out of the Eclipse Stakes at Sandown because Ian Balding's Kingsclere stable was hit by a virus. So August 15, and the 'race of the century' – the much awaited re-match between Brigadier Gerard and Mill Reef – had punters slavering. And with Balding declaring Mill Reef was recovering well, the expectation was fanned even further.

'You can take it from me that he will be fighting fit to oppose the Brigadier at York,' he said in July. Then, in the blink of an eye, it was over. Following a set-back in training, Mill Reef was out.

'Mill Reef had got the virus in force and had run in the Coronation Cup with rhinoneuritis,' Balding recalls nearly 40 years later. 'He won it in spite of that and it was an amazing, gutsy performance but it finished him.'

Being trained for a tilt at the Prix de l'Arc de Triomphe in October, Mill Reef shattered a foreleg during a routine gallop. He survived, following a tricky operation, but his racing career was over. With Mill Reef out, the race now looked to be a procession for the perfect Brigadier Gerard, who boasted a race record of 15 wins from 15 contests. Due to make his bid at York, 26 days after winning the King George VI and Queen Elizabeth Stakes at Ascot, Hislop felt the new Benson & Hedges Gold Cup was the ideal target. Not everyone felt the same way.

'An old friend of mine, with great knowledge and experience of racing, who had been at Ascot, wrote to me that he hoped we would not run the Brigadier at York,' wrote Hislop in his book, *The Brigadier*. 'He said he thought he was tired when he came in after winning the King George VI and Queen Elizabeth Stakes, but was too proud to show it, and that the race might have taken more out of him than was apparent.'

His wife, Jean, also harboured doubts but Hislop put both those concerns to one side. For a start, the one thing he certainly wasn't worried about was the opposition. Bright Beam, Gold Rod and Brigade Major, the latter owned by his wife, held no fear and neither did Hislop lose any sleep about either Rheingold or Roberto, the other two participants. That pair had fought out a rabid duel for the Derby in June with Lester Piggott practically having to pull Roberto over the line for victory.

In the Benson & Hedges Gold Cup, Piggott plumped for the Barry Hills-trained Rheingold with Roberto's trainer Vincent O'Brien uncertain whether his colt would even line up. Roberto had been dismal in the Irish Derby at the Curragh while Rheingold, in the meantime, had won the Grand Prix de Saint-Cloud in Paris and the jockey felt the colt would be suited by York's galloping surface. Then, a week before the race, O'Brien declared Roberto as a definite runner – sparking one of the more unusual moments in clerk of the course John Sanderson's stewardship on Knavesmire.

'I remember Vincent ringing me up. I didn't know him that well – I got to know him a lot better in later life and we became very good friends – but he rang me up and said "I need a hotel bedroom. It's for a jockey you see". Not only were Benson & Hedges sponsoring the race, they also sponsored an international golf tournament at Fulford, in York, and that was on the same week. There wasn't a hotel bed in York so I said "Well, there isn't one". Vincent said to me: "John, I am importing one of the most famous jockeys in North America to ride at your race meeting. Get me a hotel bedroom!" and he put the phone down.' With a begging bowl in hand, it took Sanderson hours to find that precious room. It was for the Panamanian Braulio Baeza – practically parachuted into the Minster city by Roberto's American owner John Galbreath.

Racing Stateside is no longer a mystery to well-informed punters but, back in the 1970s, few spectators knew intimately of their jockeys or, more importantly, their riding tactics. So it was hardly a surprise when Brigadier Gerard went off the 1-3 heavy favourite. He couldn't lose, could he? 'He must have been stung by a bee,' Jean Hislop would later say as Roberto and Baeza smashed out of the stalls to the front of the pack. Bright Beam tried in vain to stay with the Derby victor and the Brigadier tracked Rheingold in fourth place – six lengths behind the leading pair. Piloting Brigadier Gerard, jockey Joe Mercer moved past Bright Beam and Rheingold into the straight but there were already concerns his mount's unbeaten record might be under threat.

'One of the Stewards was Lord Allendale,' Sanderson says. 'I was standing right behind them with the binoculars in that little box past the winning post and he said 'You know, I think Joe's in trouble' as they turned into the straight. This thing was still going, showing no signs of stopping, and you knew he could get a mile and a half because he won a Derby. This wasn't a mile and a half.'

It's a long way from the turn to the line at York. That big wide, staring straight has done for many horses, and jockeys, who have timed their run too soon – too far from home. Even here with four furlongs left to run, the crowd expected Brigadier Gerard to make it. To turn on the gas and fly past the impetuous challenger. But the longer it went on, the more clear it became that Roberto was not slowing down. And would not be caught. When Mercer drew his whip on the Brigadier with two furlongs still to go, it was clear the horse was in big trouble. Brigadier Gerard got as far as Roberto's quarters but, with yards running out and the realisation the unbeaten record was shattered, Mercer eased back on the champion and Roberto stretched out to a three length win.

Hislop wrote that he knew his star was done for three furlongs out. 'There was no excuse: Roberto had galloped faster and reached the winning post first and that was all there was to it'. If Hislop was sanguine, the Knavesmire crowd were stunned into silence. Impossible had become possible.

For Sanderson, there was only the sense of huge anti-climax. 'It was bitterly disappointing. The Hislops, who owned Brigadier Gerard, were the kind of stiff upper-lip British type while the trainer Dick Hern was a proper chap. I remember going in to see Joe (Mercer) in the changing room and he was sitting, almost crying. I went and sat beside him and put my arm round him. I said "I'm sorry, it wasn't the track was it?" and he said "No". If the Brigadier had won, that was the predictable thing. What we got was this slightly iffy Derby winner, ridden by somebody nobody had ever bloody heard of, flown in, and he hit the front and never came back. That was not a standard British riding tactic – to go out and make all – and there weren't a lot of jockeys who could do it. It was quite a skill.'

Both horses broke the course record in the first running of the Benson & Hedges Gold Cup. 'Everyone was just dumbstruck,' remembers one-time *Daily Mirror* and *Racing Post* journalist Tim Richards. 'In the winner's enclosure they just couldn't believe it. People couldn't believe Brigadier Gerard was unable to get to him. What I really remember was it was just completely quiet. It was a very impressive winner but it shut everybody up, because the Brigadier was beaten. Baeza was this unknown jockey to us – coming over and riding like that. I'm not sure Roberto had ever been ridden like that before, literally pillar to post. He, apparently, had talked with O'Brien and the latter had said "Take what you like out of our conversation, I'll leave it to you" and he obviously decided that would be the best way to ride the horse. It's the biggest shock I've ever seen. It has to be. There were some shocks when I had too much money on horses but that has to be the biggest shock. You just couldn't imagine it was going to be beaten.'

Baeza, now in his 70s and the clerk of the scales at Louisiana Downs Racecourse, still revels in the glory of a race he will never forget. 'It was one of the most exciting days of my life,' he recalled. 'I was contracted to ride for Roberto's owner John Galbreath in America and about five days before I got the call telling me to come to York because Lester Piggott had chosen Rheingold. I had ridden in France, but never in England before and didn't know Vincent O'Brien, but he met me at the airport in London and we flew up to Leeds together and then drove to York. It is true that he didn't give me any instructions. He just said "You're the rider, do what you think is best" though he did say that if the pace was strong it would find out Brigadier Gerard in the last half-mile and he was right. I had Roberto up there throughout and he kept on galloping all the way to the line. It was a wonderful day for me.'

Baeza, inducted into the American Hall of Fame, would give up riding in 1976 in the face of increasing weight problems. As he led the victor home, and the Brigadier trailed in behind, Gold Rod was third and Rheingold fourth. Piggott later learned an infected cut had hurt the latter's preparation. But while there were better days ahead in the Arc, York would continue to be a miserable stamping ground for Rheingold. For the Brigadier, wins in the Queen Elizabeth II Stakes at Ascot and the Champion Stakes at Newmarket, would help ease the pain of defeat for the connections of the formidable four-year-old.

Roberto was earmarked for a York return a year later, having also won the Coronation Cup in 1973, but O'Brien pulled the colt out of the contest at 1pm on the day of the race because of soft ground. His future lay at stud.

***

SEA The Stars arrived at York with a reputation every bit as big as the Brigadier's. He was indisputably the world's greatest racehorse – and with good reason.

Having been 8-1 before storming down the Rowley Mile at Newmarket in the 2,000 Guineas, Sea The Stars had then cruised over Epsom's notorious undulating track a month later to win the Derby. When the Eclipse fell his way in July at Sandown, the horse of a generation was the name every top racecourse wanted to secure. What York offered was the richest race the track had ever staged. A prize pot of £600,000 with more than £340,000 going to the winner. Fifth place would have scooped nearly £18,000. Except there wasn't a fifth place in the 2009 renewal.

The mere threat of Sea The Stars prompted only five declarations – with just four going to post on the day of the contest. But was the brilliant horse among them? York chiefs, mindful of the record rainfall which had forced an unprecedented decision to abandon the entire Ebor Festival 12 months earlier, were once again looking nervously skywards as the meeting approached. Brows were furrowed because Sea The Stars' participation depended on York producing good ground. Oxx had already spurned a trip to the Irish Derby in the absence of ideal conditions and was perfectly prepared to do the same again – even for the Juddmonte International, a race ranked only behind the Breeders' Cup Classic and Arc de Triomphe that year.

The forecast wasn't ideal, and Oxx wasn't optimistic. 'There is a big question mark about Tuesday (race day) and we just have to hope that there is not as much rain as has been forecast,' he said the weekend before. It could be less than expected but if everything comes then it will be bad news for us.' So came the wait. But for a course which had borne the brunt of Mother Nature as much as anyone in the past couple of years, the weather was finally kind. The rain stayed away.

With Sir Michael Stoute's Tartan Bearer pulling out, five became four – and the race became a duel – a tactical affair which enthralled punters over the mile and a quarter of the Group 1 contest. Sea The Stars against the might of Ballydoyle and Irish maestro Aidan O'Brien. Their bright hope was Mastercraftsman, the Irish 2,000 Guineas and Royal Ascot St James's Palace Stakes winner. With O'Brien's Set Sail and Georgebernardshaw merely making up the numbers, pacemakers designed to help pave the way for their more illustrious stablemate, it promised to be an old fashioned match race. It didn't disappoint.

It was like a film star coming to town. Photographs of the 'celebrity' arriving in York ahead of the race were fired across the web to waiting newspapers. On race-day, Sea The Stars' arrival at the track, and his trek across to the pre-parade ring from the racecourse stables, was beamed on Knavesmire's big screens to the watching punters. No horse had ever had that kind of attention. It was reflected in the betting ring. Punters only had eyes for Oxx's hero. At 1-4, Sea The Stars was taking the money just like the Brigadier had nearly four decades previously. But a furlong and a half from home, it seemed the superstar might – just like the Brigadier – be unexpectedly beaten.

The contest began innocuously enough. Riding Sea The Stars, Mick Kinane settled the Derby hero early out the back – tracking Mastercraftsman and giving a waiting ride behind the two Ballydoyle pacemakers. The start was brisk, but Sea The Stars was patient. He was cruising. Round the bend they went, into the home straight and still everyone waited for the race to really begin. Until three furlongs from home, when the two front runners parted like the Red Sea and Mastercraftsman travelled smoothly in between and through. So did Sea The Stars. But Johnny Murtagh, in the pilot seat on Mastercraftsman, had stolen the first run and, as he went for the whip, his mount surged. Kinane took the slightest of pulls on Sea The Stars and, suddenly, Mastercraftsman had the edge. Those buried memories of Brigadier Gerard's impossible defeat came bubbling back into the consciousness.

'Now push has come to shove for Sea The Stars', said the race commentator. 'What's the champion got left in the locker?'' Plenty.

It was only in doubt for several strides, about half a furlong in fact, and then the horse, who would go on to win the Prix de l'Arc de Triomphe at Longchamp two months later, picked up and swept past Mastercraftsman. He'd had to work for it, and the distance was only a length but, despite the initial scare, it was as cosy as a mere length could be. It was even a track record time, the two minutes 5.29 seconds stripping by more than half a second the mark set four years earlier by Imperial Stride over the same distance. Not bad, given the spectre of defeat had hung in the air – if only for a couple of seconds.

'Everyone held their breath at the furlong marker,' remembers William Derby, York chief executive and clerk of the course. 'He hit a flat spot. I think the horse, looking back, was so relaxed in himself he thought it was a training gallop in a way. Then he realised it was getting serious and for a few seconds it looked like he wouldn't pick up – but then he did in good style. It was an incredible race. I've watched it a number of times and it was an elegant race. Both before and after the race, I have never known an atmosphere so focused on a horse. You get celebrities at York, great jockeys and great trainers but I have never known the focus be so much in appreciation of an equine thoroughbred. Whether it is fanciful to say it but to get a Cheltenham Gold Cup winning atmosphere on a Flat course is unusual and I think you can say we had that sort of atmosphere in the paddock and the stands. People realised this horse was very special and appreciated the fact he had run in the north of England. I don't think it is too melodramatic to say that. People appreciated his presence. The caterers at York reported that the bars were empty during that race – everyone went out onto the steps to watch and that's unusual. Everyone was spellbound by it.'

Spellbound enough to hand Sea The Stars a standing ovation as Kinane steered him back into the winner's enclosure. Waiting was a somewhat relieved Oxx, who had left the race tactics in Kinane's hands. 'He's put up a good show,' he said as his star took the acclaim of the parade ring. 'Mick Kinane says he never wins anything by much more than a length. He just does enough. He never wins spectacularly. For a while I was worried. I thought two furlongs down "How far is he going to win?" He was coasting but then he had a struggle I suspect. He dug deep and found a bit.'

It was Sea The Stars' fourth Group 1 win on the spin. That would become six when the Irish Champion Stakes and the Arc fell effortlessly to his charms. He's earned his place among the elite – in there with the Mill Reefs and the Brigadier Gerards.

***

BRIGADIER Gerard's 1972 defeat was part of a pattern which gave York's newest contest an unwelcome reputation in its early years. If you had a favourite's chance as the Benson & Hedges Gold Cup cut its teeth, then it was wise to brace yourself for inevitable disappointment. It was a graveyard for favourites.

Rheingold, a flop in the first running, was in a similar frame of mind 12 months later when – this time as the heavily backed odds-on favourite – he was trumped by Moulton and only finished third. But it was a race remembered just as much for the merry-go-round between jockeys Lester Piggott, Geoff Lewis and Yves Saint-Martin as for Moulton's shock success.

'Piggott was going to ride Roberto,' explains veteran racing reporter Tim Richards. 'But Roberto was taken out. Piggott then phoned up Geoff Wragg, the trainer of Moulton, and said he would ride his horse. Then the syndicate that owned Rheingold got together and voted. The vote went for Piggott and they talked him into riding Rheingold. Geoff Lewis was going to ride Moulton and did so and we know that Rheingold got turned over. But the person that had turned up at York Races to ride Rheingold was Yves Saint-Martin and he watched it in the stands. He arrived to find he wasn't on the horse but he was promised, I think, ten per cent of the prize money. I think he would have been pretty sick. He'd flown from France.'

What Saint-Martin watched was a decisive display. Moulton, at 14-1, was far behind the 4-6 favourite Rheingold in the favour of the punters. The outsider was several lengths down on the leaders coming into the straight but Lewis worked him into position by the two furlong marker. By that stage, Rheingold was already beaten and it was Scottish Rifle, who had made much of the headway throughout the contest, and Sun Prince who were fighting it out for supremacy. Switched away from the rails, Moulton crashed through the duelling pair and into the lead, moving away strongly to beat Scottish Rifle by two and a half lengths. Piggott, who had ridden Moulton in the majority of his races since the Derby the previous year, had inadvertently handed Lewis an expensive gift.

Moulton's win might have raised eyebrows, but there were no shocks in 1974 when one of the greatest fillies ever seen at York strutted her stuff on Knavesmire. 'She was the most fantastic filly,' says Tim Richards. 'What she achieved was phenomenal. I think she won more prize money than any European-based filly – nearly half-a-million, which was a lot of money then. She was just so bloody tough.'

Lester Piggott hadn't enjoyed his first two outings in the race, both on Rheingold, but it was third time lucky for the legendary jockey thanks to the peerless Dahlia. The only odds-on favourite to land the race in its first seven renewals, Dahlia did the business against a top class field. Snow Knight and Imperial Prince, the leading pair in the Derby, came face to face with Dahlia and Highclere, the top two in the King George VI and Queen Elizabeth Stakes, in a nine runner contest where the pace was supplied by Hippodamia.

Dahlia had been suited by the strong pace at Ascot but it was Snow Knight who made the first move at the three furlong pole. Piggott had to switch his mount to find an opening but, once the gap appeared, off Dahlia went. She hit the front a furlong and a half out and Piggott pushed her out until the final few yards. The distance was two and a half lengths and the fabulous Dahlia was worth all of it. But, if that was good, her display 12 months later was even better.

She came to Knavesmire defeated, and only third at that, in an almighty battle in the King George VI and Queen Elizabeth Stakes. Going for a treble of crowns, she had to watch on as Grundy and Bustino went toe-to-toe in front of her. Grundy smashed Bustino and he was expected to do the same to Dahlia when the pair rejoined the battle at York. Instead, it was something of an anti-climax. The 1975 Gold Cup was a gift for Dahlia. Grundy appeared to have run terribly, looking like that Ascot battle had stripped him to the very core. Dahlia, on the other hand, made all the running and won comfortably. Timeform described the race as a 'present'.

But did that do Dahlia a disservice? Piggott had, after all, executed his plans to perfection. 'Looking at the race beforehand it seemed there was nothing that would go on and make the pace, so I decided to dictate from the start on the mare,' he wrote in his autobiography, *Lester*. 'I knew she stayed much further than the ten and a half furlongs of the race, so in the circumstances making all the running seemed the obvious thing to do. The strategy worked to perfection, Dahlia winning comfortably from Card King.'

Whatever the merit of her win, Dahlia had effectively staged her last stand. It was the only time that she won that season. Continuing the slow decline which had marked her campaign to that point, in the five races following her York success she finished in the first three only twice.

***

JOHN Sanderson could have perhaps allowed himself a quiet moment of satisfaction. With the first few contests now in the record books, the Benson & Hedges Gold Cup was on the way to becoming established as one of the top middle distance races in Europe.

Partly that was down to prize money, as the £40,000 haul was naturally persuasive in attracting the best horses to run. But it wasn't all plain sailing. For every Dahlia in those early years, there was a Relkino, who sprang a massive shock in 1977 when giving Willie Carson and owner Robert Sangster their first Gold Cup wins at 33-1. The prestige of the race might have been growing by the year but Sanderson remembers that trainers weren't always so forthcoming.

'There was clearly the need for a race like that in the Pattern, but it certainly had its bad years and got a reputation of being a bit of a graveyard,' says the former clerk of the course. 'Because it was a new race as well it got a bit of a caning from the popular press and some trainers probably fought shy of it on the basis that they thought it was an unlucky race. I suppose training horses is a slightly emotional business. Not to all trainers, but to some. But what has also probably helped the development of what is now the International is the trend away from a mile and a half races. You have to remember that a mile and a half was THE distance – the classic Derby distance. In the United States, however, a mile and a half was considered to be too long for breeding purposes. That influence has been felt progressively over the last 30 years. Some people would say the obsession with speed in pedigrees has been developed. Therefore, the extended mile and a quarter is a very good race now.'

***

THEN there was Troy. The colt had a turn of speed that was a sight to behold. As races reached their climax, Troy found a hidden gear that only the very best horses could boast.

In the 200th Derby at Epsom, the Dick Hern-trained colt simply destroyed the field. There is no other word for it. Seven lengths separated the three-year-old, with jockey Willie Carson on board, from Dickens Hill – with the rest strung out down the Epsom straight. It was all the more remarkable because, at the two furlong pole, Troy still had eight horses in front of him. Sheer pace had obliterated everything else. It was the widest winning margin in a Derby since Manna in 1925.

Nothing could beat him in the Irish Derby either, Dickens Hill again trailing behind – this time by four lengths – with Bohemian Grove in third. Fast forward to Ascot, and the King George VI and Queen Elizabeth Stakes. Only seven runners turned up and Troy, starting at 2-5, had a length and a half in hand from Gay Mecene.

So to York, and the Benson & Hedges Gold Cup. That Troy went to Knavesmire at all surprised some, with the Gold Cup's ten and a half furlongs considered by experts to be too short for the Derby champion. To a point, they were right. Troy did find things a lot more difficult at York. Carson was forced to get busy almost from the very beginning. Three furlongs from the line, it looked desperate – Troy trailing a dozen lengths behind Royal Ascot winner Crimson Bleu and Lyphard's Wish at the head of the field. But he was made of stern stuff and once again produced the kind of finish usually reserved for film scripts.

Well before the line, the fevered York crowd knew the wonder horse would get there. Once again, he had found that fabulous finishing gear.

Carson might have pushed him out to the line but, despite a strong challenge from Crimson Bleu, the winning distance of three quarters of a length was merely symbolic. The rider had been able to ease up in the last few yards.

'Troy was the first Derby winner to win that race,' says renowned racing writer Tim Richards. 'There are only two others that have done it – Authorized and Sea The Stars. Troy had terrific finishing speed. That had set him apart in the Derby. He found it a bit harder (at York) because he had come back from a mile and a half to a mile and a quarter. He was considered a mile and a half horse but that would have done his stud ticket a lot of good – winning a Group 1 mile and a quarter having won the Derby.'

York would prove his final highpoint. In the Prix de l'Arc de Triomphe at Longchamp two months later, Troy – starting at odds-on – was beaten into third by the Prix Vermeille victor Three Troikas and Le Marmot. He was not the same horse. His startling turn of foot was absent. He went to stud at Highclere but, after just four years as a stallion, the seven-year-old died in 1983.

His legacy has lived on, however. Troy sired Helen Street, the 1985 Irish Oaks filly. She would produce Street Cry, who would go on to sire 2007 Kentucky Derby victor Street Sense. And Westerner, the 2005 Gold Cup winner at Royal Ascot at York, came from Walensee, the 1985 Prix Vermeille champion, who was sired by, you guessed it, Troy.

***

'YORK is definitely a special place,' says Luca Cumani. 'I had my first winner in England there – Three Legs in the 1976 Duke of York Stakes.'

But it is three big August winners which prove why Knavesmire has always been lucky for the Italian trainer. Commanche Run was the opener in 1985, the last year of Benson & Hedges' sponsorship of the race (Matchmaker and, since 1989, the current sponsors Juddmonte are the only others), and it was as a result of a Cumani plan hatched to perfection with jockey Lester Piggott.

'We discussed the race beforehand and said if there was no pace and no one wanted to make it then Commanche Run might as well,' he says. 'We just said not to chase the pace if there wasn't any. He beat Oh

So Sharp – a short priced favourite – and it was a big race to win. As a four-year-old, he developed a lot more speed than he had a year earlier. We knew he had developed this amazing new speed. He was a top class horse.'

Commanche Run's win was impressive, but his filly One So Wonderful's victory in 1998 is remembered for its controversy as much as for the thrilling finish that brought up the Cumani double. Faithful Son, Chester House and One So Wonderful were pushed to the limit with jockey Pat Eddery holding off the challengers for Cumani by a short head in a photo finish – only to be hammered afterwards in the Stewards' room. Having hit his winner 24 times to take the race, Eddery found himself on the wrong end of an eight day ban for excessive use of the whip. He wasn't the only one to fall foul. Frankie Dettori, on Faithful Son, got four days and Kieren Fallon, in charge of Chester House, was banned for three. Eddery couldn't understand it. 'You get done if you take it easy, and you get done if you hit a horse too hard. But I don't think I hit horses too hard.'

The drama lasted long after the horses had left the track. Many racing observers cite this race as the spur to rule changes which looked to clamp down on the way jockeys asked their horses for extra effort. More than a decade on, it still rankles. Cumani thought all three riders were in 'an impossible situation'.

'All three horses were running for them, they were nose to nose. They had no choice and the punishments were too harsh,' he insists. 'As for the race, I remember thinking we hadn't won it. I thought we were beaten. I was in the stands and thought she was second. I was really chuffed when the result of the photograph was announced.'

Falbrav, in 2003 meanwhile, was just sensational. 'He was the best colt I have ever trained,' is Cumani's simple assessment of his equine superstar. 'We knew a mile and a quarter was his ideal trip and he went to York having won the Eclipse a couple of races before.' What the punters liked about Falbrav was his effort, his heart and his stomach for the fight. Cumani's champion didn't always win, but if your money went on Falbrav you knew the horse would be doing absolutely everything he could to get over the line in front.

He'd already been out in the Ganay, Ispahan, Prince of Wales, Eclipse and the King George by the time he came to Knavesmire. He'd won twice and he was about to put on a show over York's ten furlongs. Nayef, winner of the Juddmonte International 12 months earlier, lined up for a second crack but it was Falbrav who was always in total control. Darryll Holland, in the saddle, tracked the reigning champ and swept through with two furlongs remaining to leave Nayef watching his fast disappearing hooves. Even second slipped away for the 2002 winner, Magistretti staying on well to get up – but this race was all about Falbrav.

Cumani recalls: 'He was slightly sidetracked in the King George, going for the Middle-Distance Championship, and that was a mistake. It was a mile and a half in soft ground and he didn't get home. But he was a very strong horse and consistent. He was able to recover from race to race and he came back as good as ever for the Juddmonte. It was very exciting to win and he put the race away with a couple of furlongs to go. It was a real privilege to have a horse like that. He won five Group 1 races and he ran in ten Group 1s from April to December. He should have won six. He should have won in Ireland in the Champions Stakes at Leopardstown and, in the Breeders' Cup, in America, he just basically didn't quite get home over a mile and a half.'

Brough Scott, in his brilliant book *Of Horses And Heroes*, wrote of Falbrav: 'York was the ultimate in redemptions. Rarely do you get a horse race with the winner looking so dominant throughout. Holland tracked Nayef...and then put him ruthlessly to the sword...this was the hailing of a champion.'

***

WHEN John Smith remembers Triptych's International win in 1987 his face instantly contorts.

'That was a hell of a day. It really was,' says York's clerk of the course from 1987 to 2002. 'It started at about three or four o'clock in the morning and I could hear the rain hammering down. I got here and it was touch and go whether we had that race that day. It really was. Racing did go ahead but the ground was desperately heavy. Then to cap it all, just as the International runners were about to leave the paddock, we had a bomb scare. The police came on and said: "We've had this tip off, that we've got a bomb. We've actually been told it's in the weighing room".

143

So they said: "I strongly advise that you suspend racing until we've carried out a thorough search". So everything was stopped and I made an announcement that racing was suspended and the police went in, and the dogs, to the weighing room and after about ten minutes, quarter of an hour perhaps, I went in and saw the senior officer. I said "How are we doing?" and he said "We're just about clear now, I think we're going to be okay". I said "Fine" and at that I went into the Stewards' room and I couldn't believe what I saw there. There was a young lady, because we always have a shorthand typist in Stewards' inquiries in the weighing room, and she was typing away. I said: "What are you doing here?" "Oh," she said. "I'm typing out the notice to say that there's a bomb in the weighing room!" I will never forget it as long as I live.'

After all that, the race was child's play. Known for her granite-like toughness – she was nicknamed the Iron Lady by star-struck racing experts – Triptych already had half a dozen Pattern races, including the Irish 2,000 Guineas and Champion Stakes, in the locker when she arrived at York looking for third time lucky. That season's Prix Ganay, at Longchamp, and Epsom Coronation Cup winner had been beaten as a three and four-year-old in York's premier race – placed behind Commanche Run in 1985 and Shardari in 1986. Another year older, Triptych, trained by Patrick Biancone, was the hot favourite this time and lived up to the billing with a spectacular waiting display under Steve Cauthen. Deposited safely in the middle of the field, he waited until just before a furlong out before shaking the reins.

Taking off, Triptych cruised past Ascot Knight in the easiest two length victory you will ever see, with Sir Harry Lewis back in third. But this wonderful story had a tragic ending. Following a second Coronation Cup win the following year, Triptych was sent to the United States and, after one start at Churchill Downs, was retired to stud at the end of 1988. That year, while in foal to Mr Prospector, she died in a freak accident when she ran into a farm vehicle.

***

SOME critics will tell you that all a jockey does is steer. You only need to look at Terimon, in 1991, to see the nonsense in that line of reasoning.

Trained by Clive Brittain, Terimon's biggest claim to fame before arriving at York had been finishing second to the incomparable Nashwan in the 1989 Derby. Terimon had been priced at 1,000-1 and 500-1 and had been backed by the each-way punters who ploughed into the bookies at Tattenham Corner. 'The police were there until 9pm sorting out the bookmakers and the punters,' Brittain laughs. 'Terimon was a bit of a character and needed a race to go his way. We had a canny jockey in Michael Roberts, the champion Flat jockey the following year, who could judge a pace. He knew what to do to save that little bit up his sleeve for the last furlong.'

Brittain was irked his grey's Epsom display was considered an oddity. But at York, Terimon proved he had real ability. 'He raced his career as a fluke but winning this Group 1 proved he wasn't a fluke,' he adds. 'We went there pretty confident. There was quite a bit of talk over who would do the work and who would lead. We just went out there and made the running. We did it in our own time and, when they came to pick him up, he quickened up and away.'

In front after a furlong, Terimon set a steady pace as he kept Quest For Fame, and the 5-6 favourite Stagecraft – another odds-on favourite to go down – in the rear view mirror. Quest For Fame still had a chance, with two furlongs left, but it was the 16-1 Terimon who quickened and ran away to a two length victory. Environment Friend, who had won the Dante that year, was fifth.

The International was very much the summit for Terimon who, despite turning out a further seven times in his career, never won again. His racing days ended at York – 12 months later – when he finished tenth of 12 when looking to defend his International title. The horse that won the day would be a hugely sentimental Knavesmire winner. But not for the horse. In 1992, it was all about the jockey.

***

HAVING given the legendary Lester Piggott his final British Classic winner in the 2,000 Guineas, the York public were willing Rodrigo de Triano to win one more for the old stager when the pair arrived for the 1992 Juddmonte International.

Fourth in the St James's Palace Stakes at Royal Ascot on his last start while not in form, the three-year-old – named, but mis-spelled, after the 15th Century Spanish explorer – was having his first run over a mile and a quarter. Having returned to the saddle after being released from jail for tax evasion a few years previously, there was the sense that time was beginning to run out for the now 56-year-old champion. But York provided a fairytale moment.

Travelling superbly, Rodrigo de Triano took up the running a furlong from the winning post and barely needed cajoling to keep Oaks runner-up All At Sea in her place a length adrift – with Derby winner Dr Devious, also trained by Peter Chapple-Hyam, only fourth. It remains the favourite York moment for John Smith, the former clerk of the course on duty that day. 'It had something special about it,' he says. 'I think his price was something like 8-1 so he wasn't the favourite. I can remember the emotion of the crowd – a furlong out – clapping that Rodrigo was going to win and there was this tremendous affection and admiration for the prowess of Lester Piggott.'

'Lester was out on his own – whether he was in front or whether he was coming from behind,' adds distinguished racing reporter Tim Richards. 'He was so strong. It didn't matter whether it was a two-year-old or a five-year-old stayer. There was finesse there, if need be. He would drop a horse, its nose in front, on the line. He could pick them up and nearly carry them over. He was a complete artist.'

It's a view shared by Graham Orange, the voice of the winner's enclosure at York Racecourse and the man who has called in the victors and conducted interviews with winning connections for more than a quarter of a century. 'If I remember rightly,' he says, 'Swinging in from the final bend into the straight he was probably stone last. In that race were Derby winners and Classic winners and he was giving them all a massive lead before coming right through and cutting them all down. I remember what stood out in my mind was just what a genius Lester was in the saddle. It was unbelievable.'

***

FOR the King of Ballydoyle, Aidan O'Brien, Giant's Causeway in 2000 was something spectacular. Nicknamed the Iron Horse by the Racing Post, he was the thoroughbred who could be relied on to provide a nail-biting finish.

Meeting an old foe in Kalanisi, the £450,000 Knavesmire showpiece was a thrilling encounter. The St James's Palace Stakes, Eclipse and Sussex Stakes had already fallen to the colt when he and Kalanisi, who had gone toe-to-toe in the Eclipse, once again squared off down the straight in the International. 'It's a bit of a macho thing with this horse,' said O'Brien of Giant's Causeway afterwards. 'He just doesn't like being passed. He's inclined to play with other horses – he lets them come to him then goes on again.'

Having got the verdict in the Eclipse, the International proved to be a virtual carbon copy victory for Giant's Causeway, who was unsurprisingly the European Horse of the Year in 2000. One glimpse in the final stages was all it took, reckoned jubilant jockey Mick Kinane. He said: 'It was only when he eyeballed the other horse near the finish and he realised he might be beaten that he pulled out a little extra.'

Pacemaker Shoal Creek ensured Giant's Causeway was given a suitable gallop but, as the latter went by at the two furlong pole, Kalanisi was wound up for his challenge. With Pat Eddery in the saddle, he actually got ahead, but in the final 50 yards Giant's Causeway refused to buckle and forced his way back to the front to secure a fourth successive Group 1 victory. There were six runners, but it had been a two-horse race. The remainder trailed in seven lengths and more behind.

**

WILLIAM Derby is convinced. 'It's one of the best I have seen here,' York's chief executive and clerk of the course enthuses when revealing the 2005 Juddmonte International is his favourite race during his time in charge.

That was the year Electrocutionist nicked it and, for Derby, it was a race which left him mesmerised. 'We had some wonderful racing that year, which included Royal Ascot at York, and the Juddmonte International was a fantastic race with Zenno Rob Roy, the triple Group 1 winner from Japan, and Electrocutionist.'

Anyone looking for clues needed to have looked no further than Electrocutionist's trainer Valfredo Valiani. The Italian had saddled precisely one previous winner in Britain, and that was at York when Super Tassa swept to the 2001 Yorkshire Oaks as a big outsider. Maybe we should have taken the hint. Electrocutionist lined up in a field of seven and started joint third favourite – behind Ace and Zenno Rob Roy. But even if Valiani's presence should have made backers confident, the horse still only had a neck to spare in the finish. He was dead last with three furlongs to go, and Zenno Rob Roy, the Japanese raider who had brought a nation's media with him to York, looked the likely winner as Ace made the running. But Electrocutionist found a sudden stride and, widest of the runners striving for the post, he prevailed from the Japanese hero, with Maraahel a head further back in third and Ace in fourth.

It was a finish which electrified Derby. 'There's a wonderful picture of them in a line, all fantastic Group 1 winners, and Electrocutionist just won it and then went on to win the Dubai World Cup. It was fantastic.'

***

FRANKIE Dettori had hit plenty of International heights before. There had been Halling and Singspiel in consecutive years in the mid-1990s, then the sensational Sakhee in 2001 and Sulamani in 2004. But one marvellous horse probably meant more – Authorized.

Peter Chapple-Hyam's Dante winner truly was one in a million. Not just because he had broken Dettori's duck in the Derby, finally giving him the victory he craved most at the 15th attempt. When he came to York for the 2007 Juddmonte International it was the first time the race boasted a million dollar prize fund. Authorized was also tasked with bucking an unwelcome trend. Not since High Chaparral in 2002 had a Derby winner gone on to win a race of any description.

Authorized's comprehensive Epsom victory meant it looked only a matter of time before that anomaly was ended but, when the colt was subsequently bested by Notnowcato in the Eclipse at Sandown in July, Chapple-Hyam came to York with the critics able to let their eyes drift towards a winner from elsewhere. Notnowcato, the 2006 Juddmonte victor, was back to defend his crown and an international field was boosted by the appearance of Asiatic Boy, a South African raider. Dylan Thomas, Aidan O'Brien's top class King George VI and Queen Elizabeth Stakes victor, also looked a potent threat in a quality field of seven runners. While they came to Knavesmire fresh and ready, Dettori, by contrast, was laid up with flu.

'Dettori didn't ride the following day but he was absolutely determined to ride in that race,' remembers William Derby, York's chief executive. 'Going into the race you could pick weaknesses in a number of the protagonists. But to have Authorized there, and to have horses of that quality targeting our races, was a great vindication of all that the York Race Committee and the board are trying to achieve.'

What they got was an imperious display. Sent off the 6-4 favourite by punters who did not share the tipsters' doubts, Authorized took a comfortable position towards the back of the field as the outsider Song Of Hiawatha made the running with a strong early pace. Notnowcato held a prominent position and took over shortly after entering the straight. Ryan Moore pushed the button on the title defender just before the two furlong pole but Dettori was wise to the Champion Jockey's move. Stationed on his shoulder, the Italian asked Authorized to respond and rousted the Derby winner to the front as Johnny Murtagh, on Dylan Thomas, also made his effort and swept into second. The pair battled all the way to the line but Authorized found the speed he had lacked in the Eclipse and prevailed by a length.

'I was saying to Frankie "Let him go" because I could see Dylan Thomas making ground and he's a hard horse to crack,' Chapple-Hyam said in the winner's enclosure. 'There was never a moment when I thought he wouldn't win. But I was wanting Frankie to let him go. He was giving him a pull and he's a galloper. He's a great horse. It's easy when they are that good.'

Dettori, despite suffering with illness, was also exultant. 'I've never seen a horse in a big race travel so well. The further he was going, the further he was pulling. In the Derby he gave a great performance and he has put the record straight today. He is a true champion. I've had the flu for two weeks but nothing would keep me away from this.'

***

HOW do you top Sea The Stars? The plan was simple; bring the world's highest rated racehorse to run the following year.

Connections of the Sir Michael Stoute-trained Harbinger paid £50,000 to supplement him in the 2010 Juddmonte International, and it was an entry which quickly got the pulse racing. Briefly. For the King

George VI and Queen Elizabeth Stakes winner, who had destroyed a top class field at Ascot by 11 lengths, was destined not to step out on the York track. Stepping up his preparations for the contest, Harbinger fractured a leg on the Newmarket gallops and never raced again. They had been banking on Knavesmire that the super horse would erase any thoughts of anti-climax the year after the Star had shone at York. Now they had to go back to the drawing board.

John Manley, the owner of Greenham Stakes and Prix Jean Prat hero Dick Turpin, tried to lighten the mood. He surprisingly stumped up the cash to supplement the Richard Hannon-trained colt, named after the notorious horse thief who was hung on Knavesmire in 1739, into the race. It pushed the Juddmonte International booty up to an eye-watering £693,000. And although Dick Turpin wouldn't be the one to shout 'stand and deliver', finishing fifth, the race would still see a 'robbery'.

It should have been Prince Khalid Abdullah's year. The owner of Juddmonte Farms had supported York's richest race for more than two decades, but had never won the flagship contest. In Byword and Twice Over there was a great chance his patience would finally be rewarded this time. There wasn't a lot between them. The pair, trained by Andre Fabre and Henry Cecil respectively, had met just once before, in the Prince of Wales's Stakes at Royal Ascot, when Byword was just half a length in front. As the Juddmonte International raced deep into the final furlong, it was still a flip of the coin as to which was the better. But what seemed certain was that the winner would come from one of these two Abdullah representatives. His moment would come at last.

With a hundred yards left, Byword and Twice Over fought side by side and stride for stride for the spoils. Neither horse, however, had accounted for Rip Van Winkle. Aidan O'Brien had won the race with Giant's Causeway in 2000 but had not tasted success at York since (Duke Of Marmalade's 2008 win had been at Newmarket after the Ebor Festival was washed out). Rip Van Winkle, the four-year-old dual Group 1 winner, had not won since taking the Queen Elizabeth II Stakes at Ascot the previous September either.

O'Brien had expressed some doubts in the run-up to the contest as to whether he would even take part but, once at York, the punters loved Rip Van Winkle and jockey Johnny Murtagh. They sent the pair off the 7-4 favourites. Held up towards the rear in the early stages,

Murtagh didn't ask Rip Van Winkle for any serious effort until three furlongs from home. Was it too late?

Byword and Twice Over were moving sweetly, but Rip Van Winkle's searing late charge was breathtaking. Murtagh knew he was going to get there – and break Abdullah's heart – and it was by half a length from Twice Over at the finish with Byword back in third. 'As soon as I got him out and on an even keel, he was really eating up the ground,' the Irish jockey said in the winner's enclosure. 'I am glad to have got there in front. I think he is a great horse. He is special. When you ride him at half speed at home he takes your breath away. He cruises over the ground. Coming here, the team was confident and it is lovely to have a big winner here at York.'

O'Brien was just as delighted. 'He's really on an upward curve,' he said. 'Johnny gave him a really good ride. He's got a lot of speed this horse. You have to say Johnny was marvellous. He just let him take his time to come into the race and let things happen.'

Rip Van Winkle was paradise for punters. In a 2010 Ebor Festival that would become renowned for big shocks and big price winners, O'Brien's horse, retired later on in the season, was one of the few that brought home the bacon for the paying public. In a contest where pre-race favourites have been downed with regularity, that's some achievement.

***

THERE are older races, contests with more history, with a greater tradition. But in just 40 runnings, there aren't that many which have burned their imprint onto the race calendar in the way the Juddmonte International has.

Comparisons with the Breeders' Cup Classic and the Arc de Triomphe aren't just for show – they indicate the sheer strength of runner, the quality of the track and the popularity of the contest. It's been hard earned. Reputations are hard to build in racing, a sport where pomp and tradition hold such great sway. But the Juddmonte International, an upstart newcomer compared with the likes of the Eclipse and the Champion Stakes, deserves its billing as one of racing's mid-summer highlights. For as long as it continues to attract the world's best middle distance horses, its success isn't in doubt.

THE EBOR HANDICAP

THE weight is immense, it buries the legs in the turf with every stride, but Sea Pigeon is about to defy it all. The pain, the odds, the severest of challenges. This is the Ebor Handicap's defining moment. For despite all of those winners, all of the prizes, it's Dawn Run and Sea Pigeon that dominate Jonjo O'Neill's career as a jockey.

The days of back-to-back Cheltenham Champion Hurdle wins are still to come. But what Sea Pigeon did in the Ebor Handicap on August 22, 1979 laid the foundations for legend. Scottish owner Pat Muldoon paid £8,000 for the son of Sea Bird II, and he had already more than paid his way long before he entered Knavesmire folklore. He was one of a brilliant set of horses trained by Peter Easterby at Malton's Habton Grange – part of a legacy which included Night Nurse and Alverton.

The famous stables are run these days by Easterby's son, Tim, and more than 30 years on, he fondly remembers the 'machine' of a horse. 'I remember his speed,' he says. 'Tremendous speed and class. But I wasn't the one guilty of settling him down. A guy called Mark Birch rode him in all his work at home. He used to pull like a train when we got him. I was lucky enough to ride him in a race. It was the Moët & Chandon Silver Magnum, which was a big stakes race at Epsom. I just had to sit on and steer – don't go too soon, that was all.'

But Sea Pigeon wasn't perfect. He had a flaw, as racing journalist Tom O'Ryan, who worked as an apprentice jockey for Easterby senior, explains. 'I'm struck by people who still come to me and say he was their favourite horse,' he says. 'He was a really smooth traveller through a race. He did everything on the bridle and had a wonderful turn of foot but when he got to the front he would prick his ears. He was the same at home. I used to ride him a fair bit and when he went a length and a half up he would prick his ears and drop the bridle.'

O'Ryan had described riding Sea Pigeon as like travelling in a Rolls Royce – a horse with a 'high cruising speed' and 'overdrive'. 'Ride against him and it was like spitting against the wind,' he wrote in the *Racing Post* on Sea Pigeon's death at the age of 30. 'A furlong from the end of the gallop, just when you thought you'd gone a good enough clip to stretch him, and he'd come sailing past, with ears pricked under a motionless pilot, as though he'd just jumped in.' No other horse at Habton Grange could get near him.

That Sea Pigeon went off at 18-1 in the Ebor reflected not his ability, but the huge amount of weight he was being forced to carry. In the Ebor's long history, no horse had conquered the one mile, six furlong stamina test with anything more than the nine stone and seven pounds endured by Gladness in 1958. Sea Pigeon was attempting the feat with ten stone. O'Neill, who had already ridden the horse in two runner-up appearances in the Champion Hurdle, was in the saddle. Birch had been his regular partner on the level but he was on another, shorter priced, Easterby contender – No Bombs – for this Ebor. O'Neill had only learned the day before he would be riding the horse at York in what was just his second appearance on Knavesmire. First, however, he had to get past the racecourse doctor.

'He'd had a fall and got broken toes,' remembers Tim Richards, the racing journalist who manned typewriters at the *Daily Mirror* and *Racing Post*. 'In the weighing room – in front of the other jockeys – as he was queuing to weigh out, he was hopping about, showing off and doing a sort of dance. He was hoping people would realise he was absolutely fine, including the doctor. In fact the doctor tested his toes. He passed him but I think he had three broken toes.'

O'Neill was no stranger to riding on the level – Sea Pigeon would turn out to be his sixth winner that year – but, even so, it almost ended in disaster. As the gates went up, Donegal Prince, the 33-1 shot, was out quickly under Philip Robinson, then a 7lb claimer, and still held the advantage two furlongs from home. Sea Pigeon was making rapid progress, however, and O'Neill took his mount into the lead inside the final furlong. He looked like winning the race comfortably, but the superstar jockey then made a basic mistake. He committed the cardinal riding sin of dropping his hands. Sea Pigeon, thinking the job was done, almost came to a complete stop. Donegal Prince flashed through and they hit the line together.

Everyone thought Sea Pigeon had lost. John Sanderson, then York's clerk of the course, remembers: 'There was stunned silence while they waited for the judge to call the photograph. The Stewards had him in – in a friendly way – but it wouldn't have been so friendly if he'd got caught. They showed him the photographs and the films of him dropping his hands. I think Peter Easterby would have shot him.'

'Apparently, Graham Lockerbie, the travelling head lad for Peter Easterby, came to greet Jonjo as he came in and said: "Peter thinks you have got beat",' added Tim Richards. 'He was terrified when he came in. He thought he had lost the race and, as it turned out, it was all right – just. It was one of the most popular victories on the Knavesmire. The place erupted. I can only just remember it but people who recall it said it was absolutely fantastic – the reception when it was announced it had won the race. Sea Pigeon was terrific. He was out of this world.'

'Jonjo rode a beautiful race up to the last four or five strides. He just eased up, thinking he had won it,' remembers Tom O'Ryan. 'He was ashen-faced. He realised he had eased up just a second too soon. The other thing about that race was ITV were on strike so there have never been any television pictures of it. You will never see a recording of that anywhere. It's always a race where you had to be there on the day.'

Luckily, for O'Neill's health, Sea Pigeon had remained in front – by nothing more than a short-head. But that he had won at all was remarkable. Donegal Prince was receiving 40 pounds, including riding allowance, from Sea Pigeon, who was also giving third placed Move Off – winner of the Ebor in 1977 – 15 pounds. The average age of his 20 rivals was less than half his own. Timeform described it as one of the highlights of the season, and ranked it the best performance of Sea Pigeon's career on the Flat. Back over the sticks, better was to come.

***

'IF you look at that race, it doesn't look like Mudawin is going anywhere a furlong out,' Luca Cumani remembers. 'But then he suddenly sprouted wings. We thought we had it and we were pipped.' Mudawin was the Ebor winner that couldn't be.

Forget the catchy name, Australian-born trainer Jane Chapple-Hyam's five-year-old wasn't so much a has-been as a never-been prior to the 2006 Ebor Handicap. The bookies hadn't looked at him, and he went off in Europe's richest handicap at 100-1. Then he pulled off not just the shock of the season, but one of the biggest shocks in Ebor history.

Mudawin was bought as a prospective Melbourne Cup candidate. He had sneaked in at the bottom of the handicap. Ridden by John Egan, there was little sense early on of what was on the cards. In a field of 19, Elusive Dream made the running at a scorching pace while, in comparison, Mudawin looked to be struggling at the back of the pack. Striding into the straight, River Alhaarth – trained by Jane's ex-husband Peter Chapple-Hyam – was sent to the front but his challenge faded almost as quickly as it arrived and the £200,000 contest looked to be a fight between Young Mick and Cumani's 13-2 chance Glistening. But now Mudawin had found his gear, and what an engine he had. With Glistening flat to the boards, Mudawin finished like a rocket and snatched the spoils from Cumani's charge by a head – with Young Mick a short head further back in third. It was hard to take in.

'We were a bit gutted,' Cumani says. 'Although Glistening wasn't that great a disappointment. He wasn't a short priced favourite – we went there with a chance, but not with a favourite's chance. It was disappointing because we thought we had it. Once we had the better of Young Mick, we thought we had the pace.'

Mudawin's victory made him one of the longest-odds winners the Ebor, a race run since 1843, had ever produced. But while it was great news for the bookmakers, it had not been such a big shock for his trainer. 'We've always thought a lot of this horse and I thought he was a crazy price,' Chapple-Hyam said in the parade ring. 'With the light weight we decided to stay out the back and hope he could run through for a place. He just thrived on the good to soft ground, which I didn't think he would.'

'Brilliant' and the 'perfect result' was how several leading bookmakers described it, but some punters were victors as well. The racecourse tote paid out £85,000 to happy racegoers, while one couple's £10 each-way bet netted them £1,500. Cumani, however, only had to wait 12 months for redemption. 'We were hoping Purple Moon could go one better,' he says. 'He was a better horse than Glistening. He was coming off a win in a Listed race and, this time, he was a short priced favourite.' The 7-2 favourite no less.

Purple Moon reunited Cumani with Jamie Spencer, who had been in the saddle on Glistening as Mudawin performed that smash and grab raid. Spencer had his own scores to settle with the Ebor. The rider, joint champion jockey the following year, had been placed four times in the race before but yearned to taste victory. A talented horse, the four-year-old Purple Moon had beaten Imperial Star by two and a half lengths in a Listed race at Goodwood just three weeks previously – a result which had, initially at least, left Cumani in confident mood.

'If you had asked me after he passed the post at Goodwood I would have said 'Why bother running the race, just send the prize money and the trophy,' he says. 'But the closer I got to the race the more I started thinking, this could beat us, that could beat us, the ground might be a bit soft.'

Those who sought to stop Cumani included Aidan O'Brien's Honolulu and the Godolphin-trained Scriptwriter. Even as Purple Moon hit the front with a furlong left, after making rapid progress in the Knavesmire straight, Cumani admitted afterwards he still was unable to relax. 'I was looking at the ones behind hoping there wasn't a Mudawin to nail me on the post like the year before. But it happens, it is horse racing. Sometimes you win it by a head, sometimes you lose it.'

This time he won it, and the emotions compared with a year previously couldn't have been more different. It was only three quarters of a length at the post, with Honolulu in second, but it had been a relatively straightforward success as Purple Moon asserted and stayed on well despite edging right in the final stages.

'It was almost a relief that he did it,' Cumani remembers. 'There was a bit of pressure but he went on to do even better. He was a progressive horse. He was a horse on the up and went on to be second in the Melbourne Cup. He also ran at Group 1 level around the world with distinction.'

***

'IT'S probably my favourite moment at York,' says Mark Johnston, the master of Middleham's Kingsley House. 'I can't think of anything that surpasses it. Despite the fact I couldn't understand all the fuss about the Ebor, it stands out mostly because of the reaction of other people. It was the reaction of people like Dean McKeown, Tony Farmer and Walter Bentley.'

The moment? The 1992 Ebor Handicap. The horse was Quick Ransom. 'There were a couple of incredible things about Quick Ransom,' Johnston says. 'He ran nine times as a two-year-old without winning and we still kept him. It wasn't something we did even then, but we were convinced he was a good horse. The following year, he started to come good and he won in the January of his three-year-old career. During that winter, there were a group of people I remember saying to, as the horse came back from the gallops, "There's the Ebor winner" – six months before he won it.'

If winning the Ebor wasn't an obsession for Johnston, it certainly was for jockey Dean McKeown. His career may have ended in disgrace, after horse racing chiefs found him guilty of a series of transgressions, but, at his height, the adopted Yorkshireman was a shrewd race rider. As a devotee of the White Rose County, he had no bigger ambition than to win York's flagship handicap.

'He was obsessed with the idea of the Ebor Handicap,' Johnston confirms. 'The plan for Quick Ransom's Ebor was "be out there". We had discussed in advance that we had to be up with the pace. Prior to that he had been renowned as a come from behind horse.'

Not this day. Quick Ransom had been tearing up the track even before the Ebor. Handicaps had fallen his way at Haydock and on Knavesmire and he had been beaten in a photo-finish at Epsom. Pressing from the front had worked at York before and McKeown shot the four-year-old out of the stalls – taking a safe position behind the leaders until it came to the endgame. Johnston recalls: 'I remember him hitting the front around two furlongs out and Dean virtually lifted him over the line.'

Quick Ransom stole a two length lead at the two furlong pole, but had to resist as the pack began to reel him in. Brier Creek made the biggest challenge but Johnston's horse held on in a finish which saw fewer than two lengths covering the first seven finishers.

'Tony Farmer, who is an East Yorkshireman from Hull, came and grabbed me by the lapels after the race and was in tears saying "What do you think about Ebors and Derbys now?," Johnston says. 'He was always telling me it was better to win the Ebor than the Derby. He really meant it. He didn't even own the horse. He just attended as one of my owners. Walter Bentley, the ex-jockey, grabbed me and exclaimed it was like the old days. It was wonderful, the reaction of the Yorkshire people, that made this Ebor day so special.'

***

FOUR races, four moments which show why the Ebor Handicap has buried itself so deeply into the minds of the racing public. York's first great race was literally that. It was given life in 1843 when Knavesmire wasn't regarded nearly as grandly as it is today. When Pagan, carrying seven stone 13 pounds and ridden by Sim Templeman, first won the Great Ebor Handicap for Col Cradock, York Racecourse was in a rut.

Walkovers were frequent in the 1830s and 40s and, on the occasions runners came to contest, competition between just three and four horses was the norm – that's if they weren't reduced to match races. Considered decadent, and in some cases even corrupt, York had been overtaken by Doncaster as the north's pre-eminent race track. It was the Town Moor's big race, the St Leger Stakes, which helped to give clerk of the course John Orton his big idea.

Orton had succeeded Walter Melrose as a race judge in March 1830, having previously been secretary to the York Race Committee, which ran the course. His early attempts to revitalise Knavesmire with the Great Yorkshire Stakes had come to little. A lack of vision and poor prize money had brought even the flagship August meeting to the brink of disaster. When only eight horses turned up for the Spring

Meeting in May 1839, Orton knew something had to be done. One columnist wrote: 'Oh York! York!! York!!! Where is now thy boasted meeting?'

Newly installed as clerk in 1842, Orton's Great Ebor Handicap, the name shortened from Eboracum, the Roman name for York, was initially contested over two miles before the distance was later cut by two furlongs. It began with stakes of £20, £15 forfeit and £200 added money. The race quickly caught on, but it took six years for the first truly great winner to emerge.

The Hero lived up to his name. He carried nine stone four pounds and was ridden by Alfred Day. As a weight carrying performance, it wouldn't be beaten for 30 years until Isonomy triumphed with four pounds more on his back. Corrie Roy, in 1883 carrying nine stone 12 pounds, was the next to tip the scales but no one has ever beaten Sea Pigeon's ten stone burden. The Hero was bred in Pembrokeshire by Allan Cresselly and, trained by John Day in Stocksbridge, he had won the 1848 Ascot Gold Cup before sweeping aside 14 rivals at York the following year. When he died in 1859, The Hero had been the victor of 29 races.

Lily Agnes, who won in 1875 at 10-1, was another popular name in the record books – a winner of 21 races including the Doncaster Cup and the Northumberland Plate and is remembered primarily for foaling the Derby winner Ormonde, who would become one of the horses of the century. The architect of a race now truly 'great', there was no happy ending, unfortunately, for Orton.

Hindsight may see him the saviour of York Races but petty jealousies drove him from his post. Lord George Bentinck, the third son of the Duke of Portland and a Parliamentarian, despised York's clerk and told the course's Race Committee he would not set foot on Knavesmire while his foe was at the helm. A great success on the turf, Bentinck brought his dominating personality to bear and, barely two years after the Ebor also began a transformation of the racecourse – brick buildings replaced wooden structures and the old horseshoe track became circular – he was dismissed. Owner of the Turf Coffee House, in York, Orton took his sacking terribly – and drank himself to death within weeks.

***

TIMES have changed as we wind through the first third of the 20th Century. The Great Ebor is merely The Ebor – renamed in 1910 – but the loss of the adjective has not diminished the contest. That's partly down to two Jacks: Flint and Brown.

No horse has won the Ebor back-to-back since Flint Jack did the trick in 1922 and 1923, winning the second of those in a downpour. Brown Jack came third in a dead heat between Gentlemen's Relish and Coaster in 1930 but was hailed a wonder winner when sweeping to an easy success the following year. In the saddle was jockey Steve Donoghue, considered the Frankie Dettori of his day. A six-time winner of the Derby, ten times champion jockey between 1914 and 1923, and first jockey to Sir Victor Sassoon, your shillings were safe with him. So they were with Brown Jack too.

Foaled in 1924, the horse raced for ten years and took every major long distance race on the calendar except the Cesarewitch. His Ebor victory nestled against Goodwood, Doncaster and Chester Cups, the legendary stayer was renowned for humping heavy weights to victory. Brown Jack was originally envisaged as a hurdler and he was good enough over obstacles to win the Champion Hurdle at Cheltenham in 1928. Switched to the more lucrative Flat, he was already a hero by the time he came to York, principally because he was in the middle of a six year run of success in the Queen Alexandra Stakes at Ascot – a race he would win every year from 1929 to 1934. When he ran there, the *Evening Standard* banners proclaiming racing at the track would simply say: 'Brown Jack today'.

Much was made of Brown Jack's Ebor weight, a heavy nine stone five pounds, but despite the horse's undoubted class the lead he carried, although burdensome, was by no means unusual. Polar Star in 1906, Lomond in 1911 and Stornaway in 1913 had all been victorious carrying two pounds more. But Brown Jack caught the public mood. 'The best stayer in the world,' was how the *Yorkshire Herald*, on August 27, 1931, regarded the horse in the aftermath of his Ebor win. 'Visitors to Knavesmire yesterday could not recall an occasion on which the winner of the Ebor had met with such an enthusiastic reception as that which greeted Brown Jack,' the paper reported. Brown Jack went off a

Above: Sergeant Cecil holds off Geordieland to win the Yorkshire Cup in 2007

Above: Jamie Spencer, right, roars his delight as Purple Moon wins the 2007 Ebor Handicap

Above: Authorized and Frankie Dettori in action during the Dante Stakes in May 2007
Picture courtesy of Louise Pollard

Below: Three months later, Authorized and Frankie Dettori are back at York to win the
Juddmonte International
Picture courtesy of Louise Pollard

Above. Jumping for joy - Frankie Dettori performs his famous flying dismount following Authorized's Juddmonte win

Picture courtesy of Louise Pollard

Above: Kingsgate Native becomes the first two-year-old for 15 years to win the Nunthorpe Stakes in 2007
Pic courtesy of Louise Pollard

Above: Flying Clarets and apprentice jockey Freddie Tylicki win the John Smith's Cup in 2008

Right: Lush Lashes makes easy work of the field in the Musidora Stakes of 2008

Below: Sesenta, in light blue, just has the measure of Changingoftheguard in the 2009 Ebor Handicap

Above: Borderlescott, wearing number 2, strides out to victory in the 2009 Nunthorpe Stakes

Above: Sariska, left, wins the Musidora Stakes in 2009 with Jamie Spencer in the saddle

Above: Sea The Stars, in yellow, gives the York public the victory they crave in the Juddmonte
International of 2009   Picture courtesy of Louise Pollard

Above: The York Racecourse stands look resplendent as Showcasing takes the Gimcrack of 2009

Above: Jockey Johnny Murtagh is delighted after Rip Van Winkle wins the Juddmonte International of 2010

Above: Sole Power springs a 100-1 surprise in the 2010 Nunthorpe Stakes

10-1 chance, but the *Herald* report reveals he was no forlorn hope for the spectators. 'He was one of the best supported winners of the afternoon,' their man at the track wrote.

Brown Jack took the lead three furlongs from home – passing the filly Wedding Favour, who had made a bold bid to make the running. The 4-1 favourite was Argonaute II, who had been last throughout much of the race but, entering the straight, tried to join Coaster in battling to stay with Brown Jack's surge. 'Both struggled hard to get to Brown Jack,' said the *Herald*, 'But the old gelding finished too strongly for both of them.' The report continued: 'There was a full-throated cheer as he galloped past the post, and, as the gallant old horse was led into the paddock with Donoghue smiling, the cheering was renewed and continued until the jockey had disappeared with his saddle into the weighing room.'

His trainer Ivor Anthony was delighted, so was Donoghue. 'It was a splendid performance in every way, and I am glad the crowd gave gallant old Brown Jack such a great reception,' the jockey said. On his retirement, Brown Jack's race record read 18 wins from 55 Flat starts, taking a touch more than £12,000 in prize money. He even had a locomotive named after him.

***

MUSEUM might be one of the greatest horses to have won an Ebor – not that the punters thought a great deal of him before he did so.

Sir Victor Sassoon's colt had already collected the Irish 2,000 Guineas and the Irish Derby before travelling to Knavesmire, but the public sent him off at 100-8 for Yorkshire's prestige race. Not even the presence of Steve Donoghue in the saddle could inspire much confidence. Victory would be considered a shock. Experts considered him to be a touch below top class, a symptom of perceived mediocrity in pre-Second World War Irish racing. Having said that, if the punters always knew what they were doing then the bookies wouldn't be rich.

In front of the largest crowd seen on Knavesmire for many years, the men with the satchels would triumph yet again. Only just, however. The *Yorkshire Herald* reported that the 'finish was as exciting as any that has occurred in the long history of the race'. It would turn into a showdown between Museum and John James.

Museum was trained by John Thomas Rogers, who had won all the Irish Classic races in that 1935 season. He didn't come to York, leaving his star colt in the charge of his son, John. The journey had been long. Leaving Ireland on the Saturday, Museum didn't arrive at the racecourse until Tuesday. But Donoghue rode a canny race. Negro, the pre-race favourite, stormed up the straight having been last in the early stages. Unfortunately, even a clear run home couldn't close the gap and he finished in a bunch behind the placed horses. John James, though, was harder to shrug off. He arrived with a sharp run inside the final furlong and, as the pair bolted past the line, some observers thought Museum had been beaten. Had the contest gone on for a couple of extra strides, he almost certainly would have been.

It was Donoghue's nous and clever tactics that built what would become a short head victory. His decision to vault Museum to the front at the two furlong marker meant that while his challengers, including John James, had to negotiate traffic, Museum had a clear run to the finishing line. It proved to be just enough. Donoghue was almost clinical in his post-race interview. The *Yorkshire Herald*'s quotes were joyless. 'I took the lead from John James about a furlong and a half into the straight,' he said. 'I was headed by one or two others but shook them off. John James then came at me again to make a near thing of it.'

Museum, the first Irish horse to win the Ebor, went back to the Emerald Isle and won the Irish St Leger, giving him the Triple Crown of Irish Classics, and adding another layer of brilliance to the fabulous Ebor Handicap.

***

GLADNESS was a horse in the Brown Jack mould – and not only because she carried a whopping nine stone seven pounds to Ebor triumph in 1958.

Trained in Ireland by the, even then, legendary Vincent O'Brien, Gladness was a superb galloper and particularly enjoyed a strong pace, which is what she got on Knavesmire. It was another step in the emerging relationship between Lester Piggott and O'Brien, who had selected the enigmatic jockey for the first time to ride Gladness in the Ascot Gold Cup earlier in the year. Gladness won that race, largely untroubled, and then easily took the Goodwood Cup before O'Brien sent her, and Lester, to Knavesmire. She brought up the hat-trick just as easily. The weight was hardly a burden as Piggott came from off the pace and the 5-1 chance claimed the spoils with something to spare.

Future York clerk of the course John Sanderson was transfixed by her performance. But it was a highpoint for the Ebor Handicap. It was about to come under attack. 'What really epitomised it was the first Ebor I ever saw, Gladness in 1958 when I was a schoolboy,' he explains. 'Gladness was an absolutely top class mare in the Dahlia class. You hadn't a prayer of attracting that sort of horse 20 years later. They were all being channelled off into the protected area of the Pattern.'

The 'Great' Ebor, then more than a century old, faced its biggest challenge in the 1970s and 80s because of the Pattern problem. The race itself was not under threat, but its credibility was. In 1965, the Jockey Club established the Pattern of Racing Committee, which recommended sweeping changes to the sport. They identified prestige races and feature contests to support the Classic tests and these formed the Pattern Race Programme – starting in 1970. The aim was to gain Black Type, the bold lettering which would accompany a thoroughbred, and its descendants, in sales catalogues. A horse with Black Type had won a contest of significance. In the pompous, selective world of racing, handicaps weren't allowed to join the gang. How did this affect the Ebor?

The Pattern races gained their significance not only from their prestige, but from their prize money. Keeping the status quo meant limiting the money a racecourse could put on for the top handicaps, of which the Ebor was the richest. That meant driving down the quality of the contest – because the very best horses would opt for the Pattern instead.

'They wouldn't let the Ebor interfere with the Pattern,' explains Sanderson, who became clerk of the course at York in 1972 and remained in post until the close of the 1986 season. 'I remember at some stage we wanted to put on a £100,000 handicap on Timeform Charity Day and Robert Sangster was going to sponsor it with his stud. They stopped it and persuaded him to put his money into the Sussex Stakes. Our hands were tied because they were trying to encourage horses that had got to a certain quality not to run in handicaps and go to the

Pattern. There was still a fairly heavy influence on the breeding side and the people who ran racing in those days in the Jockey Club were all breeders. What they were concerned with was improving the breed and handicaps were just a bit of fun. The appeal of handicaps to the betting public, both on and off the course, hadn't really taken hold in the minds of the powers that be. There was a ceiling beyond which you couldn't go – so all we could do was keep it on the ceiling. It is bound to have affected the quality of the race and it was unfair because it was anti-competitive. It was a shame because, from a York perspective, racing is a theatre and handicaps are part of the act. They are part of what you put on the stage.'

As late as 1983 Alistair Down, writing in the *Sporting Life*, chastised the Jockey Club – arguing its 'Obsessive refusal to countenance £50,000 handicaps has done a gross disservice to such races as the Ebor'. In 1979, when Sea Pigeon gave the race arguably its standout moment, the year's Timeform *Racehorses* annual complained: 'If York Racecourse, or any other, wishes to put on a £40,000 or £50,000 handicap why should they be prevented from doing so? In spite of the fall in the status of the big handicaps, the public still identifies the big meetings with the big handicaps. They don't identify the York August meeting as such – it is the Ebor meeting. These races, the big handicaps, used to be the spectaculars of the racing world...they would be so again if the Jockey Club could be persuaded to relax the rigid control it now exercises over the racing programme.' Thankfully, times would change.

***

GLADNESS was the first of five Ebor triumphs for the incomparable Lester Piggott, a figure which still sees him hold the record as the race's leading jockey. There was Primera in 1959, Die Hard in 1961, Tintagel II in 1970, but the best – for trainer Clive Brittain anyway – was the last, Jupiter Island in 1983.

'I gave 10,000 guineas for Jupiter Island and three people took shares,' Brittain remembers. 'They really stuck with him and thought they had a horse who could win the Ebor. They bought him for Lester to ride and Sam Threadwell, one of his owners, was Lester mad. He said "If Lester rides him, he wins". And he did.'

Ending that 13 year gap between Ebor winners, Piggott burst Jupiter Island through the pack two furlongs out after Abdoun, owned by the Aga Khan, had taken over the running half a mile out from the pace-maker Ribretto. It was a devastating move, typical Piggott, and led to a one and a half length victory with the jockey easing up. Secured on the 35th anniversary of his first winner, Jupiter Island proved a lucky omen for the rider. Prickle's win in the Lowther Stakes made it a Knavesmire double that afternoon and Lester then picked up the trophy as the Ebor Festival's leading rider.

Next, Jupiter Island, by York Dante Stakes and Derby winner St Paddy, became the first British trained winner of the Japan Cup. 'That showed the quality of the horse,' Brittain adds. 'He was a horse that matured and got better. After the Ebor, you wonder where to go next. He went abroad.' A winner of 14 races, Jupiter Island died in July 1998.

***

FROM the modern era, written in Ebor lore and destined to be forever remembered with the likes of Sea Pigeon and Brown Jack, is Sergeant Cecil.

'He was a wonderful horse – a once in a lifetime for me and his owner,' says his trainer Rod Millman. 'I was lucky. He was trained by a very good handler as a two-year-old, Seamus Mullins, whose reward was seeing him moved to me. When he came to us, he was just a nice horse that could easily get better in time. We took him to the next stage.'

It had been steady stuff. Cecil, as he was affectionately known by Millman and his connections, had been something of a work in progress. He made his debut on the racecourse in September 2001, finishing eighth of 11 in a Kempton maiden. But it wasn't until May 2003, and 13 races later, that the horse finally broke his duck – in a Class D handicap at Sandown. It wasn't plain sailing after that either.

Sergeant Cecil won again at Sandown two months later but, for every victory, there was also a disappointment as the striking chestnut with the headstrong nature both frustrated and delighted in equal measure. Could he fulfil his potential?

By the time of his appearance in the Ebor Handicap in 2005, now a mammoth contest worth £130,000 to the winner alone, there were no more questions to answer. The Northumberland Plate, won at Newcastle two months previously, was on the mantelpiece for a start, as Sergeant Cecil revealed his lung-busting ability to stay the two mile marathon at Gosforth Park. It was a breathtaking success given he had spent years running around in modest handicaps. Millman had worked out what made the horse tick.

'He'd done that well,' says Millman. 'We went to Goodwood next (in the Summer Season Stakes) to give him a run between races and, luckily for us, he got into a bit of trouble round the outside and finished third. That stopped him getting a penalty for the Ebor. The secret with Cecil was if he was relaxed early in a race. Once he strode off he could really produce a turn of foot. But winning the Ebor was the toughest race of any of them. It was a battle-hardened victory and he was still going up the ranks then.'

Taking the next step with the Sergeant was jockey Alan Munro, a former apprentice with York trainer Mel Brittain who had won the Derby in 1991 on Generous but had taken a four-year sabbatical from the sport in 2000 citing burnout after six years riding in Hong Kong. They were the ideal partners. Wise heads who knew the game and had both been around the block. First united at Epsom in April, the partnership did not get off to the grandest of beginnings. Cecil was 11th of 12 in the Great Metropolitan Stakes but, after Newbury and a second placed finish the following month, the pair would not be out of the top three in a race for the rest of the year.

It was the Ebor that lifted Sergeant Cecil out of the ordinary. No horse had won the Plate and Ebor double since Pillo in 1911 and the twin triumph had only ever been achieved three times in the 160 years of the two contests. The Plate, also known as the Pitmen's Derby, was one thing, but the Ebor, Europe's richest handicap, was quite another. Millman wasn't all that confident.

'Everything was fine before the race,' he recalls. 'The only thing was, walking around the paddock before the Ebor, he didn't look quite as well as I had seen him previously. I didn't know what it was. Maybe I was just being nervous. But he won it well and Alan Munro gave him a great ride.'

A maximum field of 20 lined up and, despite Cecil's heroics at

Newcastle, punters hadn't yet latched on to the Sergeant's special breed of magic. Fifth in the betting market, Millman's star went off at 11-1 with David Elsworth's Balkan Knight the 9-2 favourite. The public hadn't banked on Munro either, who gave the hold-up horse what race readers described as 'a balls-of-steel ride'.

Jagger and Odiham set the pace and Cecil, now lodged in a familiar position towards the back of the field, had only a couple of runners behind him. But even as they entered the straight with the Sergeant still carefully tucked up by Munro, it was obvious the six-year-old was travelling strongly. He ate up the ground and, as the gaps opened up, Munro took the plunge and charged through the field. Cecil had always liked passing horses, liked the thrill of burying a rival into his quickening dust. He was relentless, only getting stronger as the Ebor reached its peak. Diving between Grampian and Zeitgeist, Munro pushed his mount into the lead at the final furlong and could even ease down with a length to spare over Norton trainer Brian Ellison's Carte Diamond, with Grampian a neck back in third. Sergeant Cecil was now a history maker.

'It was a good performance and it was a very good Ebor,' says Millman. 'Carte Diamond went on to be a good horse. It was fantastic to win such a good race and he got a wonderful reception. It is the race all the northern trainers want to win. The owner, Terry Cooper, had said "I just want to win the big one". We have had good horses in the past – and I'd had the odd shop window horse – but the public had really taken to him. I thought that was as far as he would go. He would go up again in the handicap and you have to be an improving horse to carry these extra races. Then he went and won the Cesarewitch at Newmarket.'

It was a unique treble of staying contests: A Northumberland Plate, an Ebor and a Cesarewitch. A hat-trick which made Millman's horse one of the most popular in the country and his small Devon yard one of the most recognised. Victory against the odds, against the multi-millionaires. From a small trainer, and a modest owner who had named the horse after his late father.

The future for them all was bright and, at York, it was only going to get better for Sergeant Cecil.

***

IF Purple Moon was the most satisfying, then Vicious Circle in 1999 was probably the most surprising for Luca Cumani. 'He is a very backward horse,' is how the Italian trainer once described his maiden Ebor victor, who began a sequence that would bring a hat-trick of winners in just nine runners from the turn of the Millennium for the Newmarket trainer.

'He was an interesting horse,' says Cumani. 'He didn't run much as a three-year-old but he got better and better as he got older.' Vicious Circle cracked a leg at three and had run only seven times before he arrived at York as a five-year-old. It was a leap of faith for Cumani, who admits he didn't feel his resilient thoroughbred would be the one to break his Ebor duck. 'We weren't thinking of victory. We were hoping he would run well and we could have a bit of excitement. But he was a horse that deserved his success.'

The race developed late and it wasn't until a furlong from the finish that Vicious Circle surged to the front against the far rail under Yorkshire rider Kevin Darley and beat Travelmate by two lengths. Mowbray was a length further back in third with Eminence Grise, who had been hampered near the line, in fourth. It was still comfortable as Vicious Circle virtually trotted home while everything else was flat to the boards.

It was another five years, 2004, before Cumani returned to the Ebor winner's enclosure with Mephisto but this time it was in the most controversial of fashions – and it still rankles the saddler today. It was settled not on the track, but in the Stewards' Room and, subsequently, by appeal. Cumani's horse had beaten Toby Balding's Gold Ring by a short head in a thrilling finish before a 20 minute inquiry took some of the magic off the contest for the Italian. There was contact between the two horses. Mephisto's rider, Darryll Holland, was suspended for one day for careless riding after his horse veered left towards the final furlong and gave Gold Ring a nudge before coming out on top in the gripping duel. Tension ruled with the Stewards before Mephisto kept the race but Toby Balding, trainer of Gold Ring, appealed against their verdict.

With £130,000 on the line, he had to. But the result stood and, although Cumani says he can 'enjoy it now for what it is', he adds: 'It's not particularly satisfactory if you can't celebrate immediately at the winning post. There's the emotion of the race, the emotion of the Stewards' Inquiry and 20 minutes out. It takes a bit of the gloss away and then of course the appeal was another worry. Luckily it stayed in the record books.'

***

BUT the Ebor isn't just about magical moments on the track, it can also change the course of a career. Take the cases of Amanda Perrett and James Given.

'It helped us attract new owners and we very much pushed on after that,' says Perrett of Give The Slip's 2000 Ebor triumph while, for Given, Hugs Dancer's 2002 success marked the time 'I stopped being Mark Johnston's former assistant'. Two trainers, two very different horses, the same result. A vocation made better by an Ebor victory.

Perrett's problem in the run up to Give The Slip's Ebor race had been which jockey to choose. Mick Kinane or Pat Eddery. Eddery had ridden the horse all year but Kinane had taken the mount in the Gordon Stakes at Goodwood on a three-year-old Perrett knew was 'a classy horse'. In the end she plumped for Eddery's nous for what had, at first, only been a speculative Ebor entry. But if Perrett was concerned about the draw, or the fate of three-year-old runners in the Ebor Handicap – 'It's quite tough for a three-year-old to win the race,' she says – her jockey was supremely confident.

Remembers Perrett: 'I think we were drawn 16 but Pat was very confident he was going to win. He wanted to make all the running and he gave him a brilliant ride. It was thoughtful and it was a great thrill. We talked about the race beforehand and Pat said "There isn't a plan B". That was what he was going to do and it was great. The horse had natural speed and ability – to get from a bad draw to the front – and Pat was masterful from the front on a track which is great for front runners.'

Eddery tacked over from his wide draw to lead the field in what observers would describe as a 'vintage ride'. Boreas, the race favourite, looked ready to make his challenge in the final furlong but, sticking tight to the rails, the canny Eddery had not exhausted the reserves of Give The Slip and the market leader was repelled by three quarters of a length. It brought up another century of winners for Eddery, his 27th ton in the previous 28 seasons. Give The Slip was bought by Godolphin and went on to become a pacemaker for Fantastic Light. The fate of Hugs Dancer, on the other hand, was a little different.

'We took him to the Melbourne Cup and the Australians recognised what I saw in the horse,' James Given says. 'He has retired there and is working on a sheep farm in Australia. We had bought him out of Sir Michael Stoute's yard as an unraced two-year-old. We didn't get him an owner until the middle of his two-year-old year. Eventually, we got someone to buy him but it wasn't an auspicious start. In three seasons, though, he went up a stone in the handicap three years in a row. He started in claimers and ended up in Group 1s. He was a bit of a monkey early on. We used to run him in headgear – visors and so on – and he was able to improve steadily. He was never pushing himself to the limit but there was nothing ungenuine about him. He was a great horse to have – a horse who used to come to work and enjoy his work. He loved it and wanted to do it.'

Given wanted to win the Ebor badly and felt good about his chances, until he saw the draw. Drawn in box 20, with just two to his outside, it looked an impossible task for the five-year-old gelding. At 25-1 in the market, the betting public agreed. But they hadn't banked on Dean McKeown, the jockey with the Ebor passion who had enjoyed his only previous win in the race a decade earlier on Quick Ransom.

'It was one of Dean McKeown's, and the horse's, finest performances to be able to overcome those disadvantages,' Given adds. 'The horse was quite quick in his starts and he had won up to two miles five furlongs at Goodwood twice. It was a great moment for him (McKeown). I remember him saying in the interview how winning the Ebor for a northern jockey was like winning the Derby.'

It was a masterful piece of race riding. Taken to the inner early on, chasing the leaders, the pair travelled steadily towards the front of the pack before McKeown shook the reins and implored his charge to take the lead at the furlong marker. Driven clear, he held on gamely by three quarters of a length from Pole Star with Barathea Blazer a neck back in third. It was the start of McKeown's last hurrah. The rider, then aged

42, had ruminated about retiring and had been forced to sell mortgages during a lean spell two years previously.

Ebor victory delayed his decision to hang up his boots and, riding Collier Hill, he would win the Canadian International and, in 2006, the Hong Kong Vase. Perhaps he should have called it a day then. In the event, he had no say in the matter – being warned off by the British Horseracing Authority in October 2008. That may have tarnished the memories for some, but not Given's recollection of a wonderful race. What he remembers most are the spectators.

'The York crowd are very appreciative of their racing,' Given explains. 'I remember parading the horse down the track after the win – going down the Knavesmire was a totally special moment. My younger brother was a good rugby player – a double blue at Cambridge – and he ran out onto the pitch at Twickenham and to the enormous atmosphere of a full house. He said you felt the sound rather than heard it and that was my experience of Knavesmire that day. It's a moment I will never forget.'

***

GIVEN may never forget Hugs Dancer, but punters had every reason to sweep the 2009 Ebor right under the carpet – all, that is, except champion Irish trainer Willie Mullins and apprentice Gary Carroll.

After the entire meeting was washed out 12 months earlier amid unprecedented August rainfall, the sun was out for the showpiece of a new four-day Ebor Festival – but it was the backers who got burned. A bucket load of cash came for Aidan O'Brien's Changingoftheguard and the three-year-old, backed in to 15-8 favourite, would have forced a £5 million payout from the bookmakers had he done the business. It wasn't to be. From the second the stalls opened, the portents didn't look good as Changingoftheguard, ridden by the experienced Group 1 winning campaigner Johnny Murtagh, reared when the gates went back and fell to the back of the field. The Ballydoyle contender was still chasing half a mile from home and repeatedly found his way to the front impeded with Murtagh trying to weave his way through the pack. Meanwhile the 25-1 outsider Sesenta, piloted by young Irish claimer Carroll, enjoyed a much smoother passage. The top weight

Warringah had set a fair pace early on and tried to crank up the pressure in the home straight. It looked like he might just do it as well, sticking in front well into the final furlong. But with victory tantalisingly close, Sir Michael Stoute's runner was swamped and had nothing left to give. As Warringah dropped back, it was Sesenta who surged through with Changingoftheguard – now switched left and finally coming through that wall of horses – desperately trying to make up the yards. It was a vain effort and Carroll had just enough in hand – a head at the line – to give Willie Mullins, a man more used to reigning in the National Hunt sphere, an unlikely superstar.

'She's the smallest animal I have in the place,' said Mullins in the winner's enclosure afterwards. 'She's only 16 hands, but she's been at every cock-fight all season, from Fairyhouse to Cheltenham. She's just an extraordinary mare that keeps pulling it out and keeps looking fresh and well. With her size, you look at where you can get her in at light weights. We knew she would stay a mile and three quarters no problem. I didn't ever think that we'd win it though.'

Irish eyes smiled again in 2010, thanks to Dirar. Trainer Gordon Elliott had won a Grand National when Silver Birch cleared Aintree's famous fences in style to win in 2007. But he believed Dirar's Ebor victory to be just as special. It established him, at just 33, as a training force – a horse handler who had already won the world's most famous race, and Europe's richest handicap, in the space of just three years. For Dirar's rider, Jamie Spencer, it was another precious moment. Spencer, who has enjoyed a love-hate relationship with the Ebor, was exultant at the line – shouting in celebration and pumping his fist in triumph – as the 14-1 shot was switched to the rail with a furlong to go and eased past Rosika. It's a feeling all those who have won the Ebor well know.

***

'IT'S only a handicap but it is OUR race. Everybody associates the Ebor with York.' So says former clerk of the course John Smith of the flagship contest that never fails to bring the Knavesmire crowd to life. From 2011, it was only set to get bigger.

After York and Ripon came to agreement over fixture difficulties, the Ebor Handicap was due to form the final feature race of a thrilling four-day Festival – moving from its traditional Wednesday berth to a Saturday and adding another big-race weekend card to the fixture calendar. Manna from heaven for those at the top of the racing chain, with the chance of a bigger weekend television audience and maximised betting turnover.

The Great Ebor Handicap was originally conceived as the race to save the historic York Races from extinction. Now those in charge of securing its legacy hope a Saturday Ebor spectacular will not only secure its place as Europe's richest Flat handicap, but improves its status on the world stage. John Orton would have been proud of that.

THE GIMCRACK STAKES

IT'S the worst ground you've seen. Staff poke the sodden track with forks in the hope it will somehow magically move the deepening puddles. The divots, ploughed into the turf by the pounding hooves of the day before, haven't yet been filled in. They look like potholes. It's a squelching quagmire.

Today, they wouldn't think twice. The meeting would be abandoned. After all, would you subject a top-class racehorse to this? Mill Reef is only two and, down at Ian Balding's Kingsclere stables, they already know he is going to be a star. But in the 1970 Gimcrack Stakes, on that desperate ground, they are about to take an enormous gamble with his future.

***

MILL REEF was bred in the United States, at the Rokeby Stables in Virginia, by his owner Paul Mellon. He was named after the Mill Reef Club, situated in Antigua where the Mellon family maintained a home. Mellon, a philanthropist, was co-heir to the Mellon Bank fortune and was believed to be one of the richest men in America.

Mill Reef was foaled in 1968, a son of Never Bend, and it was felt

174

early on in his life that his running action would suit the turf tracks of Europe better than the dirt surfaces of America. So Mellon sent him to England in December 1969, and to Balding, who was establishing his burgeoning training empire. 'He was in a class of his own,' says Balding. 'He was the best horse I have seen and the best I have seen since him is Sea The Stars. Even Paul Mellon knew he was the horse of his lifetime and the best thing that ever happened in his life. He was quite astonishing.'

Mill Reef began in scintillating fashion. He won by four lengths on his debut at Salisbury, beating the 2-9 favourite Fireside Chat, before sweeping to a six length success in the Coventry Stakes at Royal Ascot in a canter. 'He then had an unlucky defeat to My Swallow in the Prix Robert Papin,' Balding adds. 'He was dead unlucky. There were about 20 runners and he was drawn on the very outside at Maison Lafitte. He had to get across and get in front of My Swallow and covered a lot more ground. He wasn't at his best either and looked awful.'

Some members of the fourth estate were still to be convinced. 'It was during the May meeting at York when Mill Reef won at Salisbury on his debut,' remembers former *Daily Mirror* racing journalist Tim Richards. 'We were shocked because we thought there was a good thing in that race and then Mill Reef won it. I don't think when he won there, although he did so very easily, that we were all jumping up and down with a view to the Classics. We might have regarded it as a bit of a fluke.'

At the Gimcrack, the question was not whether Mill Reef was of Classic potential, it was whether he ran at all. 'We came to the Gimcrack and this was the first time Paul Mellon had seen him run. He was over from America and was staying with Lord Halifax at Garrowby,' Balding remembers. 'It poured down with rain. I think the Gimcrack was on the Wednesday then and the previous day it had poured. I just did not think it was suitable for a high class horse to work on. I walked right down to the six furlong start and, with much dread, I went to get Paul Mellon out of lunch with the Stewards. I said "I really hate to say this but I've walked the track and, you know how much it has rained, I don't think it is for a high class horse like this."'

John Sanderson, clerk of the course at York from 1972 to 1986 was assistant to his uncle, Major Leslie Petch, for that Gimcrack. 'You would question today whether we would be allowed to race on that ground,' he says. 'The sort of ground you could race on and what was acceptable in those years – the jockeys wouldn't ride on it today. I can remember being on the track that morning. The old man, who had suffered a heart attack the previous year, was back and I used to shadow him. I remember being on the track with a gang of men with forks – in front of the stands – forking the puddles to get the surface water down below. But Mill Reef belonged to Paul Mellon, who was a great personal friend of Lord Halifax. I think actually, I have to say, that counted for a lot in terms of getting him to York and running on the day. I think Mellon had come over and was staying with the Chairman at Garrowby and he was going to run unless it was absolutely catastrophic.'

Flash back to Balding, however, and the trainer is pitching entirely the opposite course of action to his American employer. 'I said I couldn't see Mill Reef liking the soft ground because he was so good on the fast ground at Ascot,' Balding says now. 'But we didn't have to make a decision until [Mill Reef's jockey] Geoff Lewis had had a ride in the first race. So he said: "Let's leave it until after the first race" and went back to his lunch. We then had this famous meeting outside the weighing room after the first race with me, Paul Mellon and Geoff Lewis. Geoff had this stammer and he said: "Mr Mellon, if the horse was mine I definitely wouldn't run it" and I said: "I hate to say it but I feel the same way". Paul Mellon said: "Well, I really appreciate very much how much you obviously care about this horse and I totally understand but I just have a funny feeling that everything will be all right. We should run and I will take the responsibility." Thank God Paul Mellon was there. If he hadn't been we definitely would not have run – no question.'

Balding still has the Gimcrack race on film. He calls it 'the most amazing thing I have ever seen'. Timeform, the racing annual that analyses every horse in training, wrote that it was a performance that 'had to be seen to be believed' in their review of the year – *Racehorses of 1970*. Even today, the sight lives on. Writing in his book, *Of Horses And Heroes*, the racing commentator and journalist Brough Scott said Mill Reef's display 'remains one of the most remarkable things ever seen on a British racetrack'. This was the classic definition of a one-horse race. Mill Reef absolutely hacked up. 'He won by ten lengths and one of the judges said he was going so much faster at the end of the race than anything else that if it had been another 100 yards he would probably have won by 20 lengths,' Balding says.

Lewis had promised not to take the stick to Mill Reef, fearing the horse wouldn't be at home on the squelching ground. He didn't need to consider it. Mill Reef was never off the bit. Once he got to the front inside the last two furlongs, he left the rest of the field, headed by Green God, in his mud-splattered wake.

'It was the most amazing race and look at some of the opposition that he beat – Green God was the champion sprinter the next year and very good on soft ground,' Balding states. 'It wasn't as if he beat rubbish. Some of the horses there were pretty useful two-year-olds. Luckily for us, Paul Mellon made that occasion and, when he ran his first race as a four-year-old, the Prix Ganay was on ground that was very soft at Longchamp. He won by 20 lengths and I have never seen a Group 1 horse win a race easier. We never would have known, were it not for Paul Mellon, how he was on soft ground.'

Mill Reef had won the Derby by then, having gone to Epsom and scored easily by two lengths from Linden Tree. You won't find many Derby winners in the modern era who have also won a Gimcrack.

'He sluiced up, in more ways than one,' jokes Sanderson. 'It was fantastic for the race and for York that he went on and did what he did the following year as a three-year-old. As a winner of the Gimcrack, it was one of the most extraordinary things. He was a hell of a horse, there was no question about it. He was a fantastic athlete and clearly the ground didn't disadvantage him. I know, from my own riding days, that some horses go better feeling their feet rattle with the sun on their backs and some enjoy the mud. He was pretty adept in both. One of the things I think that sets a great horse apart from the run of the mill ones is that they will actually perform on almost any ground. Mill Reef was one of those.'

***

MILL Reef's victory in 1970 is the highlight of an odd quirk in York's history that gave a race its hero: Gimcrack. The grey is a legend on Knavesmire but, and this is where the oddity arises, only ever ran twice at York and failed to win on either occasion.

Foaled in 1760, Gimcrack was by Cripple – a son of the Godolphin Arabian who is one of the founding lines of the modern thoroughbred racehorse. He was small, standing at barely a quarter of an inch above 14 hands, but what he lacked in size, he made up for with an abundance of ability. In a career which spanned some seven years, Gimcrack won 28 of his 36 races. These weren't over the relative sprints that comprise the race distances we are used to today. Contests in the 18th Century were invariably run in heats and were usually between four and six miles each. No wonder Gimcrack quickly gained a reputation as the iron grey.

He first came to York in August 1768, by this time an old horse, and ran in the Great Subscription Plate of £298 10s 0d over four miles. He finished only fifth of eight runners, beaten by the 2-1 favourite Pilgrim – the horse of Lord Rockingham, twice the Prime Minister and a founder member of the Gimcrack Club. Originally owned by Sir Charles Bunbury, Gimcrack had passed into the hands of Lord Grosvenor when he returned to York for the final time the following year. Again, the Great Subscription Plate – this time for £361 10s – was the objective and the horse was the 5-4 favourite. Two were better this time as Gimcrack finished third behind Chatsworth and Tortoise. And that was it for Gimcrack and York.

So why was the horse so special? And why did members of York's Race Committee feel obliged to name a club, hold a yearly dinner, and stage a race after an animal who, despite his brilliance, had done precious little on Knavesmire?

It's thought the Gimcrack Club, founded in 1767, was named because the grey was simply the greatest horse in training at that time. Little is known either about the origins of the club – formally known as the Ancient Fraternitie of Ye Gimcracks – who brought it together or who its original members were. It met at least once a year for an annual dinner at the old Punchbowl Hotel but, aside from that, the society remains secret. No archives are left to unravel the mystery.

Reginald Teasdale, secretary of the York Race Committee in the 1930s, told the pre-eminent northern racing historian John Fairfax-Blakeborough that he believed the Gimcrack Club never existed as such. 'It is commonly thought that those who meet at the Gimcrack dinner to perpetuate the memory of Gimcrack are for the time being the successors of "The Ancient Fraternitie of York Gimcracks" and I suppose that those few hours constitute a gathering of the club,' he revealed.

Whatever the reasons behind the club, the influence of the little horse and his legacy continued to grow in the ensuing years. It might have originally been little more than a drinking club at first but, in 1846, a greater tribute was established. Like the foundation of the Great Ebor Handicap, the Gimcrack Stakes may have been another attempt to lift the prestige of York Races, which had been badly hit by the rise of Doncaster and by poor prize money. The new race, which today forms such a key part of York's four-day Ebor Festival every August, was almost certainly the brainchild of one R M Jaques, of Easby Abbey, Richmond, who was a prime mover in the resurgence of the track in the middle of the 19th Century – pumping extra prize money into the races. Another theory suggests that a number of racing clubs, which were formed in the first half of the 1800s and gave money to races in their name, disbanded and then endowed what became the Gimcrack Stakes.

Whatever the motivation, the new contest first appeared in the racing calendar of 1845 as: 'The Gimcrack Stakes of 10 sovs. each, with 100 added by the members of the York Gimcrack Club, for two-year-old colts 8st. 7lbs and fillies 8st. 2lbs, the winner of the Prince of Wales's Stakes to carry 3lbs extra, the second horse to receive 25 sovs. out of the stakes, and the third horse to save his stake. The winner to give three dozen champagne to the York Gimcrack Club. One mile.'

Eleven went to post for the first Gimcrack Stakes in 1846 and it was Ellerdale, ridden by Middleham jockey Tommy Lye and trained by town compatriot Tom Dawson, who won. An apt Yorkshire victory. Jaques, himself, tasted success in the race he had helped to found when Mildew, who he owned, took the honours in the fourth running of the contest. But history had to wait ten years for the first brilliant winner of the race – Blink Bonny in 1856.

Trained by William I'Anson at his Spring Cottage Stables in Malton, Blink Bonny had won a stack of races – including the Sapling Stakes at Manchester and the Tyro at Newcastle – before starting favourite and winning the Gimcrack. She won eight of her 11 races as a two-year-old, but got even better the next season A rarity, a filly who won the Derby, she also doubled up with the Oaks and finished fourth in the St Leger – despite having such a serious dental problem she could barely chew her food. Blink Bonny was a 5-6 favourite for her Gimcrack and beat Lord Zetland's Skirmisher by two lengths.

As the race became established, and animals like the great Thormanby (1859) – who won ten of his 15 races in his first season and was another to win the Derby – were added to the roll of honour, the powers that be at York gradually altered the conditions. In 1897, the race was first run over the straight six furlongs – a distance it continues to be contested over today. The prize money for the race had rocketed to £200 in 1883 and to £1,000 by 1902 but, at the start of the 20th Century, it had become almost as important to win the race for the invitation it brought to the Gimcrack Club dinner as the glory of the success itself.

The winning owner, to this day, occupies the position of chief guest at the annual occasion and is invited to speak at length on turf matters. These have sometimes been the scene of fireworks. None more so than in 1887 when Lord Durham, an influential steward of the Jockey Club, created a storm which resulted in Sir George Chetwynd taking him to the High Court. Durham made allegations about the running of horses in a certain stable and remarked at the conduct of its chief patron. Despite mentioning no one by name, all at the dinner knew it was Chetwynd to whom he was referring. The accused's first reaction was to challenge Durham to a duel but the matter instead ended up in court – mainly on the grounds that those present at the dinner argued that Chetwynd could not restore his reputation merely by winning the man-to-man contest. In the law courts, Chetwynd was shown to be a professional punter. He won the day but it was a hollow result. He had demanded £20,000 in damages. He got one farthing – the judge showing his obvious displeasure at the case. Chetwynd resigned from the Jockey Club.

In more recent times, Sheikh Mohammed, in 1997, used the address to threaten to pull his Maktoum family out of British racing if the sport's finances were not improved. Through his advisor, Michael Osborne, dinner guests were told that the country's ranking of 35th out of 40, measured in terms of costs recoverable through prize money, was a 'desperate plight for a nation with the finest racing in the world'.

Modern dinners are set at a horseshoe table as the sport's great and good gather for what is effectively Flat racing's state of the union address.

***

JUST three years into the 20th century and the Gimcrack Stakes has already revealed its leading jockey and trainer. John Osborne Jr had ridden the race winner a stunning nine times by 1880, thanks to the likes of Exact (1852), Lord Of The Vale (1865), Holy Friar (1874) and lastly Simnel, while William I'Anson Jnr – son of Blink Bonny trainer William Snr – saddled seven winners. Pursebearer (1881), Castor (1885) and Royal Stag (1890), the last coming with Barbette in 1903, constitute his winning tally. But while they all have their place in history, we have to wait another 30 years before a truly special Gimcrack winner hits the radar. The horse was Bahram.

He was foaled in 1932 at the Aga Khan's stud farm at the Curragh, in Ireland, where he was quickly identified as being an outstanding prospect. Racing experts were agog at his flawless conformation. He would enjoy a brief, but also flawless, career on the track. Wins in the National Breeder's Produce Stakes and the Rous Memorial Stakes were achieved before Bahram arrived at York for the Gimcrack in 1934. He came up against another unbeaten colt, Consequential, on Knavesmire but little was to stop the Aga Khan's brilliant thoroughbred maintaining his perfect record on the track. Bahram took up the running early in the contest and, though Consequential tried to make a race of it, once the reins were shaken the victory was achieved in a decisive manner.

The Middle Park Stakes was quickly won after that appearance on Knavesmire and, the following year, he achieved the British Triple Crown of Classic wins: 2,000 Guineas, Derby and St Leger. After just nine races, Bahram was retired to stud at Newmarket – where he carried out his duties with equal brilliance. A leading sire in 1940 and 1941, producing the 2,000 Guineas winner Big Game and the St Leger victor Turkhan, he later went to America and then Argentina, where he died at the age of 24 in 1956.

Palestine, meanwhile, was another top class Gimcrack horse owned by the Aga Khan – so good only one dared face him. A winner of 11 of his 13 racecourse outings, York's prestigious juvenile contest fell into his lap in 1949. The Aga Khan sent his son Prince Aly Khan from Deauville to check on his prize and waited on the end of a telephone in France to hear news of the result. The Prince saw a quirky race, worthy of note in the modern era, because the unbeaten colt squared off in what was effectively a match race. Only Foxboro lined up to oppose him and it was literally a canter for Palestine and his legendary jockey Gordon Richards. But Palestine was a worthy winner. He would take the 2,000 Guineas the following season before retiring to stud in 1951. He was also the silver lining in a cloud of post-war Gimcrack victors.

'If you actually analyse the post career of Gimcrack winners over a period of years it sometimes doesn't read too well,' admits former clerk of the course John Sanderson. 'Before Mill Reef, Bahram was the best and after 1970 it would be more than 30 years before Rock Of Gibraltar turned up.'

Gimcrack winners were precocious, full of promise but equally capable of fading into obscurity. Many winners became sprinters, others simply failed to train on into their three-year-old careers. But some, like the 1948 winner Star Kingdom and the 1960 victor Test Case, would make their mark off rather than on the track. Star Kingdom, who raced under the name Star King, won nine races in 16 starts and during his two-year-old season only Abernant, who would scoop back-to-back Nunthorpe Stakes in 1949 and 1950, was thought to be a better English sprinter. The Greenham Stakes, the Jersey Stakes and the Hungerford Stakes would be claimed in 1949 before, two years later, he was shipped to Australia and acquired the dom suffix.

After a slow start at stud, Star Kingdom's progeny exploded into winning life in the late 1950s and he became the country's leading sire for the first time in 1959. It was a feat he would repeat on a further four occasions before 1965 and he would produce the first five winners of the Golden Slipper Stakes. Todman, one of the greatest Australian racehorses and a prodigious talent at stud himself, was the first of Star Kingdom's five Slipper successes, while the likes of Melbourne Cup winner Sky High in 1961 and Australian Derby winner Skyline only added to his reputation. Star Kingdom would stand at Barramul Stud for 16 years before dying at 21.

Test Case was a grandson of the 1937 Ascot Gold Cup winner Precipitation and was distantly related to Chamossaire, the 1945 St Leger winner at York. Trained by Jack Jarvis at Park Lodge Stables in Newmarket, he was a son of Supreme Court, the first winner of the King George VI and Queen Elizabeth Stakes. In the Gimcrack, he started at 100-7 with Floribunda, who had crushed him at Royal Ascot in the New Stakes, the unsurprising favourite. It had been touch and go whether he would even run, having been cut following a kick at the starting gate but, despite being outpaced early, Test Case came through strongly to win by two lengths from Prince Tudor. Floribunda finished in third.

When his racing career came to an end without the Classic success for which every Gimcrack or any big two-year-old winner, for that matter, longs, Test Case was exported to New Zealand. At stud, Test Case sired the country's dual Derby winner Ben Lomond, along with a Wellington Derby and Wellington Oaks winner and a host of others. Good on the track, better in the barn.

That was also true of Royal Applause, the 1995 winner. Trained by Barry Hills, and ridden by Walter Swinburn, he had taken a maiden at Newbury on his debut and the Coventry Stakes at Royal Ascot and came to the Gimcrack as the 4-6 favourite. Facing just four rivals, Royal Applause was restless in the stalls, nervous for the fight, but settled well – tracking the leading group before Swinburn took him to the front at the two furlong marker. It would not be that plain sailing. With 200 yards left to travel, he was attacked by Tumbleweed Ridge and both went all out. Royal Applause didn't crack, but Tumbleweed Ridge did, edging left just enough under pressure to fail by a head. It was a game performance and capped an unbeaten juvenile season for Hills' youngster, which climaxed with the Middle Park Stakes at Newmarket. But like so many other Gimcrack victors Royal Applause struggled as a three-year-old, failing to land a blow either in the 2,000 Guineas or in the King's Stand Stakes at Royal Ascot.

A five-runner event in Doncaster proved his only victory and Royal Applause's career could have faded there into obscurity, yet another name on an inglorious roll of honour. But he exploded back into form at four, and became champion sprinter following a run which brought wins back on Knavesmire in the Duke of York Stakes, the Cork and Orrery Stakes at Royal Ascot and the Haydock Park Sprint Cup. The

Breeders' Cup Sprint – the final race of Royal Applause's racing career – proved too much, but a 14th place finish couldn't take the gloss off the rejuvenated colt as he embarked on his new life at stud.

A lifetime record of nine wins in 15 starts made him a hot property when he went to stand at the Darley Stud. Acclamation, placed in the Nunthorpe Stakes and a winner of Ascot's Diadem Stakes, along with Lovelace, a Group winner at Baden Baden, Finjaan and Battle Of Hastings are just some of the talented performers to arrive from Royal Applause's profitable period as a stallion.

***

WERE it not for Sir Ivor, Petingo's place in racing history would surely have been more assured. The Sam Armstrong-trained colt won the Gimcrack Stakes in 1967 and, the following year, was also victorious in the Craven Stakes, the St James's Palace Stakes at Royal Ascot and the Sussex Stakes at Glorious Goodwood. That alone puts the horse, who was owned by the Greek ship owner Marcus Lemos, high up the list of quality Gimcrack winners.

He was, undoubtedly, a top miler. But Petingo might also have won the 2,000 Guineas in 1968 had he not come up against Sir Ivor, the fabulous thoroughbred who would also go on to win the Derby a couple of months later. Lester Piggott, who rode Sir Ivor in both the Newmarket Classic and at Epsom, knew all about Petingo. Lemos was a good friend of the brilliant jockey and both owner and trainer had high Classic hopes for the horse. Piggott, however, was torn. He had ridden Sir Ivor in the Grand Criterium at Longchamp and the pair had won so easily it was clear the colt was extremely talented. Armstrong, on the other hand, was Piggott's father-in-law – the jockey having married his daughter Susan. It was a question of family.

In the Gimcrack, Petingo had also proved his ability. Sent off the 7-4 favourite, Piggott observed in his autobiography, Lester, that his mount 'absolutely slaughtered his rivals, winning by six lengths'. The son of Petition had even shown greenness over the six furlongs but had hardly come off the bit. The Middleham-trained Dahban was in the lead at the halfway mark and with two furlongs to go Cheb's Lad took over at the front. But Piggott was merely biding his time. He swept into the lead a furlong out and raced clean away from his rivals, Cheb's Lad meekly tottering home in second with Scipio in third.

It was Piggott's third Gimcrack win in five years, having also claimed the prize on Talahasse in 1963 and Young Emperor in 1965. When Petingo then went on to win the Middle Park Stakes, he looked an excellent 2,000 Guineas prospect. Which one to choose was a tough decision for Piggott. He opted for Sir Ivor, telling Armstrong in the winter of the pair's Gimcrack victory. The choice may have temporarily hurt his popularity with the in-laws but it would prove to be the right decision. Piggott believed Sir Ivor to be the greatest horse he ever rode and, while Joe Mercer won the Craven Stakes at Newmarket by four lengths, when Petingo was despatched by a length and a half in the Guineas there were no more questions to answer.

Petingo was never going to stay in the Derby, another factor Piggott had considered when making his choice about which horse to ride in the Classics. Sir Ivor was hardly assured to get the trip either, his breeding suggested a mile was his best trip, but Piggott tucked him up at Epsom and beat Connaught by a length and a half. The jockey had the best of both worlds as well. He rode Petingo in both the St James's Palace Stakes, when the horse was the 10-11 hot favourite, and at the Sussex Stakes. A great horse, but just edged out in Piggott's affections by one who was even better.

***

FIVE horses lit up three decades of Gimcrack Stakes. Rapid River, Music Boy and Nebbiolo in the 1970s, Horage in the 80s and Turtle Island in the 90s. Rapid River was the son of Forlorn River, the Arthur Stephenson-trained colt who won the Nunthorpe Stakes in 1967. Stephenson also held the reins when his offspring hit the track. He proved to be a chip off the old block.

'No two-year-old had as many performances of a high order to its credit as Rapid River,' said the annual Timeform *Racehorses of 1972*. Rapid River proved aptly named in the Gimcrack of that year, which he won with a devastating turn of pace. He came into the contest on the back of victory in the Seaton Delaval Stakes at Newcastle a couple of weeks before. It was his first real performance of note.

Rapid River had been swiftly away that day but he was tardy when the starting stalls opened at York. A hundred yards into the race and he was five lengths adrift – almost always a fatal blow in a six furlong contest. He had not been fancied beforehand either. At 8-1, six of his eight opponents were preferred to him in the market. The slow start proved merely a minor inconvenience. Three furlongs later, he had not only caught the others but swept past them into the lead. No one, not even the late running runner-up Prince Chad, could get near Stephenson's speed machine. It was a performance which made an impression on Timeform's racing experts.

'The speed with which Rapid River made up the ground he had forfeited out of the stalls, and the manner in which he carried through with his effort right to the post, impressed everyone,' they wrote. 'There seemed good reason to believe that he would go on from there and prove himself the fastest of his age.'

Ayr's Harry Rosebery Challenge Trophy, despite giving plenty of weight to all his rivals, was claimed the following month before Rapid River found one too good when The Go-Between beat him by two and a half lengths in the Cornwallis Stakes at Ascot. With strength and speed in abundance, Stephenson's colt was expected to come back stronger the following season. Instead, he fell slightly flat.

He won impressively at Haydock on his reappearance and would also have success at Leicester and back at Haydock, in October, where he put two talented northern sprinters to the sword. But, alongside those victories, he was beaten in the Prix de l'Abbaye and failed to give a good account of himself in the Nunthorpe Stakes at York – starting as the favourite but only able to finish fifth behind Sandford Lad despite having Lester Piggott in the saddle.

***

MUSIC Boy was the horse who began a racing dynasty. So important was the 1975 Gimcrack winner to the start of what is now the formidable Cheveley Park Stud that a bronze of the horse stands at the massive farm in Newmarket. Having bought a place which was in receivership, David and Patricia Thompson, along with their business partner Ken Mackey, stood the York winner at the stud in 1977.

The horse that started this racing revolution was trained in North Yorkshire by Stanley 'Snowy' Wainwright and the Gimcrack was an epic victory for the handler, who trained out of Malton. An oil painting of his number one horse now takes pride of place above his bed at his home in Ganthorpe and Music Boy's performance on Knavesmire would fulfil a long-held dream. He had been close before, Burlington Boy finishing third behind Rapid River in 1972 and Continhugh trailing Giacometti by three lengths in fifth 12 months later.

Wainwright had longed to win the Gimcrack, ever since he had led in Captain Bill Elsey's Be Careful as a stable lad when the horse won the race in 1958. Music Boy was bought as a yearling at Doncaster Sales for just 1,800 guineas – the horse with the white blaze down his face catching the eye of the experienced handler. Mackey, his new owner, wasn't initially as keen about his prospects but the horse was cheap enough. Wainwright was taken by his appearance and, in particular, his strong and muscular physique. He proved to be an absolute bargain. So much better was the juvenile than the other thoroughbreds at Wainwright's Blinkbonny yard that the horse had to be sent down the gallops alone. He was simply too fast for the others.

Johnny Seagrave rode him to victory at Ripon on his debut and when the horse won again at Catterick two weeks later it was clear Wainwright had a potential star on his hands. The trainer chose to step him up in class next time out – electing to send him to York for a five furlong contest. Seagrave wasn't on board this time. His regular rider was unwell so Snowy sent for Lester Piggott. The jockey who had won it all might even have secured the ride on Music Boy in the Gimcrack Stakes had he and Wainwright not had a spectacular falling out on Knavesmire. The trainer considered that Piggott had ignored his instructions and, with Lester reportedly deciding to hold the horse up, Music Boy was beaten for the first time on the track.

Snowy was furious with Piggott, famously announcing to the world that: 'Lester will never ride for me again'. It brought an immortal retort from Piggott. Told of Wainwright's forthright views, Piggott replied: 'I had better pack up then'. Wainwright's anger with Piggott paved the way for Seagrave to step back up to the plate. 'He only had two speeds, very slow and very fast,' said the jockey when remembering one of his best ever mounts. 'To win the Gimcrack on him at York in front of my local crowd was great. It was a special day.'

By then, he had claimed the Great Surrey Stakes at Epsom and the Windsor Castle Stakes at Royal Ascot in a photo finish. But the Gimcrack provided a different test for Music Boy. Having shown his superiority over five furlongs, he now had to do it over six – a distance over which he had never won. Then there was the quality of the field. It featured the Coventry Stakes winner – the unbeaten Galway Bay – the July and National Stakes victor Super Cavalier, along with the Richmond Stakes champion Stand To Reason. Add the promising Delta Song, a $40,000 yearling who had won a maiden at Goodwood the previous month, and Hittite Glory into the mix and it was a formidable gathering. These were pressing reasons why Wainwright's horse was sent off at 14-1, fifth in the betting market.

Wainwright decided to grasp the race by the scruff of the neck, telling Seagrave to go out and give it everything from the beginning. His tactics were clear – batter the opposition early on and make the question of an extra 200 yards an irrelevance. It was perfect. Music Boy blasted out of the stalls and had already won the race by the time that extra furlong came into play. He was helped by being well away from some early drama, caused when Hittite Glory swerved at the start and badly hampered Delta Song. It caused a mini-domino effect, the latter horse then bumping Stand To Reason, who also lost a few lengths. It wasn't race defining. Music Boy was already clear and asking his opponents serious questions. By the time Stand To Reason recovered to make a late challenge, the race was in Seagrave's grasp. The pair won by a length, with Galway Bay a head further back in third. An astonishing turn of pace and an unrelenting gallop had secured Wainwright the race he craved. His greatest triumph, won on his local track.

Wainwright considers Music Boy the greatest horse he ever handled but his success was not confined to the track. At the end of his Gimcrack winning season, Snowy took Music Boy down to Cheveley Park Stables, which had been bought by Mackey along with David Thompson, his business partner. It was not a success for the trainer. Having been settled at Malton, Wainwright found it difficult to adjust to new surroundings and different facilities. He lasted barely two months and, when he came back up north, Music Boy did not come with him, remaining in Newmarket trained by Brian Lunless. The horse – who would go on to win the King George Stakes at Goodwood under the Cheveley Park Stud name – and a 23-year-old Forlorn River were the hopes of the new enterprise.

But Music Boy was a spectacular success as a stallion. From 17 foals, he was the leading first season sire and his offspring would go on to earn more than £2.5 million. He has been followed by the likes of Never So Bold and Polar Falcon, with Pivotal, born and bred at Cheveley Park, the real stunning success of the operation. But it all started thanks to Wainwright's eye for a bargain.

***

NEBBIOLO, the winner in 1976, would give Irish trainer Kevin Prendergast his first big international victory when winning the 2,000 Guineas in 1977. Unsold at 1,900 guineas as a yearling, Nebbiolo was ridden at both York and Newmarket by Gabriel Curran.

One of five successes in his juvenile season, the Gimcrack was taken despite opposition from the Coventry Stakes winner Cawston's Clown, the triple-scoring Royal Diver and the four time victor Mr Nice Guy. It was the first two named who took on the lead as the race got under way but, regardless of the strength of the field, none caused Nebbiolo, a 2-1 chance, the slightest concern. At four furlongs Curran came through to the front pursued by Forty Winks and, for a moment, it looked like the crowd might see a race as the jockey had to draw his whip and get to work. He was hard at it until the last 100 yards when Forty Winks held up a white flag of surrender and Nebbiolo drew away to a two and a half length victory. Had the race been that good?

Nebbiolo was caught in the Middle Park Stakes and the racehorse guide Timeform reckoned he had a bit of work to do before he could be regarded as being in the highest echelon. His performance at Newmarket the following May, however, firmly put him in that league. He had to overcome his Middle Park conqueror Tachypous and Vincent O'Brien's soon to be dual Classic winner The Minstrel in the Guineas. It was Curran's greatest moment, and it wasn't bad for Prendergast either.

Speaking after crowning his illustrious career with his 2,000th winner, the now veteran trainer said: 'I suppose if I had to pick one moment it would have to be when Nebbiolo won the Guineas. He was up against The Minstrel who was supposed to be a wonder horse and, of course, he was trained just down the road. That stands out as The Minstrel then went on to win the English and Irish Derbies.'

***

DREAMS can come true. Look no further than Horage in 1982. Trainer Matt McCormack is struggling. Two seasons into the job and the winners have hardly been flowing. He has barely a handful to his name. On a trip to Doncaster Sales, McCormack takes a chance and spends £42,000 on eight yearlings.

One of the youngsters he buys is a colt by Tumble Wind for 8,000 guineas. He's named Horage. But the yearling comes with immediate problems. The people McCormack has bought him for decide not to go ahead with the deal and it looks like he is going to be left to foot the bill. So enters a hero. Lebanese businessman Abed Rachid hasn't come to McCormack's stable to look at Horage but ends up buying him anyway. There's something about the horse which compels him. As on a whim decisions go, it would turn out to be one of the best Rachid would ever make. For when the two-year-old took to the track, he went on to do something quite extraordinary.

It started at Ayr in the Hillhouse Stakes. Six runners and the 6-1 Horage broke his maiden immediately, winning by three lengths. When he subsequently found the winner's enclosure at Pontefract, and then at Ascot – beating two other undefeated colts in the process with such ease that he finished five lengths clear – McCormack must have realised he had a prospect on his relatively novice hands.

Victories four and five were in the record books when Horage took the trainer to the Coventry Stakes at Royal Ascot, a festival he could only have dreamed of attending at the start of the year. With a blacksmith having pricked his foot when shoeing him the day before the race, causing him to go slightly lame, it made his display under Pat Eddery all the more brilliant. Despite reportedly feeling his foot, changing his legs a couple of times, Horage put in a top-drawer performance – beating off a persistent Kafu to win by a length and a half.

When McCormack came to York for the Gimcrack Stakes, Horage had won eight on the spin with the trophies from Newmarket's July Stakes and, just five days before his Knavesmire test, the Washington Singer Stakes at Newbury in the cabinet. He could not have been in better heart. He was ridden in York's premier two-year-old contest by Tony Murray, who had taken the ride in his previous win after Eddery had been claimed to ride in Ireland. At 8-13, he was one of the warmer favourites in Gimcrack history and did not disappoint. He made all. Rock 'N' Roller, who finished second, never looked at any stage like upsetting the favourite although Horage was pushed along for a furlong before quickening away to a four length success.

In truth, the calibre of his opponents means it is a Gimcrack that probably won't live on through the ages. Four of the runners started at odds of 33-1 or greater and the second favourite, Sayf El Arab, hadn't been seen on the track for nearly three months. But the York victory brought up Horage's ninth win on the spin and had earned his owner more than £100,000 in prize money. It was a phenomenal achievement.

Unfortunately for the film script writers, Horage could not go through the campaign with a perfect ten. His unbeaten record was lost in the Mill Reef Stakes at Newbury where, again as a pre-race favourite, he finished fourth of the five runners and, as he came to start his three-year-old career, some experts felt he would struggle against the improvement of a couple of his juvenile rivals. What did they know? If McCormack needed any further proof that this stunning story was assured a happy ending it came in the St James's Palace Stakes at Royal Ascot the following June.

The racing review, Timeform *Racehorses of 1983*, would argue his victory was 'one of the bravest front running performances seen all season'. He was not fancied. In fact, Horage was the outsider of the seven runners who lined up at the Berkshire track at 18-1. His season had not begun promisingly when, to be frank, he had been thrashed in a race at Thirsk in April. A minor injury, a sore heel, had reportedly kept him from challenging for Classic glory in the 2,000 Guineas and the runner-up, Tolomeo, was among those pressing ahead for St James's Palace glory. But Steve Cauthen, the enormously talented

American rider who would dominate British racing over the following few years, crashed Horage out of the gates, had a four length lead by the turn and kept on the pressure to the line. Tolomeo came with a fast late run but Horage had his measure – by just a head.

Of the top two-year-olds of the previous year, Horage was the only one to win a top class contest at three. He could not quite live up to his Ascot form in his final three races before being retired to stud. Beaten in the Hungerford Stakes and the Prix du Moulin at Longchamp before ending his career with a fourth place finish in the Queen Elizabeth II Stakes at Ascot, he was sent to the Ballygoran Stud in Ireland's County Kildare. Horage was the racing dream brought to life.

***

TURTLE ISLAND, meanwhile, won't be remembered for his Gimcrack victory in 1993. It will be for the way he destroyed the field in the Irish 2,000 Guineas at the Curragh the following year. Fifteen lengths over Guided Tour made him one of the most comprehensive winners of as Classic contest but the colt had signalled his talent in York's famous two-year-old contest.

Owned by Robert Sangster, Turtle Island had won a Group 1 at Leopardstown and the Norfolk Stakes at Royal Ascot before taking on the Gimcrack and, though he wouldn't need this virtue in Ireland, his showing on Knavesmire revealed he was as hard as nails. It was an approach which matched his trainer Peter Chapple-Hyam's 'unorthodox' approach when watching his horses in action. Most handlers are restrained, binoculars fixed, studying every nuance, each tiny detail, of a race. Chapple-Hyam was anything but. As Turtle Island fought hard to keep up with Unblest up the York straight, the trainer cajoled. After James Fanshawe's juvenile was worn into submission, by just a head at the finish following a frantic duel from the two furlong marker, Chapple-Hyam entered the winner's enclosure with clenched fists. Newspaper reports claimed he was 'close to growling'. He had never even contemplated defeat. 'Even when they came upsides him I knew he'd win,' he declared.

Interestingly, Turtle Island beat a useful field which included Mister Baileys, the 15-8 favourite, who would be the following year's 2,000

Guineas winner. Timeform said it was one of the best performances in the race in recent years. Turtle Island appeared three times more on the track after he had cut a swath through the Irish Classic contenders – gaining podium places in the St James's Palace Stakes at Royal Ascot and the Celebration Mile at Goodwood before finishing down the field in the Queen Elizabeth II Stakes back in Berkshire.

After six wins in 13 starts, Turtle Island was sent off to stud, where he would sire the 1999 2,000 Guineas winner Island Sands for Godolphin and the Prix Cleopatra and Prix d'Astarte filly Turtle Bow three years later.

***

NEVER comfortable in the glare of publicity, John Magnier had a brainwave when Mull Of Kintyre won the Gimcrack Stakes in 1999. The chief of breeding empire Coolmore chose to nominate a friend to make the speech to the Gimcrack dinner on his behalf that December. His pal was Alex Ferguson.

There had been nothing controversial about Mull Of Kintyre's display on the racetrack. Attracting nearly £100,000 in major bets, the latest Aidan O'Brien superstar left the opposition lagging way behind – as the 4-5 favourite. Ma Yoram, three lengths adrift, had been Mull Of Kintyre's closest challenger. But the Irish-trained horse disputed from the very start, led at halfway, and just kept getting quicker on the way to the finish. He won without ever really needing to be hard ridden.

Magnier's choice of Ferguson to make the Gimcrack address ruffled feathers in the York Race Committee. The idea had been pitched to John Smith, the clerk of the course at York from 1987 to 2002, and had been enthusiastically received. Magnier's motives were pure enough. Ferguson's Manchester United had won the treble of Premier League, FA Cup and European Cup the previous season and the Coolmore boss rightly felt the sport would gain widespread publicity if one of the country's most high-profile sporting figures gave the address. He could give racing the shot in the arm its critics felt it sorely needed.

Smith had the task of putting it to the committee, but found they weren't as pleased as he was with the plan. 'They said "Well, we do prefer somebody who has got a direct interest in the horse" rather than a personality like Sir Alex. That was the reason they turned him down,' he says. 'It was because he wasn't directly involved – he hadn't even got a share in the horse – but he was a name. Wasn't it the same year he had just won the European Cup? So I thought he was good for the course. But I could see the Committee's point of view. I didn't have to break the news to John Magnier. The man in the middle of all this was Mike Dillon, of Ladbrokes. He was very friendly with Alex Ferguson, Ballydoyle and the Magniers. It was he who said the Committee would prefer to have somebody directly involved with the horse.' But Magnier took umbrage.

In his book about Ferguson, *If You're Second You Are Nothing,* the national newspaper journalist Oliver Holt wrote that it was Lord Manton, a former chairman and still a powerful figure on the Race Committee, who threw out the suggestion. Holt wrote: 'He [Magnier] regarded the decision as an affront and a short-sighted and snobbish snub to Ferguson. He was determined to make York bend to his will and decided he would put Ferguson's colours on his top horse each year just before the Gimcrack until Ferguson won it.' They couldn't stop him making the speech then.

Juniper, the following year, was first up for the new axis but failed – beaten narrowly into third place. Rock Of Gibraltar, in 2001 however, was a different story. Listed as a co-owner, Rock Of Gibraltar ran in Ferguson's red and white racing colours. Mick Kinane rode and the two-year-old, taking in just his fourth race, went off at 11-4. Kinane made most of the running on the stand rail and, as the race reached its climax, surged away to win by three lengths from the 33-1 shot Ho Choi. Ferguson wasn't there, watching the race on television before taking his Manchester United team to a Premiership match at rivals Blackburn Rovers. However, Ferguson was at York that December and rose to speak at the 231st Annual Gimcrack Dinner. In front of an illustrious audience, Ferguson gushed: 'Being committed to enjoying this marvellous sport almost inevitably means being in love with York as a racecourse. York's reputation as a wonderful place to savour the glories of Flat racing has never been higher. York flourishes as the result of a magnificent team effort.' It was the summit of the Manchester United manager's involvement in the racing world.

Rock Of Gibraltar turned out to be a hell of a horse. The accusations hurled at some Gimcrack winners about just how good they were could never be levelled at 'the Rock'. York proved the beginning of a brilliant journey. His racing career was pitifully brief, just two seasons to be precise. But in that time he shone. He would set a record of seven consecutive Group 1 wins before Domedriver got the better of him in the 2002 Breeders' Cup Mile. The Dewhurst Stakes, 2,000 Guineas, Irish 2,000 Guineas, the St James's Palace Stakes at Royal Ascot, and the Sussex Stakes at Glorious Goodwood – all fell to this machine of a thoroughbred.

Landseer got the closest to him, falling by a short head in the Dewhurst, and Hawk Wing tested him to the limit before succumbing by a neck in the 2,000 Guineas. He wasn't called 'The Rock' for nothing. With a host of championship belts, a career as a stallion would always see him leave the track earlier than the racing public might have liked. His passage to stud was also to end Ferguson and Magnier's racing partnership, the pair famously falling out in a dispute over shares of breeding rights when Rock Of Gibraltar took up his place at Coolmore's studs in Ireland and Australia.

**

BUT marvellous and mediocre continue to taint the Gimcrack. Tony James, the 2004 winner for example, was no Rock Of Gibraltar. Clive Brittain's colt took the glory in a stamina sapping race on soft ground but would never claim another victory.

The horse that followed him into the winner's enclosure 12 months later, though, would not suffer those criticisms. He was Amadeus Wolf. Training at the secluded, but beautiful, Hambleton Lodge stables at the summit of North Yorkshire's Sutton Bank, the star of diligent trainer Kevin Ryan was rising inexorably. He had a particular talent with young horses – nurturing them to great things on the racecourse. Amadeus Wolf, whose Gimcrack win would bring Ryan his first domestic Group race success, was the first major winner in what would turn out to be a brilliant run. Ryan had already won the Listed Acomb Stakes with Palace Episode on the opening day of the Ebor Festival, and he was hungry for further success.

Amadeus Wolf, starting at 7-1, was a son of Mozart – the champion sprinter who won the July Cup and the Nunthorpe Stakes in 2001 before dying in his first season as a stallion. He began with a bang, winning a maiden at Ayr, before finishing third on his next start: the Coventry Stakes at Royal Ascot at York. A podium finish at Chester followed before Amadeus Wolf returned to Knavesmire to take on his Coventry conqueror Red Clubs in the Gimcrack. There had been three lengths between the pair in June, as jockey Neil Callan hadn't been able to get his horse anywhere near the Barry Hills-trained victor. This time, in the Gimcrack, he was to turn the tables. Ryan's stable jockey was happy to be back in the saddle, having missed Palace Episode's victory because of a ban.

Tracking the leaders early on, Callan asked Amadeus Wolf to go get the race at the two furlong marker. He was still behind Red Clubs, who chased and got himself into a potentially winning position with 200 yards left to travel, but, while his rival could find no more, Amadeus Wolf strode on and swept a length and a half clear at the finishing line. Ryan said: 'It's a great thrill to win, particularly at York. We've always thought he was a very good horse and he's rubber stamped it.' Amadeus Wolf would become the apple of his eye.

After Gimcrack success, he marched straight on to Newmarket and secured the trainer his first Group 1 winner when crushing Red Clubs again in the Middle Park Stakes. Michael Hills, Red Clubs' rider, must have been cursing. A victory like that naturally put Ryan's horse in the frame for Classic contention the following season. But his colt could only finish seventh in the 2,000 Guineas at Newmarket in a race dominated by another Aidan O'Brien-trained star, George Washington. Amadeus Wolf would continue to perform admirably on the highest stage despite that setback, picking up places in three Group 1 races in 2006 – the Prix Maurice de Gheest at Deauville, the Nunthorpe Stakes at York and the Sprint Cup at Haydock. He would find the winner's enclosure only once more, however, and fittingly it was back at the scene of his Gimcrack triumph.

The battle was the Group 2 Duke of York Stakes at the climax of the May meeting in 2007. Ryan's star was the 3-1 favourite and, with Callan in the pilot's seat as always, it was an eye-catching display from the four-year-old. A length and a quarter was the distance between Amadeus Wolf and old foe Red Clubs after Callan led his mount to the front at the furlong marker. Expectations had been high and they remained so afterwards with Ryan targeting Royal Ascot glory.

The Golden Jubilee Stakes was a step too far for Amadeus Wolf who, following two further defeats – including finally being trounced by Red Clubs in the Betfair Sprint Cup at Haydock – howled his last on the track and was retired to the Irish National Stud. 'He was a lovely horse to train,' Ryan told the author after he headed across the Irish Sea to start a new life in County Kildare. 'He had a great temperament and he was very uncomplicated. We will be lucky if another one like him comes along.'

***

THE Gimcrack Stakes is a strange race. It's founded in memory of a horse who never actually won on the track and, even today, its winning owners can sometimes be more excited about addressing the annual dinner held each December than they are about their horse having won. With that in mind it is perhaps no surprise that, of York's great races, the Gimcrack is the one that has experienced both glorious highs and worrying lows.

Bahram, Mill Reef and Rock Of Gibraltar form its summit, horses of breathtaking majesty who have left an indelible mark on the racing landscape. But you can also take your pick from any number of one-hit wonders through the years to see the other side of the coin. The conditions of the race determine that this will always be the case.

Sometimes, just as in every other walk of sporting life, promising juniors don't live up to their early billing. And so with every Gimcrack winner, like the 2010 champion Approve, a waiting game ensues. Will they go on to fulfil their undoubted promise? Or will they become just another also-ran – a wannabe who turned out to be a nobody?

Whatever happens, the stories are still fascinating in the making.

THE YORKSHIRE OAKS

CONDESSA crosses the finish line but no one is cheering, less still watching the Musidora winner claim Yorkshire Oaks glory. Their gazes are in the distance, eyes fixed, up the Knavesmire straight. At the stricken figure of Willie Carson.

A sudden fall, a horse flailing in agony, and the four-time champion jockey lies utterly still. Crumpled and unconscious, he is seriously injured. Carson was confident Silken Knot, who was trained by Major Dick Hern and had been in and out of form that season, would win the 1981 renewal of the contest. But it would not be for another big race victory that the popular jockey would remember August 18.

Warning signs may have been present before the stalls even opened in the mile and a quarter event. The filly had seemed reluctant to run. Coming round the final turn and into the straight, Carson now found out why. Negotiating the bend, the Royal rider suddenly heard Silken Knot's foreleg snap. As the injured filly stretched out her other leg in a desperate bid for balance, that broke as well – sending horse and Carson tumbling into the turf. She had been ideally positioned near the front so, as the jockey hit the deck, he fell right into the path of the chasing pack. It was an 11 runner race. He was trampled by at least five horses, fracturing his skull and breaking vertebrae along with his left wrist.

In the panic of the aftermath, the life of the 38-year-old Scot had seemed in danger. Racegoers rushed to his aid before ambulance crews swept onto the track to tend to the rider. Only his helmet had prevented Carson from suffering even more serious injuries. Miraculously, as he regained consciousness still lying on the turf waiting to go to hospital, the racecourse public address system revealed his injuries were not life threatening. The cheer that followed was the biggest of the day.

Six days later, when he felt up to talking about the accident, the effects were still clearly evident – and not just the headache and the broken bones. 'I'm also deaf in one ear,' he told the *Yorkshire Evening Press*. 'There was blood coming out of it when I was brought to hospital but I think it's only temporary. I was in a good position coming round the final bend into the straight when I heard one of the filly's legs snap. Then I was thrown to the ground, and remembered no more about it until I was in the ambulance.' His head injuries meant the doctors could not give him an anaesthetic when he arrived at York Hospital. 'They had to set my broken wrist without it. It was very, very painful, but it helped take my mind off other things. I was fitter than usual this year, thank goodness, and that's helped my recovery. I've lost count of the broken bones I've had in my career and I had a lot of near misses before last week. But I've never had a fractured skull before and I wouldn't know how long it will be before I'm really my old self again.'

It was not an easy road. Depression, tiredness, the need to be lifted out of a bath, Carson revealed in his autobiography *Up Front* that, 12 years later, he still suffered from headaches. It became known as 'that race', the moment Carson became synonymous with Knavesmire. Despite riding many victories, and horses of the quality of Dayjur, it was the moment which stood out above all his others at York. It also swamped Condessa's moment of triumph.

Jim Bolger's three-year-old had been impressive when winning the Musidora in May – leaving the odds-on Fairy Footsteps trailing in her wake. It was argued the soft ground at York that day had proved decisive in her victory and, after finishing only eighth in the Ribblesdale Stakes at Royal Ascot on her next appearance, the assumption appeared only more decisive. A runners-up spot in the

Irish Oaks had confounded that to some extent, and she was subsequently sold just a few weeks before her York adventure to the American owner Craig Singer for what Bolger called 'a very big amount'. It was reported to be more than half a million dollars.

He is quite clear on why Condessa was able to step up her performances when it absolutely mattered. 'The real key to her was to get a run in her within seven days of the main event,' he reveals. 'She had run at Lingfield just before the Musidora and she had run on the Curragh four days before she ran in the Yorkshire Oaks.'

When Silken Knot sent Carson sprawling, the surprising 5-1 shot Condessa had plenty to do. Firstly, she had to get out of danger – moving round the injured Carson as both he and the fatally injured horse hampered those running behind. As Condessa began the long journey to the finishing line down the Knavesmire straight, it looked a hopeless task. 'Jack Doyle was the agent (for the sale) and turning into the straight she was either last or second last,' remembers Bolger. 'Three furlongs down she was still last and Jack was up at the furlong marker – I don't think he thought anyone was around – and he put his two hands in the air and said "Please God don't let her get beat".' His prayers were answered.

Jockey Declan Gillespie still had three lengths to find on Leap Lively, who had won the trial which proved Condessa's warm up at Lingfield, Home On The Range and Fiesta Fun. Four others were either level, or just in front, as Gillespie tried to get something extra out of his filly. But something remarkable was happening. With every passing yard, Condessa was eating up the ground on the leaders. She moved so quickly, she caught Leap Lively with 50 yards still to go. Almost breezing past – as much as you can by a neck – she sealed a brilliant win going away. Albeit a victory marred by Carson's crash.

'We knew Carson was seriously injured and that put a dampener on everything,' Bolger says. 'That aside, it was obviously very pleasing to go to York and win.' Condessa could not repeat the trick. Third at the Curragh on her comeback, and failing to impress at Doncaster in the Park Hill Stakes, she went on to Longchamp and the Prix de l'Arc de Triomphe but never featured.

Her American owner took her to race in the United States where she ran at Woodbine and Aqueduct before eventually going to stud.

Carson's immediate memories of the horrors of that 1981 Oaks would also be soothed in the very near future. Back riding in the race the following year, he would add to his success on Dibidale in 1974 by winning the Oaks back-to-back in 1983 and 1984 with Sun Princess and Circus Plume and in 1989 and 1990 with Roseate Tern and Hellenic.

***

SO what did Willie Carson nearly die for? The Ebor is York's oldest race but the Yorkshire Oaks isn't far behind its bigger brother. It was established six years later, in 1849, and was originally restricted just to three-year-olds. In fact, it wasn't opened to older fillies and mares until nearly a century and a half later. Only since 1991 have the generations been able to clash over a mile and a half at York in this race.

Its origins lay in the renaissance which pulled York Racecourse up from the abyss in the middle of the 19th Century – a time when the track was mired by poor prize money, poor racing and dwarfed in the shadow of its rival on Town Moor in Doncaster. A meeting of the York Race Committee in 1842 proposed to establish a racing fund to revitalise the decayed track and, as a minute book of the year shows, to 'restore the City of York to its ancient position in the annals of British racing'. It was in this climate that the Yorkshire Oaks became established.

It aimed to be a county version of the Epsom Classic. Its first winner, in 1849, was Ellen Middleton, owned by Lord Zetland. The first to achieve the Epsom and York double was Brown Duchess 12 years later. She was the daughter of The Flying Dutchman, the Derby winner who had beaten Voltigeur in that thrilling match race at York in 1851. Brown Duchess was one of only two Classic winners produced by The Flying Dutchman – the other being the 1853 Derby victor Ellington – and she finished third in the 1,000 Guineas before beating Lady Ripon by a neck at Epsom to take the Oaks. She beat a field of seven quite easily to add the Yorkshire equivalent before going on to win the Park Hill Stakes and dead-heat in the Doncaster Cup. The 4-9 favourite at York, Brown Duchess saw off Tattoo, drawing clear decisively after being held up early on.

Meanwhile, more than a century after achieving the feat, Fred

Archer remains the Yorkshire Oaks' most successful jockey. Between 1875 and 1886 he won the race a staggering eight times. Of these mounts, three – Spinaway (1875), Jannette (1878) and Wheel Of Fortune (1879) – took the Epsom and York Oaks doubles.

Equally as dominating in the latter part of the 19th Century was the trainer Matthew Dawson. Saddling nine Yorkshire Oaks victors between 1868 and 1884, he was responsible for seven of Archer's successful rides. But while no jockey has got near Archer's magnificent eight, Dawson's tally of nine has been matched in the modern era by an equally brilliant trainer – Sir Michael Stoute.

The Epsom-York double wasn't terribly uncommon as the race wound its way through the 1860s, 70s and 80s. Of the 22 horses to have managed the feat in the race's history, eight came between Brown Duchess in 1861 and Reve d'Or in 1887. There would only be a further four in the next 72 years. La Roche was the first, getting the 20th Century off to a cracking start when winning in 1900 but there followed another two decades before Love In Idleness took the glory in 1921. Frieze's brace came in 1952 and of Petite Etoile's Oaks and Yorkshire Oaks double of 1959, we shall see more shortly.

***

NASH Light and Will O' The Wisp will always live on in Yorkshire Oaks folklore. Not because they were particularly special fillies, but because in 1932 they shared what is the only dead-heat in the race's history.

Will O' The Wisp, ridden by the brilliant jockey Gordon Richards, was the 13-8 favourite and looked justifiably so when coming down the straight with a handy advantage. But Fred Rickaby, who was riding the joint 6-1 second favourite Nash Light, did not know when he was beaten. Crucially, Will O' The Wisp would soon give him the impression she had gone too quickly, too soon. As Richards put his mount at the head of affairs straight from the off, Rickaby held up Nash Light to the extent where, coming round the turn towards home, the whole field was in front of his filly. But down the straight he urged her into action and she responded, flying through the field in pursuit. Rickaby's encouragement came from the actions of his formidable rival up front.

Richards was casting his gaze backwards – not because he had all the time in the world, but because he could feel his filly weakening.

'It seemed when the straight was reached that nothing could beat Will O' The Wisp and Richards appeared to look over his shoulder,' reported the *Yorkshire Herald* the day after the contest. 'The filly was, however, obviously tiring and as the post got nearer she pulled up as though she had had enough for one day.' Rickaby rode a 'splendid finish' catching the favourite right on the line, the *Herald* reported. With an extra couple of yards, they had no doubt Nash Light would have won. With no photo finish to rely on, none of the technology that can decide a result in a flash today, the judges decided they could not split the pair.

But while foiled of outright glory on Will O' The Wisp, Richards had nothing to stop him three years later when he piloted Trigo Verde. She had finished second to Coppelia at Newmarket on her last start the previous month and was installed as a hot 11-10 favourite at York. Trigo Verde justified the confidence. She did not win narrowly, she trounced a decent field by three lengths. The lead had changed hands several times before the horses approached the straight. Then Fairlead, owned by King George V, struck the front. 'Someone on the stands remarked to Willie Jarvis, the King's trainer, "Yours is in front",' the *Yorkshire Herald* reported in its race write-up. 'Quickly came the rejoinder "Yes, but the winning post is up here".'

Jarvis's fears were well judged. The field had barely begun its path towards the line when Trigo Verde took the lead. She would not be overtaken. While Fairlead failed to live up to her name, dropping back down the pack, nothing could challenge Richards' domination. It brought up his fourth Yorkshire Oaks victory. The legendary rider, who had also claimed the spoils in 1927 on Gioconda and Glorious Devon in 1930 would win the race three more times – thanks to Sculpture in 1937, Sea Parrot in 1951 and, finally, Kerkeb two years later.

***

LESTER Piggott would come to regard Petite Etoile as one of the greatest fillies he ever rode and by the time she came to Knavesmire for the Yorkshire Oaks in 1959 he had no doubts about her ability. But it hadn't always been that way.

She had won two of her four appearances on the track as a two-year-old but the legendary rider was not greatly enthused, describing her in his autobiography, *Lester*, as 'nothing particularly out of the ordinary'. In fact, her racecourse debut had been remarkable only for the fact that she got loose before the race, galloped around aimlessly, and was subsequently smashed by eight lengths in a two horse race.

Even though the winter had done wonders for her, perhaps, with that indifferent juvenile form to draw on, it wasn't that much of a surprise when the jockey – with the pick of the Classic potentials at Noel Murless's yard, where he was employed as stable jockey – opted not to ride Petite Etoile in the 1,000 Guineas. He plumped instead for Collyria, and chose the wrong one. Petite Etoile won and Piggott never made the same mistake again. She was third favourite for the Oaks at Epsom, winning without having to get into top gear, and had also taken the Sussex Stakes at Goodwood before the Yorkshire Oaks beckoned. At 2-15, she wasn't quite the hottest favourite in the race's history – that honour went to the almost unbackable Winkipop, a 1-8 favourite in 1910 – but she was very close. Now already the greatest filly to have run since the end of the Second World War, Petite Etoile eased past Mirnaya by three quarters of a length.

On the track she was brilliant, but at home she was famously quirky. Murless described her as a 'bloody monkey' and it is said she always had to have a grey horse in front and behind when walking in the string. Petite Etoile remained unbeaten throughout her three-year-old career after winning the Champion Stakes. Later, she would twice win the Coronation Cup at Epsom and had 14 career victories.

Elsewhere, Homeward Bound (1964), Lupe (1970) and Mysterious (1973) were a trio of talented fillies who would also emulate Petite Etoile – taking an Epsom and Oaks double. The first of these was trained by the authoritarian John Oxley at Newmarket's Hurworth House Stables and was ridden by Greville Starkey, who had his first major retainer with the hard hitting handler. Although Ebor, the *Yorkshire Evening Press*'s racing reporter, revealed there had been a lot of money pre-race for the Irish-trained Ancasta before the Yorkshire contest, he wrote that 'neither she nor anything else had any chance from the moment that Greville Starkey decided to make a move on Homeward Bound'.

She had been sent off the 2-1 favourite and, with six rivals to contend with, it was Lester Piggott on board Amfissa who showed the way. Tracked by Siesta Time, she was in front until long into the straight when Ancasta struck the front before the two furlong marker. 'But Starkey was just biding his time,' reported Ebor, 'and getting Homeward Bound into a nice challenging position on the rails. He sent her on just over a furlong out and she forged clear for a good victory.'

Beaufront chased but had to settle for second, three lengths adrift, in what was a marvellous performance. Lupe, meanwhile, was still unbeaten when she took on the Yorkshire Oaks test six years later. She was the first of three winners in four years for Noel Murless, now coming into the twilight of his career. His charge was a 4-6 shot – partly because of her undoubted talent having won at Epsom but also because there were only two other runners: Highest Hopes and Christine. Ridden by Sandy Barclay, Lupe was a comfortable leader in a slowly run contest all the way round the course until they reached the halfway point of the straight. Then, as Ebor reported, trouble looked to be ahead. 'Joe Mercer ranged alongside on Highest Hopes about two and a half furlongs out,' he wrote. 'Highest Hopes was about half a length up on her but she rallied splendidly for Sandy Barclay and ran on in most determined fashion to regain the lead and win by two lengths.' Christine trailed in third, some 15 lengths adrift.

Highest Hopes got her revenge when beating a field including Lupe in the Prix Vermeille at Longchamp the following month. Lupe would have a trial race for the Epsom Oaks named after her at Goodwood until it was rebranded, in 2007, as the Height of Fashion Stakes in honour of the dam of Nashwan and Nayef who had won the Lupe Stakes herself in 1982. And three years later, Mysterious, also trained by Murless, repeated Lupe's trick. This special filly won the 1,000 Guineas as well. By Crepello, the 2,000 Guineas and Derby winner in 1957, Mysterious ran only once as a two-year-old and showed inexperience despite winning the Cherry Hinton Stakes at Newmarket by a length and a half.

Murless's juvenile was expected to do better the following year and she didn't take long to prove that potential. The trainer would come to the opinion that only Petite Etoile was better than this filly, who opened her account in 1973 when winning by three quarters of a length from Grasse in the Fred Darling Stakes at Newbury in April. The Guineas was next and if there were still doubts about her talents, they were dispelled when Mysterious won by an easy three lengths from Jacinth over the Newmarket mile. Good, but better was to come.

Her second Classic, the Oaks at Epsom, came in even more dominating fashion. While every jockey behind her was flat to the boards, whips cracking in desperate pursuit, Geoff Lewis, on board Mysterious, did not even have to move on the going away filly. She beat Where You Lead, who had won the Musidora at York, by four lengths. That meant she was 1-2 on her next start, the Irish Oaks, but found Dahlia – a very special filly in her own right – far too good and fell by three lengths. Her unbeaten record gone, the Yorkshire Oaks would be some sort of redemption. She won by two and a half lengths, coasting past opposition which included the French filly Virunga, who had finished in the frame in the French Oaks.

It could easily have been even more emphatic. Held up towards the back of the small field of five coming into the straight, Mysterious was still on the bridle when she ranged up alongside the leaders and cantered to the winning post. Had she wished, she could have won by a whole lot more. Virunga trailed in well behind her, with Cheveley Princess a further seven lengths back. It was the last time Murless would win the Yorkshire Oaks. The Warren Place-based Newmarket saddler retired in 1976 – handing his yard over to Henry Cecil.

***

FAIR Salina began a dynasty for Sir Michael Stoute. Barbados-born, Stoute came to Britain as a 19-year-old in 1964 and learned the trade as an assistant to the redoubtable Pat Rohan at Malton. Setting up on his own eight years later, he would experience success quickly and one of the first of countless major wins came at York when Blue Cashmere won the Nunthorpe Stakes at 18-1 in 1974. Though he can't have known it then, Fair Salina, four years later, was the start of a love affair Stoute has enjoyed ever since with the Yorkshire Oaks.

Stoute has claimed no other top class race as many times as he has taken the fillies' and mares showpiece on Knavesmire. That is in a career which has included five Derby wins, seven Lockinge Stakes, seven Nassau Stakes and five International Stakes. All trail his nine Yorkshire Oaks crowns.

Fair Salina was another to have triumphed at Epsom before stamping her authority, if it was needed, on York's fillies' 'Classic'. She had also won the Irish version but had done so in some controversy, and it was a result which set up a thrilling sequel at York. For it matched Fair Salina once more with Sorbus, who had something of a score to try to settle. Sorbus had actually won the Irish Classic, with a length separating her from Fair Salina at the line, but Stoute's jockey Greville Starkey complained – arguing that his progress had been checked when Sorbus veered left. The Stewards agreed and gave the contest to Fair Salina.

Interestingly, she was a 5-1 outsider when race time arrived at York. Sorbus was just in front at fours with Relfo, another who might have snatched the Irish crown with a bit more luck, considered the filly to watch at 7-4. Starkey looked to take command from the outset and he did so with a dominating ride. He pushed Fair Salina clear of the pack with fully six and a half furlongs still to travel. With two furlongs to go, she was still well in front but Sorbus, ridden by Raymond Carroll, tried to run her down. The chasers had encouragement. Fair Salina, her stride shortening, was getting tired. But she had enough in hand, holding off Sorbus by a length and a half. It was a brave decision by Starkey, who had opted to go for glory so far from home, but it had paid off.

Fair Salina went on to the Prix Vermeille at Longchamp a month later and was beaten after trying to take charge of the race from the moment the stalls went up. She was then retired – as the first filly to win all three Oaks crowns. Stoute, as has been the case in his career generally, would prove to be the man with the Midas Touch. Sally Brown (1985), Untold the following year, Hellenic in 1990, Pure Grain five years later, Petrushka at the start of the new Millennium and Quiff (2004) would join the fabulous Islington in completing his sensational roll of honour. It is a record that will take some beating.

***

DIMINUENDO had a big effect on former York clerk of the course John Smith. He liked the filly so much, he named his cat after her.

'I was taken with Diminuendo,' says the man in charge of

Knavesmire from 1987 to 2002. 'It was Steve Cauthen's era and he was a great jockey, and a great personality. 'He was very articulate. It was always a pleasure to have him around.'

By the time Diminuendo came to the Oaks she was already arguably the top class filly of 1988. As we have seen, Sheikh Mohammed's filly had won the Musidora Stakes at York in May, before impressively winning at Epsom the following month and then dead-heating in the Irish 1,000 Guineas. That had been considered a lacklustre display, but there was not to be a repeat back at York in the Yorkshire Oaks. The bookies definitely feared her, bringing the Henry Cecil-trained three-year-old into 3-10.

Jockey Steve Cauthen was again on board and a field of five lined up to oppose including Andaleeb, who had won the Lancashire Oaks, and Sunday Sport Star who, with Sudden Love, had run a futile effort to catch Diminuendo at Epsom. Diminuendo passed Sudden Love with such ease at the two furlong marker it was as if the latter had just stopped. She had been held up at first and was sixth coming into the straight before moving impressively and sweeping away from the rest of her competition. Sudden Love managed to hold on to second spot but Cauthen's brilliant filly coasted in. It was five lengths and she had been eased down close to the finish. Her time, of two minutes 25.79 seconds, established a new race record which still stands. What would her time have been had she been really asked a serious question? Group 1 races were not supposed to be this easy.

Now, having proved her superiority over the three-year-old set, Diminuendo went hunting the men and her elders. It was a step too far. Starting the favourite for the St Leger at Doncaster the following month, a brave effort brought her just a length short of Minster Son, while she could only finish tenth at Longchamp in the Arc. That should not colour her achievements. Diminuendo was an enormously talented filly, and one still referred to when a new pretender emerges.

***

TOUGH, willing and always game – that was just User Friendly's jockey George Duffield. The filly, who trainer Clive Brittain reckons is among the greatest he has ever trained, and the veteran jockey were perfect partners through an amazing journey in 1992.

Duffield, for so long a hard-working, committed, yet journeyman jockey was enjoying the kind of Indian summer of which riders dream. He had won thousands of races in his long career but the truly big prizes had largely escaped him. Then he was given the ride on the daughter of Slip Anchor ahead of her racecourse debut in a fillies' maiden at Sandown in April. Even that had come about fortuitously.

'It was through Michael Roberts,' Brittain explains. 'I knew I had a nice filly in User Friendly, not necessarily a Group filly certainly, but he came and rode work and agreed she was good. Anyway, Henry Cecil had asked him to ride some horses for him and he had a filly who was one of the favourites in this maiden race at Sandown. We had no contract, it was just he rode for the stable. I thought he was making a mistake because I thought the filly (User Friendly) was really good. I said if he got off it would be very difficult for him to get back on. George came along and in this race she was hopelessly drawn on the mile and a quarter track – wide on the outside. I said "Just drop her in and she will still stay". She was 25-1 in that maiden at Sandown. It was a big field, she won and I knew then that we had a filly of class.'

It was a major transformation. At the yearling sales at Newmarket in 1990, User Friendly had failed to meet her reserve price and was subsequently not raced as a juvenile. But having initially been backward, she had improved tremendously – as she showed Brittain at home. 'We only gave her one good piece of work', he says. 'She actually worked with Terimon (who won the Juddmonte International Stakes the year before). She had one gallop and it was the only one she ever did that was in anyway searching. We got a lead horse and another decent filly and she just cruised past them. We went to Lingfield for the Oaks trial knowing we would take a lot of beating.' Starting favourite, and facing four rivals, Duffield waited early on User Friendly, the 2-1 favourite, before bringing her to the front in the straight and beating Niodini by two and a half lengths.

Next was the big one. Epsom, the Oaks, and Duffield's first Classic victory. 'We weren't the favourite but we beat the favourite and then people realised what a good filly she was,' Brittain states. 'It really made George. Well, not made him but it was the icing on the cake. He had worked so hard and travelled so many miles.' In a small field of seven, including the Musidora Stakes first and second All At Sea and

209

Perfect Circle, User Friendly won by three and a half lengths with the chasing Musidora victor twenty lengths clear of Pearl Angel in third.

Adding the Irish Oaks to her impressive CV, the horse, who had now won all four of her starts, then came to York with the Yorkshire version – and a treble – on the mind of Duffield. She was backed as if defeat was not an option, starting as an almost unbeatable 8-11 favourite. But while talent had got her through to this point, it was the Yorkshireman Duffield who would now show off his own brilliance in front of his home crowd. Brittain always had faith. 'To maintain that momentum, running like she did, there is a certain amount of pressure,' he explains. 'I have every belief in the horses I train. I couldn't see anything in my mind that could beat her.'

Perhaps we should have asked him that question again halfway down the York straight. Firstly, a shaken Duffield had suffered a near death experience in the skies when the light aircraft taking him, Lester Piggott, Michael Hills and Philip Robinson up to York for racing was almost struck by a fighter pilot – flipping the plane and momentarily sending it plummeting. Robinson told reporters that day: 'I was in the front next to the pilot when we noticed some activity among some fighter planes and suddenly one appeared right in front of us. He could only have been feet away and his slipstream flipped our plane over. We all thought we had been hit and the pilot sent out a May-Day signal.'

You could have forgiven the rider for having been shaken by the near miss and Duffield himself wrote in his autobiography, *Gentleman George*, that he did not believe he had been as focused as he would have liked. Neither did it help that a problem with malfunctioning stalls resulted in a false start and, when the race finally did begin, User Friendly completely missed the break – losing five lengths on the field. It meant Duffield had to get to work much earlier than he wanted and York's fast ground appeared to be hampering his filly's action. Then, as the pace picked up into the last half mile, User Friendly was pinned to the rail and looked in big trouble. So just like the pilot who had averted disaster in the skies that morning, Duffield took evasive action. Hitting the brakes, he pulled out and swung wide into the centre of the track to try to steer the filly through the traffic.

'It was his class and his knowledge of the track,' Brittain says of Duffield's quick thinking. 'He knew that he wasn't going to get a run and he had to get out and get out quickly.' Even then, User Friendly still had a lot to do. But she ground down her seven rivals, taking the lead at the furlong pole, and seeing off Bineyah by two and a half lengths. Having looked beaten halfway down the straight, it was some comeback.

If User Friendly had ability, she also had guts in abundance – a trait she shared with her jubilant jockey. Duffield would continue feeling the benefit. Having won his first Classic on her at Epsom, she would provide his second when winning the St Leger at Doncaster the month after her York exertions. She would then go down narrowly to Subotica in the Prix de l'Arc de Triomphe at Longchamp in October. Back in training as a four-year-old, she would take Duffield to Paris glory with the Group 1 Grand Prix de Saint Cloud but would not successfully defend her Oaks crown – finishing third to Cumani's 'special' filly Only Royale.

***

ONLY Islington nearly a decade later has matched what Only Royale did in 1993 and 1994. In the long history of the Yorkshire Oaks, those two sparkling fillies are in a very select bracket. The only horses to win the race twice.

'She was very special,' says Only Royale's trainer Luca Cumani. 'She was a filly that was difficult to train and it was hard to keep her form for very long. But I rate her quite highly. She is among the best I have trained.'

The daughter of Juddmonte International winner Caerleon had won five of her six races as a three-year-old but had yet to bag a big race before coming to Knavesmire in August 1993. Rainbow Lake, having won the Lancashire Oaks at Haydock, was the 13-8 favourite and we have already seen the fate of the previous year's heroine User Friendly. A Group race may not have been pocketed before the Oaks but Only Royale had shown what she was capable of when finishing second in the Nassau Stakes at Goodwood a couple of weeks before her trip north. At York, even at the big price of 10-1, she would reveal exactly what she could do.

In the final stages, jockey Ray Cochrane had so much in hand he could afford to virtually stand up in the saddle to take a look back at her despairing chasers. Travelling well, Cochrane shook the reins at the furlong marker and just held on as the filly moved easily clear. Dancing Bloom was a distant three and a half lengths away in second.

Having now broken her duck, Only Royale next won the Prix Foy at Longchamp in a small field and ended the campaign with a decent fifth place showing in the Prix de l'Arc de Triomphe. Remaining in training for the 1994 campaign, it is somewhat ironic that the Yorkshire Oaks would be the only race she would win that season. Frankie Dettori was in the saddle on this occasion but the race finish was strikingly similar to 12 months previously – Only Royale striding away leaving her competition for dust. Again it was Dancing Bloom, the distinctive filly with the white blaze on her face, who was leading the stragglers. This time, Cumani's horse was six lengths better. It had taken one shake of the reins, one slap of the whip, for Dettori to unleash Only Royale's power. At 15-2, a price which relied heavily on her under-par performances at Goodwood and in the Coronation Cup at Epsom, she was arguably one of the bargains of that year's Ebor Festival. And, until Islington came along, she was unique.

The Arc remained elusive for Only Royale, in 1994 she would finish seventh, but she had reserved her best displays for York and had given Cumani another high profile success at one of his favourite tracks. 'It's a great track and is very fair,' he says. 'I like it. I just wish it was a bit closer to Newmarket.'

***

RAMRUMA followed Fair Salina, Diminuendo and User Friendly in becoming the fourth filly to win the Epsom, Irish and Yorkshire Oaks treble in 1999. Henry Cecil's horse also tried to win the St Leger that year but, like Diminuendo and User Friendly before her, found it a step too far and finished second.

Ramruma was out of the 1978 Musidora Stakes winner Princess of Man and she had demolished her opposition at both Epsom and the Curragh. York's Oaks saw her remain in fine fettle. She was up against ten rivals, making up the race's biggest field since it was opened to older horses eight years previously. Among those was Zahrat Dubai, who had won the Musidora at York in May and had claimed the Nassau Stakes at Goodwood. Ramruma had beaten her at Epsom and, rather comfortably, would do so again on Knavesmire.

Ridden by the multiple champion jockey Pat Eddery for the first time, she was on the premises from the very start. The 5-6 odds-on favourite took to the front with only a couple of furlongs of the race's mile and a half distance having elapsed, eclipsing her rival Mary Stuart, and simply stayed there. Eddery gradually increased the pace and then got after her with three furlongs left to travel but she was never really threatened. Ramruma briefly wandered about but the challenges came and went with Cecil's filly remaining comfortably ahead. The 33-1 chance Ela Athena was the nearest to her, finishing second a length and a quarter away, Silver Rhapsody was third with Zahrat Dubai back in fourth.

'She was out on her own for much of the race and is very lazy but she wouldn't have let anything come past her,' said her owner Prince Fahd Salman, who had already made the decision to keep her in training the following year. 'It was a smashing performance today. She ran on her own and wouldn't let anyone after her.'

Ending a 22-year wait for a Yorkshire Oaks win – his previous two had been May Hill in 1975 and Busaca in 1977 – Eddery said: 'She was doing nothing in front but waiting, and when she saw another horse out of the corner of her eye, she found that bit more.' Twelve months later, Ramruma was back to defend her crown.

Having finished last at Newmarket on her reappearance in the Jockey Club Stakes in May, not much was expected of her and she went off a 15-2 outsider. It was a valiant, but ultimately, unsuccessful effort. Her third place finish, behind Stoute's Petrushka and Henry Cecil's Love Devine had, however, restored her reputation. Ramruma finished her career the following month with a podium place in a Listed race at Ascot.

***

ISLINGTON, the super filly who is the only other horse to match Only Royale's back-to-back Yorkshire Oaks double, ruled the roost in 2002 and 2003. She would give trainer Sir Michael Stoute both his seventh and eighth successes in the race, and he would match Matthew Dawson's record of nine with Quiff the following year.

Islington came along at a golden time for jockey Kieren Fallon. Never a figure far away from controversy, Fallon was nevertheless at the height of his riding powers in the early part of the decade. Matched with Stoute's powerful Newmarket yard, the rider ruled the sport with an iron whip – winning the champion jockey title three times in a row between 2001 and 2003 and bagging a host of Group race prizes, including the Derby on Kris Kin. In Islington, he had a perfect companion.

A daughter of Sadler's Wells and Hellenic, the 1990 Yorkshire Oaks winner, Islington, as we have already seen, was a length too good for Spinnette in the Musidora. But returning to York she had a pressing question to answer. It came in the shape of Godolphin's Kazzia. She had won both the 1,000 Guineas and the Oaks and had been bought by Sheikh Mohammed's Dubai operation after being spotted winning a pattern race in Italy the previous year. A neck better than Snowfire at Newmarket, she had travelled to Epsom and beaten Quarter Moon by half a length with the rest of the field barely in sight. That made her the 7-4 favourite for Knavesmire's Oaks showpiece.

Islington, who had only finished eighth at Epsom, had bounced back well to win the Nassau Stakes at Goodwood but there was the obvious question mark as to whether she would stay a mile and a half. In a field of 11, Islington was the 2-1 second favourite. The 100-1 shot Starbourne went off quickly but, always travelling well, Islington stalked Kazzia and Fallon sent her to the front just before the two furlong marker.

'I decided to ride her positively, but I took a chance when I did go, probably a bit too soon, but I didn't like to disappoint her when she was going so easy,' Fallon said after the race. He need not have worried. Islington soon went clear and galloped away well, beating the 20-1 chance Guadalupe by five lengths with Sulk, runner-up to Islington in the Nassau, in third. For Kazzia, who could only finish fourth, the aura of invincibility had been smashed. She had been humbled. Islington had put on an exhibition. 'She was a bit special today,' said Stoute.

Fallon felt there was still more to come from Islington. But it would be York, a year later, before the defence of her crown would see her put another win on the board. Following a decent fifth in the Arc, Islington was third against top drawer opposition in the Breeders' Cup at Arlington, the Prince of Wales's Stakes at Royal Ascot and was down the field in the Eclipse at Sandown, won by Falbrav, before York came calling once again. Could she get back to the top?

Fallon thought it would be tougher. Islington had apparently been impressive in Newmarket gallops but, with the Epsom Oaks winner Casual Look and a promising Irish filly in L'Ancresse in the field, the jockey was cautious. 'This is probably the toughest Yorkshire Oaks for a long time,' he said. 'There are some very good fillies in the race.' He was right to a point. It was closer this time for the 8-11 favourite. But she still won. Tracking the leaders once again, Fallon stretched her legs over two furlongs and she stayed on well. Watching on, however, Stoute was having kittens. 'I don't know why Kieren did that to me,' he said of the jockey's early move for home. 'I didn't want to see her go on that far out.'

Ocean Silk, the mount of Jimmy Fortune, came with a late run inside the final quarter of a mile but she could not wear down the champion, who prevailed by a length. Islington had always been doing enough. She was back to her best – her problems were fully behind her. Fallon said: 'She was travelling sweet throughout. Obviously, I got to the front a bit sooner than I wanted and she was just idling in front, but when Jimmy came to me she picked up again. It is nice to ride a horse who is so genuine and tries so hard. She likes this track and was very impressive when she won the Musidora here last year. You can have horses for courses and this filly likes this one.'

After a podium place in the Irish Champion Stakes, Islington lit up the Breeders' Cup at Santa Anita when beating L'Ancresse by a neck in the Filly and Mare Turf. She would end her racing career in mid-division at the Japan Cup in Tokyo that November and was retired to Ballymacoll Stud in County Meath.

***

ALEXANDROVA, the most recent of the fillies to win both the Epsom and Yorkshire Oaks in 2006, was always destined for stardom. At least her price tag suggested so.

In the world of breeding, money is no guarantee of success. But when John Magnier, Michael Tabor and Derrick Smith – the trio behind the thoroughbred world-dominating Coolmore Stud – paid 420,000 guineas for her as a yearling at the October Sales in Newmarket in 2004, they were clearly expecting a substantial return on their investment. Well bred, by Sadler's Wells out of Shouk, she was named after a Russian ballerina and certainly looked the part. On the racecourse, she would act like it too. Her somewhat delicate frame belied by her guts, determination and breathtaking ability. She won only one of her four outings in her first season – a maiden at Tralee – but was always expected to improve in her second campaign.

Alexandrova re-emerged at York, for the Musidora Stakes, where she was the well-backed 8-15 favourite. But it was not to be her day. Clipping heels and stumbling in the opening stages of the race, the off-balance three-year-old was out the back of the field until Kieren Fallon, her rider and then stable jockey for her trainer, Ballydoyle's Aidan O'Brien, brought her through to lead three furlongs out. The effort she had been forced into expending to get back into contention seemed to have taken its effect, however. When she moved right at the furlong marker – a sign of tiredness – and was headed by Short Skirt, Mick Kinane galloped on and shocked Alexandrova by a length and a quarter.

A disappointing result certainly but, afterwards, O'Brien was in a sanguine mood – with both trainer and jockey of the opinion that she had needed the run. 'It wasn't a surprise that she got a bit tired towards the finish, but we're very pleased with her and she'll come on for the run,' O'Brien said. 'The Oaks is the plan.' Decent ground was the key for that challenge, with O'Brien adding her running action - 'she does bend her knees' - would mean a firm surface would rule her out.

At Epsom, for the Oaks, the ground was perfect. So was Alexandrova. A decent field, which included her Musidora conqueror, was beaten out of sight. Rising Cross, the nearest to her, was six lengths behind. Short Skirt was another length and a quarter back. Easy was the only way to describe how the 9-4 favourite had secured a brilliant Classic win. A little over a month later and she had another one. The Irish Oaks, at the Curragh, fell just as easily to her charms. This time Scottish Stage was the one seeing only her backside. Four lengths was the difference.

Onto the Yorkshire Oaks and, in a slowly-run race, her jockey Mick Kinane played a waiting game, almost toying with the field, as he kept Alexandrova last of the six runners until the three furlong marker. She was detached. Once he let her off the leash, however, as at Epsom and as in Ireland, there was no doubt where the crown was headed. She cut through the pack, strolled in front with a furlong left to travel, and moved away with some style from her beaten rivals – confirming her place as the best filly of her generation and the first in seven years, since Ramruma in 1999, to win the Oaks treble. O'Brien was thrilled.

'They went slow but it was no worry at all,' he said in the winner's enclosure. 'She is a fantastic filly and is very exciting. She has unbelievable class. When they go slow like that and then kick from the front, it can be hard to pick them up but she has that extra gear.' It was a victory for the generations too. Alexandrova's usual rivals, like the runner-up Short Skirt, were in the field but so were three four-year-olds – Exhibit One, a Group winner in Italy, Irish Noblesse Stakes winner Sina Cova and the dual Group victor, and Gran Premio di Milano holder, Shamdala.

For those at the track, Alexandrova provided welcome relief of a sort. At 4-9 she relieved the bookmakers of some of the cash from their overflowing satchels barely half an hour after Mudawin's 100-1 Ebor Handicap win had stunned the crowd into silence. 'She's a very special filly,' said O'Brien – never normally someone to get carried away with a winning performance.

Alexandrova was seen once more on the track before she took her place at stud. She finished third in the Prix de l'Opera at Longchamp, pushed along and not quite finding her top gear for Kieren Fallon. Not the glorious end O'Brien would have hoped for perhaps, but it was still a glorious career – particularly at York.

***

SARISKA was all the rage at York in 2009. While the International, the boys, had Sea The Stars that year, the girls had the English and Irish Oaks heroine who looked ideally placed to join those select fillies to have gained a treble by winning Knavesmire's Yorkshire Oaks.

One significant obstacle stood in the way: Dar Re Mi. John Gosden's filly, owned by Lord Andrew Lloyd Webber, had found Lush Lashes too good during her three-year-old career – twice finishing behind her in the Musidora and in the Yorkshire Oaks which, in 2008, was held in Newmarket after torrential rains wiped out York's Ebor Festival.

At four, she reappeared on Knavesmire but went down by a short head to Crystal Capella in the Middleton Stakes when sent off the heavily-backed 4-5 favourite. But she bounced back when winning the Group 1 Pretty Polly Stakes at the Curragh the following month and so arrived for the Yorkshire Oaks in the best of form. She was a big outsider – compared to Sariska anyway. While Bell's super filly was the 4-11 favourite, the bookies priced Dar Re Mi at what would turn out to be a rather generous 11-2. Bell certainly thought Sariska was up to the task and said victory could even see her take on Sea The Stars at the Arc. 'She's very good. She's improving rather than going backwards,' he said in the run-up to the contest. 'She never does anything wrong and she is getting better.'

That kind of confidence made Dar Re Mi's success all the more stunning. There were questions over whether the ground was too firm for Sariska, but a gracious Bell would offer no excuses afterwards. In truth, Sariska, who was meeting older horses for the first time, was under pressure three furlongs from home in the premier fillies' contest. Dar Re Mi had made a bold bid for victory and Sariska just could not get anywhere near her. The former had three quarters of a length in hand at the finish. The victory seemed even more impressive when Gosden revealed afterwards that Dar Re Mi had come through a far from ideal preparation.

'Our filly got a little wound up because we were going to lead her across and then Johnny Murtagh came off Roaring Forte after winning the Addleshaw Goddard Stakes. She had a loose horse go past her three times when she walked across. That got her a bit edgy and her jockey Jimmy Fortune said down at the start she was already in a race,' he said. 'She has settled and done it well, but she was a bit more revved up than would be normal. She's a very progressive filly.' In 2010, under William Buick, Dar Re Mi would win the money-laden Dubai Sheema Classic at the fantastic new Meydan track in Dubai.

What of Sariska? Well, Bell had hardly been discouraged by her performance at York. 'Obviously we are a bit deflated post-race, but she is still second in the Yorkshire Oaks, beaten by a Group 1 winner,' he said. 'We came to win. It's not the end of the world. She has lost something in defeat, you can't deny that, but give her credit. We didn't quite get away with it.' Thoughts of tackling Sea The Stars were abandoned. She ended her three-year-old career on Champions Day at Newmarket in October, where she trailed in third to Twice Over in the Champions Stakes.

Sariska reappeared at York the following May and regained her track crown with an impressive victory over Midday, who had won the Filly and Mare Turf at the Breeders' Cup the previous season, in the Middleton Stakes. It was a small, but classy, field of four who lined up – the other two contenders being Godolphin's Flying Cloud and Alan Swinbank's Honimiere. Despite her Yorkshire Oaks upstaging, no one had lost faith in Sariska and she went off the 10-11 favourite. For those who backed her, it was money well spent. Her jockey, Jamie Spencer, had a length and three quarters in hand over the Henry Cecil-trained Midday and, after finding only Fame And Glory too good in the Coronation Cup at Epsom, Bell brought Sariska back for the Yorkshire Oaks with the aim of righting the wrongs of 12 months ago. With Midday the principal opposition, a horse who had already been comprehensively beaten by Sariska once, it appeared the 85-40 favourite's time had come.

With Oaks glory waiting, however, Bell's filly would reveal the flaw which would shortly end her racing career. Ushered into the stalls with no problem, when the starting gates opened Sariska refused to budge. No amount of urging from Spencer, her jockey, could move her and it was Midday who was left to take control – speeding away from English and Irish Oaks heroine Snow Fairy after asserting at the three furlong marker.

Cecil, who was claiming the Yorkshire Oaks title for the first time since Ramruma 11 year previously, said: 'It was a great performance. She was always going so easily, and she went and won her race. It was a pity Sariska didn't join the troop. But the second is a very good filly. I would say that's as good as she's ever been and it was her best run.'

Bell would shrug off another bout of Yorkshire Oaks disappointment, arguing that 'nobody's died'. But when Sariska repeated the trick at the Prix Vermeille, once again staying lodged in the stalls, the Newmarket trainer knew the game was up for his brilliantly talented, but now obviously quirky, filly. She was retired almost immediately.

***

QUEENS of the turf stride out in the Yorkshire Oaks, and it is a race which is deserving of its hype. Since its conditions were altered to allow the participation of older fillies in 1991 it now offers a real clash of the generations – the chance to see the best of the three-year-old brigade take on their elders over a Classic distance.

The 2010 edition, which featured the Epsom and Irish Oaks winner Snow Fairy, the double Oaks heroine Sariska and the back-to-back Nassau Stakes winner Midday, was undoubtedly the fillies' race of the year. Class invariably tells. In the last 30 years, only twice has it gone the way of a filly or mare priced at bigger than 10-1. It attracts its winners from all over the globe – stars who have added the York prize to Classic victories. Quite simply, it is York's diamond.

THE NUNTHORPE STAKES

IF you miss the break, you're finished. If you are drawn badly, some would say you might as well stay at home. You can barely afford to lose a length. In the five furlong sprint, racing's equivalent of the 100 metres, everything has to go right. These thoroughbred giants – quirky, temperamental – hit speeds of more than 40mph on a desperate dash for the finishing line. When the blur of colour flashes by, it's only the very best, the toughest, that prevail.

Like Borderlescott. With a string of horses barely in the twenties, Robin Bastiman shouldn't have been downhearted when his six-year-old sprinting sensation won the 2008 Nunthorpe Stakes. But while there was joy at Group 1 success, there was also a tinge of disappointment. Because it wasn't at York.

They had never seen rain like it on Knavesmire that August and it completely wiped out the four-day Ebor Festival. Bastiman, and Borderlescott, marched instead to Newmarket and won but the trainer – based in Cowthorpe just ten miles from the track and those skyscraper-like stands – ached to do it again at his home track. The pundits thought his chance had passed. Look in the newspapers in the week before the race and you'll see little mention of the defending champion. Instead, the column writers and reporters dwelt on a former conqueror, the durable Kingsgate Native, and Radiohead, the fresh face looking to do what John Best's four-year-old had done two years previously – win the Nunthorpe Stakes as a juvenile. It irked Bastiman.

'You would have thought it was a two horse race,' he recalls. 'The horse had won the race the previous year but it was all about Kingsgate Native and Radiohead. Scottie was running against the same horses and you have got to have everything in your favour. We went to Goodwood (for the King George Stakes on his last run before the Nunthorpe and finished fourth) and he was so wide he was in a field. He needs cover. I think he's a pro. He's just a one off. You know exactly what he wants to do. He gets out there and he wants to beat them. He has this turbo charge and he just picks up.'

Those in the know might have forgotten Borderlescott's rocket finish, but they had noticed Bastiman's decision to change jockey. Pat Cosgrave had ridden the horse at Newmarket, and in many of the super sprinter's previous races. But Bastiman had an ace up his sleeve in Neil Callan. 'It is an old trick,' he explains. 'I've been training a long time. I felt as though a change of hands would be good. It was nothing more than that. I didn't know whether he would be past his best next year. I thought "This is the time". Neil Callan rode it really well. I was pleased for him. He did it exactly how I wanted him to do it and as long as the jockey does that you can't complain.'

What he did was deliver Borderlescott at the right moment. For the seven-year-old had an interesting quirk. He needed to be buried in the pack – protected, shielded against the barging and shoving – and allowed to build up a nice head of steam. Get him to the front too early and he would down tools, believing the race was already won. Produce him too late and he would not get there in time – the line would blunt his inevitable surge. So Callan had the toughest of tasks, and the weight of Bastiman's expectations on his shoulders. He also had to forget about the pain.

Callan had to be passed fit by a doctor after being unshipped from Rodrigo de Torres the day before in the £300,000 DBS St Leger Yearling Stakes. The press might not have believed, and the punters weren't too convinced either given they sent the reigning champion off at 9-1, but Bastiman's faith never wavered for a second. 'He's right,' he said a fortnight before the York duel. 'Put it this way, providing he gets a decent draw at York there will be no excuses. He only comes to himself at this time of year. That's his time. He's around 10-1 and that's not a bad each way bet is it? He'll be thereabouts. I'm sure he will. I am looking forward to it and just hope everything goes right with him. This is the race. As far as I know, he's as well as ever. So we go for this.'

'Cover', as Bastiman insisted was required, was what Borderlescott got as Callan popped his mount in the centre of the pack as they fired out of the stalls. Tax Free, the speed machine from Dandy Nicholls' renowned stable of sprinters, got out quickest and scorched down the straight circuit, along with Henry Candy's Amour Propre. But Borderlescott kept in touch and, as Tax Free and Radiohead went for everything inside the final furlong, Callan did as he was instructed and brought the old stager to the front, down the centre of the track, and unleashed that tremendous speed late inside the final furlong. It was the daring move that was required and it was just enough, by a neck from the fast-finishing Benbaun, to give Bastiman stunning back-to-back Nunthorpe wins. It was the first time in more than a quarter of a century that a champion had defended his crown.

'Every race he gets better and better,' Bastiman says. 'The horse has got such a following. It was a great victory for a small yard. It proves I can do it.' Twelve months on, another year older, Borderlescott looked to emulate what only two others, Tag End and Sharpo, had managed – a hat-trick of Nunthorpe wins. It looked an insurmountable task. Bastiman knew the odds were against him and Borderlescott from the outset. 'The Nunthorpe's going to be a hard race for the old boy to win this time,' he admitted in early July. But he will definitely take his chance.'

Bastiman felt a bit more confident following the Group 2 King George Stakes at Glorious Goodwood. Borderlescott had opened the campaign with a runners-up spot in the Palace House Stakes at Newmarket and followed up with three successive third placed finishes in the Temple Stakes at Haydock, King's Stand Stakes at Royal Ascot and the City Wall Stakes at Chester. Returning to Goodwood, where he hadn't won since clinching the Stewards' Cup four years previously, the old man lit up the festival. Taking the mount for the first time, former champion jockey Kieren Fallon got a brilliant tune out of the veteran and delivered him to the line with a precision which thrilled the trainer. Group Therapy and Astrophysical Jet, taking the minor honours, were half a length adrift. It might as well have been half a mile. 'Bring on the Nunthorpe now,' declared Bastiman. 'I think he is better now than ever.'

But, as Bastiman celebrated in the parade ring, disaster struck. His star horse had gone lame. 'He tries too hard in his races and he might have taken a bit of bone off his pelvis,' he said. 'We boxed him up and as soon as he came out of the horse box he felt his near hind leg. It is the muscle in between his hip and down to his stifle. It's just a nightmare. We got him right for the Nunthorpe – maybe next year.' Bastiman pulled him out of the Nunthorpe Stakes. Borderlescott was yet to join Tag End and Sharpo in Nunthorpe legend. Or so it appeared.

Religious sceptics take note. It seems a miracle happened at Bastiman's Cowthorpe yard. A week before the race, the eight-year-old had sensationally recovered. His lameness was gone. Bastiman, not a man who looks like a modern day messiah, came to the conclusion he must have merely tweaked a muscle. 'Animals can't talk but they can jump and kick and he wouldn't have done that in the horse walker unless he was fine,' the trainer said. 'We got a saddle on him, had a gallop and, if he had stiffened up, he wouldn't have been right. We are happy with him, it's whether he is good enough now.'

So Borderlescott would get the chance to join the legends after all. But there were dangers all around him. Starspangledbanner, the Golden Jubilee Stakes and July Cup winner saddled by Irish winning machine Aidan O'Brien, was trying to succeed over five furlongs for the first time in Europe. Equiano had the Palace House Stakes and Royal Ascot's King's Stand Stakes in the locker before arriving at York, while Kingsgate Native, the 2007 Nunthorpe winner, also posed a serious danger. It would have been a real collector's item had Borderlescott done the job – but the old stager finished sixth, his trademark blistering turn of speed missing on this occasion. We still got a rare triumph, and it was a victory no one could have anticipated.

It had only happened once before in a Group 1 race, in 1975 when Hittite Glory won the Flying Childers Stakes at Doncaster. So Sole Power joined a very select club when he caused the biggest upset in Nunthorpe Stakes history. In 88 years they had never seen anything like it. It will be probably be another century before we see it again. A 100-1 winner.

Talk to Irish trainer Edward Lynam and he will tell you they had always rated the three-year-old who, until the Nunthorpe, had only ever won before on the all-weather at Dundalk. In his last four starts, his highest finishing position had been fourth – in the Group 3 Palace House Stakes at Newmarket. Fifth in a Listed race at Tipperary the last time he had appeared on the track, it was hardly the sort of form that puts you in the frame to win one of Europe's premier sprints. But Lynam had seen something in the Kyllachy gelding, owned by Sabena Power – mother of Irish betting mogul Paddy Power. 'We always rated the horse,' he said with the shock of victory resonating round the winner's enclosure. 'He's a very, very fast horse but he has been immature. We thought this race would suit him. I'm not saying we thought he'd win. The last time I had a Group 1 winner someone woke me up.'

If Lynam wasn't saying he would win, the bookmakers definitely weren't. At 100-1, he was tied with Piccadilly Filly as the rank outsider of the 12 runners. But Sole Power was about to turn the form book upside down. It was Rose Blossom, trained locally by Malton's Richard Fahey, who set a fierce gallop in the early part of the contest. Sole Power was held up in the face of this blistering pace. Around him, though, strange things were happening. Starspangledbanner, sent off the 6-4 favourite, was soon driven along after jockey Johnny Murtagh raced him down the stands side. He looked outpaced by the fierce gallop. Equiano, second best backed at 7-2, was also struggling while Kingsgate Native was finding life cramped when he tried to make some headway at the two furlong marker. In the midst of these difficulties for the fancied runners, Sole Power swept past his 100-1 rival Piccadilly Filly and to the front inside the final furlong.

Murtagh tried everything to get Starspangledbanner near the leader but to no avail. Sole Power hit the line a length and a quarter ahead. Cue absolute silence. Except from a frantic winning jockey, Wayne Lordan, and the victorious connections of a horse who had just stunned 16,600 people. 'I didn't think I'd have much of a chance,' admitted the jockey afterwards. 'It was a surprise. He is just speed. I was in a car the last time I went that quick. He ran well at Newmarket earlier in the year and I thought he might be a horse who might take his chance next year. It's hard for a three-year-old against older horses but they went very quick and he's picked up and done it well.'

He was celebrating, and so were the bookies, but the punters mainly went home miserable. There were a minority that had taken the plunge. One picked up £3,500 after putting £30 on the horse through the Tote but only around £400 of bets were taken at the course. The biggest winner was Sabena Power. Her smash and grab Nunthorpe Stakes raid banked her £136,000. And a place in racing history forever.

***

FOR a contest which has witnessed some of racing's greatest sprinting performances, the Nunthorpe Stakes had very humble beginnings indeed. Named after an area of York located close to the racecourse, the first version of the race was staged in 1903 but it was initially a low-grade seller – a shadow of the colossus it would become. Not until 1922 did it evolve into the race it is now and Two Step, the first victor, is a name that has now slipped into memory.

That opening decade was dominated by two horses, Highborn II and Tag End. The former became the first horse to win the race twice, in 1926 and 1927, and his trainer Ossie Bell remains the contest's leading trainer. Greenore (1932), Concerto (1933) and Ipsden (1937) gave Bell five victories, a total that still stands. Tag End went one better than Highborn II – scooping the contest for three consecutive years from 1928 to 1930, a feat only one horse, Sharpo, has matched in the intervening 80 years.

While the hat-trick might have been a lofty ambition, dual winners were by no means unusual in those formative years. Linklater managed it during the middle of the war years (1942 and 1943), albeit away from York which was closed during the conflict, while the flying grey Abernant (1949 and 1950), Royal Serenade (1951 and 1952) and Right Boy (1958 and 1959) all successfully managed to retain their titles. Abernant was considered by many to be perhaps the greatest sprinter of the 20th Century. Trained by Noel Murless and ridden by Gordon Richards, he was sired by the 1941 Derby winner Owen Tudor. A dominant juvenile, Abernant won five of his first six starts, including the Champagne Stakes and the Middle Park Stakes in 1948. Considered unbeatable between five and six furlongs, he only narrowly lost the 2,000 Guineas – over a mile – to Nimbus by the shortest of margins. But once he was dropped back in trip again, the major successes fell somewhat easily into his grasp.

Fourteen wins from 17 starts shows his class. His first Nunthorpe, in 1949, followed the King's Stand Stakes and the July Cup. At four, the horse would also win the King George Stakes for a second time as well as defend his Nunthorpe crown. Going to stud, his winners included the 1962 1,000 Guineas victor Abermaid. Royal Serenade, meanwhile, may be remembered more for his export to America where, following his two Nunthorpe wins, he would win the Hollywood Gold Cup at double the York distance.

Youngsters had their time in the early fifties, High Treason becoming the first two-year-old to succeed in 1953, followed swiftly by My Beau (1954) and Ennis (1956). But it was not a trend which would catch on. The next juvenile to triumph would be Lyric Fantasy nearly 40 years later in 1992. Right Boy only cost 575 guineas as a yearling and was initially trained by Bill Dutton. When Dutton died in 1958, his son-in-law Pat Rohan took over his Yorkshire yard at Malton and stewardship of the rising star.

Right Boy had already won the King's Stand Stakes in 1957 but his association with Lester Piggott – who rode the colt on both his Nunthorpe Stakes victories – saw the two combine for 16 victories. Piggott triumphed five times on Right Boy in 1958, and he started at 8-100 for the Nunthorpe that year. In his autobiography, the legendary jockey wrote the grey was all out to win by half a length but rated the speedster as the best sprinter he ever rode – citing his explosive speed and tremendous consistency. It was a trait he proved again when, a similarly priced 4-9 favourite, he won another Nunthorpe 12 months after the first. Alongside the Nunthorpe, Right Boy would also take the Cork and Orrery Stakes at Royal Ascot and the King George Stakes at Goodwood in successive years. Great horses, great winners who, by the start of the 1960s, had elevated the Nunthorpe Stakes to one of Britain's premier contests.

***

IN the mid 1970s, Easterby was the name on the lips of every racing fan. At Habton Grange, near Malton in North Yorkshire, Peter's dynasty was approaching its glorious height.

Night Nurse had just won the Champion Hurdle, while Alverton and Sea Pigeon were set to reach the very top. But while Peter was hitting the headlines, a few miles down the road in Sheriff Hutton, his brother Mick had a very special horse of his own in 1976. It was the kind of purchase the younger of the Easterby brothers was becoming renowned for – a bargain.

'Lochnager cost next to nothing,' remembers northern racing journalist Tom O'Ryan, who was an apprentice based at Peter Easterby's stable in the mid-70s and familiar with the yards of both siblings. 'He was as good a sprinter as a lot of people have ever seen. In 1976, he won the King's Stand Stakes at Royal Ascot. He won the July Cup. He was European top sprinter that year. He was given typical Mick Easterby preparation in that he came through the handicap ranks. He was just an outstanding horse with an outstanding ability and temperament. He came from rags to riches and that makes a horse very popular.'

But for the first time since its inception, the race in which Lochnager starred wasn't the Nunthorpe Stakes. From 1976, until reverting back to its original title in 1990, the contest was sponsored by bookmaker William Hill and was known as the William Hill Sprint Championship. What the backing brought was cold, hard cash. Added money increased significantly so, by 1981, it was worth £5,000 more than the King's Stand Stakes at Royal Ascot – attracting a better field to boot.

The first year of their backing, the race carried a first prize of £18,660 which made it the most valuable sprint of its type in Britain. Lochnager took advantage. His reputation was such that he was as short as 5-4 in the betting market. Ten opposed him, including eight of those he had seen off in either the King's Stand Stakes or the July Cup. The form suggested he wouldn't be beaten. He wasn't but, even though the victory gave him the sprinters' championship, the experts at Timeform felt it was the least impressive of his wins.

It was stablemate Polly Peachum who provided the most trouble, sticking tight to Lochnager and jockey Edward Hide, along with the three-year-old Faliraki. Hide was forced to go all out on the sprinting sensation and he got there with only half a length to spare over the wide ridden Faliraki, with Polly Peachum a neck further back in third. It was his last appearance on the track. A tilt at the Prix de l'Abbaye at

Longchamp had been envisaged but his connections decided instead to give it a miss. He was retired to Malton's Easthorpe Hall Stud.

'It was very special for Yorkshire people to see a horse of that calibre dominating the sprinting division as he did,' says O'Ryan. 'He was a horse with a great following and again he found York lending itself to his talents. A special one.'

***

BUT not as special as Sharpo who, between 1980 and 1982, emulated Tag End in winning the Nunthorpe three times. Foaled in 1977, Sharpo first came to prominence when winning the Temple Stakes in 1980.

The colt seemed to have a particular liking for York in a career restricted by a tendency to perform better on softer ground. Trained by Jeremy Tree, he was ridden by Pat Eddery in his first two attempts at York's premier sprint test with the American dynamo Steve Cauthen taking over in 1982. Owner Monica Sheriffe almost sold Sharpo but lot 320 was withdrawn shortly before the 1979 Newmarket Autumn Sale. The chestnut had run just once to that point – finishing well down the field in a Newbury maiden – a race where he fractured a bone in a hind leg after leaving the stalls awkwardly. The injury healed, the sale was averted and connections must have been very relieved when the horse became something of a sensation in his three-year-old campaign.

Having smashed his opposition in the Temple Stakes in May as a 33-1 outsider, in what was only his second outing on a racecourse, he was second to Kearney in the Cork and Orrery Stakes at Royal Ascot. Moorestyle beat him in the July Cup at Newmarket, over six furlongs, before York loomed large. With his Newmarket conqueror not entered on Knavesmire, he was up against Valeriga, who had won the King George Stakes at Goodwood and the Palace House Stakes but had been behind Sharpo in the Cork and Orrery, along with the Royal Ascot King's Stand Stakes winner African Song.

Moorestyle's absence may have taken a touch of the shine off Sharpo's display but, nevertheless, it was still a hammering. Racing towards the stand side of the track, Valeriga went to the far side and Tree's horse destroyed him. Held up early, Eddery pushed Sharpo to take the lead from Valeriga with a furlong and a half left to run and, once he saw daylight, he accelerated away. It was two and a half lengths at the finish. Eddery had not needed to resort to the stick. Hands and heels was all it took. It was one of the most impressive sprinting performances of the season. Valeriga was well beaten.

Sharpo's triumph was part of a superb Eddery treble. He also won the day's other big race, the Gimcrack Stakes, with another Jeremy Tree runner, Bel Bolide. Twelve months later, however, and the champion was the forgotten horse. You could get 14-1 on him in the ring before the contest, with King's Stand Stakes winner Marwell odds on and Moorestyle, who defeated Sharpo again in the previous year's Prix de l'Abbaye and now finally at York, the second favourite. Sharpo had disappointed in the King's Stand Stakes, his previous outing, finishing second last but there were valid excuses. The hard ground at Ascot had hardly suited the colt and his participation at York had been in doubt until Tree knew there would be some give in the track.

With the ground in his favour, Sharpo put on a sensational show. Eddery initially tracked Moorestyle, with Standaan setting the pace but, a furlong and a half from home and switched to the outside, Sharpo turned on the gas and swept past Marwell into the lead. Once again, Eddery didn't need the whip – guiding his mount to the line again with just hands and heels for a two and a half length win. The filly Marwell brought home the stragglers with Moorestyle in third, a length and a half further back. Sharpo had dispatched some of Europe's top sprinters in desultory fashion and he would be back again for a third go. This time, as the evens favourite, no one would take him for granted. Steve Cauthen described Sharpo as the quickest horse he had ever ridden. But his joy in 1982 was Pat Eddery's misery. As Sharpo went for the treble, Eddery wasn't in the driving seat – forced to miss the race with a hand injury he had picked up on the opening day of the Ebor Festival. But one man's loss is another's gain, and Cauthen was determined to stamp his mark on the contest.

The American was already a riding superstar. The son of a Kentucky farrier, Cauthen rode Affirmed to the Triple Crown of Kentucky Derby, Preakness and Belmont Stakes in 1978, the youngest jockey – at just 18 – to achieve the feat. He moved to Britain in 1979 and he was an immediate smash. By the time of his arrival at York three years later, Cauthen had already won two Classics in the 1,000 and

2,000 Guineas and would go on to win the Champion Jockey title three times, along with two Derbies, three Oaks and three St Legers.

Sharpo's bid for the hat-trick was helped because Marwell and Moorestyle weren't there in 1982, both having retired to stud the previous year. And while new faces emerged, the likes of Soba and Indian King among them, they weren't in Sharpo's league. After taking the July Cup at Newmarket, the now five-year-old came to York and won imperiously. It was an insult to even call it a test.

The filly Chellaston Park wandered in two lengths behind as that acceleration once more took Sharpo to the front inside the final furlong. An awestruck Cauthen, like Eddery before him, could afford to ease off at the winning post. 'I'd like one of those every day of the week!' he said straight after the contest. 'I have never been on a faster horse either here or in America. Sharpo's got terrific acceleration.'

Sharpo had one more act of greatness to perform before finally being sent off to stud. His racing career would end gloriously as Europe's foremost sprinter thanks to victory in the Prix de l'Abbaye at Longchamp. But not only did he have the gift on the track, he also passed on his talents as a stallion. By his death in June 1994, his progeny had won 216 Flat races worth a total of $1.7 million.

***

HABIBTI brilliantly won the 1983 William Hill Sprint Championship but it was a race mired in controversy. Not that it affected the winner in the slightest. Trainer John Dunlop would brand his flying filly the best sprinter he had ever trained – 'and definitely the fastest' – and her breathtaking performance was crowned in a length and a half win over Soba.

David Chapman's rival horse, trained ten miles from the track at Stillington, carried the Yorkshire money but was relegated to last place by the Stewards after the race. David Nicholls, later to become a master of training sprinters, rode her and picked up a five-day ban after the Stewards judged she had interfered with Crime Of Passion soon after the start. Fine Edge, who finished six lengths behind Soba, was promoted to second with the old campaigner Chellaston Park, second to Sharpo a year earlier, in third. Nicholls felt he was hard done by. 'I don't think I was really to blame,' he said. 'As for poor Soba they have been very hard on her by placing her last.'

Even with the drama of Soba's demotion, nothing could take away the splendour of Habibti's performance. Held up early, she went three lengths clear before jockey Willie Carson eased up – giving her a second York win following her crushing defeat of Royal Heroine in the Lowther Stakes as a two-year-old. Soba had actually got away the quicker but was collared by Habibti in the final furlong – before the drama that took even a runners-up spot away from Nicholls and Chapman.

The result looked closer than it had been. Meeting in the July Cup the month before, Habibti had been a two and a half length winner while, by the time of the Prix de l'Abbaye, she was beating Soba for a fourth time. It was her finishing speed that was so devastating and which made her one of the top horses of her generation.

***

'EVERY so often comes an occasion on a racecourse when those present count themselves fortunate to have been there. Nunthorpe day at York was one.'

From the racing experts at Timeform, this was praise indeed. But the comment, closing the account of Dayjur's season in the firm's *Racehorses of 1990* book, was not an exaggeration. In full flight, the son of Danzig was poetry in motion. 'Dayjur, visually, is the most impressive sprinter I have set eyes on,' states racing journalist Tom O'Ryan. 'It was just awesome to see him winning the Nunthorpe in 1990. It was one of the most impressive displays of sprinting you will ever see. He was a hugely talented horse.'

'Dayjur was the top,' adds former York clerk of the course John Smith. 'He had to be the top. Cadeaux Generaux was a great horse as well but Dayjur was something very special. He was a flying machine, he really was. Dayjur must be the best sprinter I've seen here.'

In a race dedicated to the pursuit of speed, Dayjur is the fastest of them all. No horse has ever travelled quicker than the 56.16 seconds which the Dick Hern-trained star produced to scorch down York's five furlongs that August. He was so quick, he lowered the course record –

set by Committed in 1984 – by more than a second. At York, he was approaching the height of his powers.

It was a career which had begun with victory in a Newbury maiden and then a runner-up spot in a Listed race at the same track. Dayjur began his three-year-old season in dubious fashion – seventh of ten in the Free Handicap at Newmarket in April 1990. But that was over seven furlongs and Dick Hern, about to find out he had another marvellous horse on his hands, dropped the colt back in trip – first to six furlongs for his next two starts and then to five, where he would really show his devastating pace.

Priced at 11-2 for the Group 2 Temple Stakes at Sandown, Dayjur beat Tigani by two lengths in straightforward fashion. But it wasn't just the distance which had changed. Having being held up or in contention in his previous five racecourse encounters, Dayjur, piloted by Willie Carson in every one of his races, now set out to smash the opposition. He would always look to make all.

It had worked a treat at Sandown and it was an identical story at Royal Ascot in the King's Stand Stakes. A comparative outsider at 11-2, given his Temple display, Dayjur was just as emphatic. Once again, he and Carson took charge immediately and two and a half lengths was the gap which separated Hern's horse and the runner-up, Ron's Victory. The Nunthorpe Stakes, reverting to its original name after being known as the William Hill Sprint Championship since 1976, would be Dayjur's first crack at a Group 1 contest. Those opposing were well aware of his tactics – blast off and turn on the rocket-boosters. The question was could any of them keep up?

Some of his eight rivals were familiar. Statoblest had already been beaten by Dayjur both in the Temple Stakes, where the former had been the 9-4 favourite, and the King's Stand Stakes – Luca Cumani's sprinter trailing in a distant seventh. Lugana Beach, trained by David Elsworth and ridden by Steve Cauthen, had been third at Royal Ascot, while Blyton Lad, fourth at Sandown, again resumed hostilities. Unfortunately for them, however, this was a procession for Dayjur, the 8-11 favourite. As was now the plan, Dayjur and Carson bolted out of the blocks. Statoblest was prominent, Pharaoh's Delight, who finished third under Ray Cochrane, ran on well but nothing in the field could keep up with Dayjur's blistering pace. He led by two lengths at the halfway mark, with Statoblest the best of those vainly trying to catch the rapidly accelerating colt. The gap was a length with a furlong to go but that was as close as Statoblest would get. Carson shook the reins and Dayjur found an even faster turn of foot – capping an extraordinary performance by recording a four length triumph.

Dayjur was the last in the long line of great horses trained by Dick Hern, a man who had won 16 British Classics, and had handled many of the best horses ever seen: Brigadier Gerard, Troy, Henbit, Nashwan, Bireme and Bustino to name just a few. 'What a trainer he was,' remembers the former *Daily Mirror* and *Racing Post* writer Tim Richards. 'I found him very good. A lot of people didn't get on with him at all but he was a really kind sort of chap. I always found him very helpful. He was quite deaf, which made things a bit difficult for him. He didn't always hear things but maybe some of those things he didn't want to hear. He was a brilliant trainer and if you asked him a sensible question you would get a sensible answer.'

The annihilation of his rivals at York was part of a five-race winning sequence for Dayjur that only ended on his final run. Even then, it took a freak result to beat him in the Breeders' Cup Sprint at Belmont, two months after his Knavesmire exploits. With the race at his mercy, yards from the line, the colt inexplicably jumped a shadow and was overhauled by Safely Kept by a quarter of a length. He went to stud, standing at his owner Sheikh Hamdan Al-Maktoum's Kentucky Shadwell Farm, for a $50,000 fee. Hayil, the winner of the Middle Park Stakes in 1997, and Tipsy Creek, who won the Norfolk and Temple Stakes, are among his progeny.

***

LOCHSONG was the filly with lightning in her legs. Brilliant, but volatile, the York public saw both the best and worst of her in the Nunthorpe Stakes of 1993 and 1994. She was trained by Ian Balding, whose Kingsclere stable had been blessed with another amazing talent to shine on Knavesmire: Mill Reef.

Balding would soon be convinced by her ability. But he admits that, at first, he wasn't keen on his soon-to-be legend. 'Her owner Jeff Smith hadn't long had horses with me. Lochsong had been in training as a two-year-old with Lord John FitzGerald in Newmarket,' he remembers. 'Jeff said: "I've got this filly, she's very well bred and I'm anxious to win a little race with her then she can come back to stud and become a broodmare". She came second in her opening race and hurt herself. Next time, Ray Cochrane knocked spots off her to win at Redcar over six furlongs. As it happened, Jeff was in America and I said to Ron Sheather, Jeff's racing manager: "Do you suppose Jeff would mind if we gave Lochsong one more run in an apprentice race?" She was a very difficult filly in training and we had this apprentice, Francis Arrowsmith, and we said we would get her in this apprentice race at Newbury and she could run and go straight home afterwards. She won the race. Francis was the only one who could get on with her. He rode her and just hung on and she won by a short head. So she goes home and, midway through the winter, Jeff Smith rang and said: "I've been thinking about Lochsong. When you think about it, she's had three races and won two and was second in the other, I think we ought to train her next year". And I'm thinking: "I don't want this horrible filly back again" but I heard myself saying "What a great suggestion, I'd love to have her back". She came back and was the star handicapper the next year. Her rating went up 30lbs. It was extraordinary. I think she was the first animal to win the Stewards' Cup, Portland Handicap and the Ayr Gold Cup. That was her four-year-old career.'

Now Balding knew exactly what he had in his yard and, as a five-year-old, she was to improve beyond belief. But it was a balancing act. For all her brilliance she was tough to handle – unless she had everything her own way. 'I had an old hack called Quirk who was instrumental in her success,' Balding adds. 'She wouldn't go anywhere at home without Quirk. I had to lead her everywhere she went – with Francis Arrowsmith still riding her every day. We would go down to this all-weather gallop – now called the Lochsong Gallop – I would lead her on to it and away she would go, flat out to the top, and then she wouldn't move until Quirk had come up. She just fell in love with him and adored him and wouldn't go anywhere without him. She was very difficult – not easy to train – but she was some racehorse. She was absolutely amazing.'

On the day of the 1993 Nunthorpe, Lochsong was running in a Group 1 race for the first time. That she was a mare continuing to be on the up could not be in doubt, however. She had won the King George Stakes at Goodwood, a Group 3, but this was another league again. Could she respond?

Frankie Dettori had the mount but wasn't the slightest bit concerned. He knew he was on board a freak of nature. The days of Godolphin glory are still ahead for Dettori, and he had recently endured a high profile split with Luca Cumani when Balding asked him if he would commit to riding Lochsong. Willie Carson had ridden the filly in the past but, with his commitment as first jockey to Sheikh Hamdan, Balding was looking for a regular rider who could get to know Lochsong's foibles. Writing in his autobiography, Dettori said the key to keeping Lochsong sweet was to simply let her get on with it. She would dictate the race, its pace, her position. He would merely steer in the right direction. Her speed would be decisive. In the Nunthorpe, that's exactly how the race went. She beat Paris House by a length and a half in a race she completely controlled from the second the starting stalls went up.

Paris House, trained by Jack Berry, was no mug. Group victories in the Flying Childers Stakes, Palace House Stakes and Temple Stakes where, on both the latter occasions he had beaten Lochsong, made the iron grey a crowd puller. In Lochsong, however, he would eventually have his match. Balding's filly had bested Paris House on their most recent match up, in the King George Stakes, when, receiving 11 pounds, she had repelled him by a head. At York she got just three pounds, and this time she trounced him. Sent off at 10-1 – more than twice the price of Paris House – and trailing favourite College Chapel by even further in the betting market, Lochsong, like a bullet, shot straight to the front. By halfway, Paris House was the only challenger not to be off the bridle, and even he could not stand the pace. It was a wonderful performance. Not bad at all for a girl who suffered from dodgy joints. 'The Nunthorpe that day was the most amazingly emotional occasion that I have ever known on the racecourse. She just flew down there from start to finish. I was so incredibly excited and thrilled by it,' Balding enthuses.

European horse of the year that year, Lochsong was champion sprinter in the next – her six-year-old season. The Palace House Stakes, Temple Stakes, King's Stand Stakes, King George Stakes and the Prix de l'Abbaye, for the second time, all fell effortlessly to the unstoppable heroine of the racetrack. But not the Nunthorpe Stakes. There, in front of an expectant York crowd, Lochsong erupted. As they paraded in front of the stands, the buzzy and brittle mare boiled over – and took Frankie Dettori for a ride.

'She was a difficult lady,' recalls Balding. 'I said to Frankie (as we were going out for the parade) "For God's sake don't let her out of a canter". We led her onto the track and as soon as I let go she plunged twice and then was gone. No one could hold her. I was worried about her running into the starting stalls. It was pretty horrible.'

The image of Dettori, vainly trying to bring Lochsong to a stop, is still remembered by York clerk of the course John Smith, who was in charge at Knavesmire from 1987 to 2002. For a start, the sight of the bolting mare flying off wildly down the track brought changes. 'I always remember, she was the reason for parades being changed for sprinters because they are so wound up,' he says. 'I can see him now. Poor old Frankie Dettori, trying to restrain Lochsong as she went down to the start. It was an impossible job. She took off. It's amazing how these jockeys can control them at such light weights. She was flying, she really was.'

Lochsong was brought to a stop, eventually, but her race had already been uselessly run. She lined up anyway, even though Balding felt it was a pointless exercise, and her early speed raised brief hopes she could achieve the impossible when leading after a couple of furlongs. But, gassed out, the field swamped her at halfway and rather than push the tired horse any further Dettori let her roll in last. It was an enormous disappointment for Balding but, for her owner Jeff Smith, the afternoon was about to get even worse when his Blue Siren, also running in the Nunthorpe, was demoted to second behind Piccolo. 'Sickening' is how Balding still describes it.

Lochsong, volatile temperament or not, was still an unforgettable performer. The same can't be said of her sister Lochangel – a Nunthorpe winner who has failed to hold the same sway in Balding's memory. 'She was not in the same class, as a racehorse, as her sister,' he says of the 1998 victor. 'I said to Jeff Smith, her owner, 'This is the one that's going to be the better broodmare' but actually Lochsong has done better as a broodmare. It can't have been one of the more memorable races. What I do remember about Lochangel is that she was one of Frankie's magnificent seven at Ascot. She ran over seven furlongs then – I was running her over the wrong distance again!'

It can't have been that memorable for Frankie either, who also rode her at York. Lochangel gets a page in his autobiography, but for her Ascot exploits in 1996. Her Nunthorpe win doesn't merit mention.

***

THE starting stalls open, and you feel the surge of acceleration beneath you. You're into stride, the power is sensational, and the wind whistles past your ears as you hit top speed. But you don't feel the rush. It's something else. Fear. It only lasts for a second. Then your instincts kick in. It's unexpected, but you know what to do. And you fight – the speed, the gravity pulling you towards the ground. You do anything. Anything to get that horse home first.

The bit snapped almost immediately as jockey Kevin Darley steered Coastal Bluff out of the gates in the opening seconds of the 1997 Nunthorpe Stakes. Try to imagine what that means. With no bit, and no reins, Darley had no means of either steering or controlling his mount. Snapped tight to the horse's back, the veteran horseman had only Coastal Bluff's mane to cling onto as he careered down Knavesmire's straight. Hair is hardly a substitute. How do you move the horse if it hangs left or right as that speed saps every muscle and sinew? More importantly, how on earth do you stop?

'At the time you didn't realise what had happened to Kevin Darley. It was an incredible feat of riding that was,' says John Smith, the York clerk of the course on that amazing day. 'To ride a horse without a bit and just at a canter is one thing but to do it at that speed and have the courage and the guts to do what he did was unbelievable.'

Darley's efforts on the David Barron-trained horse were so outstanding that the ride is considered one of the greatest of all time – coming 16th in a national poll of the best. 'I think that race shows the competitive nature of jockeys when something like that happens,' Darley told local newspaper *The Press* almost a decade after the gripping contest. 'It was certainly not the kind of ride you have very often. I immediately thought 'What's happened?' As soon as I stood back to take a pull it all came off. At first I thought it would get tangled up in the horse's legs and that it could bring him down. Thankfully, it did not. It might have been different if it had been a long distance race. Sprinters tend to run in a straight line and the horse was still running straight. 'Because he was doing that, I thought "I'm still in with a chance".'

That Darley was thinking of winning the race at all says a lot about his drive and ambition. These virtues would bring him some 2,500 winners in a 30-year career and the champion jockey title in 2000. He would enjoy Classic success on Bollin Eric in the St Leger in 2002 and with the fabulous filly Attraction three years later in the English and Irish 1,000 Guineas. But he still considers the ride on Coastal Bluff to be one of his best. All of his skill was required, and not just because of the riding difficulties. He had a history maker to contend with. For as Coastal Bluff drove on towards the finish, matching him stride for stride was Ya Malak.

Both horses were trained near Thirsk – Coastal Bluff by Barron at Maunby and Ya Malak by David Nicholls at Sessay. The latter was ridden by Nicholls' wife, Alex Greaves, who was bidding to become the first woman to win a Group 1 contest in Britain. As the pair hit the line at the conclusion of the five furlong feast, no one knew who had won. Despite the drama with the bit, Coastal Bluff led strongly at the furlong marker but Ya Malak bore down on him with every stride – and caught him right on the finish. Two reprints of the photographs could not help the Stewards separate the pair. After 20 minutes, racecourse judge Jane Stickels decided they could not be split. The race was a dead-heat.

It was redemption of a sort for Nicholls, who as a jockey had seen a runners-up spot in the race snatched from him when Soba was disqualified following Habibti's win in 1983. The trainer won the race again with the nine-year-old veteran Bahamian Pirate in 2004, while Darley could also look forward to another Nunthorpe success on board Reverence in 2006. But this was Greaves's moment. 'Smart Alex', the headline yelled the following day but the rider said it was about getting the chance rather than striking a stunning blow for equality.

'To win on a local track on such an historic meeting as the Ebor was a little bit special,' she reflected that evening. 'The win was down to the whole yard, not just me and David – it was a team effort by all the staff. Usually women don't get as many rides as men and don't get as many opportunities, but personally I've managed to get on and make a career out of it. I think it was a question of being in the right place at the right time – it's getting the chance more than anything. A few years ago I would have to change in a caravan at races, but now they have proper changing rooms. When you first start you have your hard times, but I've got to know most of the jockeys now and get on all right.'

Greaves, who retired in 2005 and became assistant trainer to her husband, rode more than 300 winners in a 15-year career and paved the way for the revolution which sees the likes of Hayley Turner and Cathy Gannon now at the top of the sport.

***

THE record books say Dayjur is the quickest, but don't mention that to Lord Teddy Grimthorpe. He insists the true record belongs to the 2003 winner, Oasis Dream.

'When he won the Nunthorpe it was a record time mainly because I think it was five yards further than Dayjur's – the distance of the race was slightly different,' he points out. 'It's a fact, if you look in the Racehorses it is there actually – apart from the fact that Richard Hughes (jockey) was looking at himself on television.'

Grimthorpe, a member of the York Race Committee and racing manager to Prince Khalid Abdullah, was quibbling about four hundredths of a second. That's all that separated Dayjur and Oasis Dream, whose time of 56.20 for the five furlongs was still nothing short of electric. 'Oasis was really one of those rare horses that did exactly what it said on the tin in that he looked like he was built like a sprinter,' adds Grimthorpe.

Out of a mare by Dancing Brave, the John Gosden-trained colt left some fast horses trailing in his wake on Knavesmire. Victory was expected. At 4-9, he was one of the heavier backed Nunthorpe favourites in the race's history and he never looked like disappointing. The Tatling was the closest to him, two and a half lengths back, but that winning distance hardly reflected his dominance. Rider Richard Hughes always had the three-year-old travelling at the head of affairs and as soon as he moved out of first gear the contest was finished as a spectacle. Gosden, a man used to handling thoroughbred superstars, was flabbergasted. 'I've never trained anything as fast as this horse,' he cooed in the aftermath.

Oasis Dream's career was fleeting. That York victory, his fourth, was also his last. After a run at Haydock and a tenth place finish in the Breeders' Cup Mile at Santa Anita, the horse was retired to stud following a career which saw just nine visits to the racecourse. As a stallion, he has also been highly successful. Standing at Juddmonte Farms, he has so far sired half a dozen Group 1 winners – including Midday, Arcano and Aqlaam. In fact, no sire in the history of the European pattern has more two-year-old pattern winners from his first four crops.

***

CROUCHED round a telephone, straining to hear the call on loudspeaker, this probably wasn't how John Best envisaged winning his first Group 1 with the 2007 Nunthorpe Stakes. His two-year-old tank, Kingsgate Native, was about to do something precious few juveniles had done before. But the master of Scragged Oak Farm in Kent wasn't at Knavesmire to witness the feat. He was thousands of miles away in Florida. It is hardly the worst of places to pass away the hours but when there is no English racing on the television at the American sales ring, it might as well be the desert.

'We were trying to get it so we could watch it but we were failing miserably,' Best remembers. 'We ended up listening to it around the phone. There were about four or five of us sitting in one of the offices huddled round it – with the phone on loud speaker. In some ways it was a nice way to do it and we were leaping around and shouting and screaming. But it was frustrating not being able to watch. It was my first Group 1 winner and I wasn't there.'

Did that reflect the two-year-old's chances? Lyric Fantasy was the last two-year-old to win a Nunthorpe Stakes and she had done it 15 years previously. Youthful winners had not been exactly abundant in the pages of Nunthorpe history. What was attractive about the prospect of running a juvenile that could take on his elders was the weight-for-age allowance. When Kingsgate Native lined up, he was receiving least a stone and a half from every other runner in the field. Even with that huge advantage, the press were virtually united – Best's horse couldn't win.

They had some reason to be confident in their predictions. For a start, he had yet to even win a maiden. But the instant dismissal of his chances annoyed the trainer. 'The thing was that I knew the horse, both physically and mentally, was very mature,' Best adds. 'Everyone said to me: "You wouldn't have picked him out as a two-year-old among the older horses". That's what he was like at home. He was always a horse that fitted in with all the other horses. It was a gamble to run him in the Nunthorpe and I took it fairly early on. I entered him just after Ascot – having had his first run there. The owner John Mayne said : "What have you done that for?" He was still a maiden and he's the only maiden to have won it. I should have kept all the papers. Coming up to it, all the press – particularly the racing press – and I am not criticising them, they were generally saying to me and writing, "Why on earth is he running a two-year-old in this race? Two-year-olds can't win this race". They were saying it was mad to do it. Immediately afterwards, it was "But the weight-for-age is all wrong". There were five previous Group 1 winners in that race so you can't even say it was a sub-standard Nunthorpe.'

In that field was the previous year's winner, Reverence, the Diadem Stakes winner Red Clubs along with the Middle Park Stakes winner Amadeus Wolf and Desert Lord, both trained by locally-based favourite Kevin Ryan. If the press weren't convinced, neither were the punters. They sent Kingsgate Native off at 12-1 with Dandy Man the 9-4 favourite.

'The nice thing was that his rider Jimmy Quinn managed to get cover pretty quickly on him,' Best says. 'He'd only run two times before and he was pretty sharply out of the stalls. Jimmy was able to drop him in and get a bit of cover. He was following the pace and I keep seeing the race and watching it and he doesn't just beat them – he beats them well. When Jimmy pulled him out and hit the front it was all over in half a furlong.'

Kingsgate Native strolled past Desert Lord and even though he wasn't asked a question until a furlong out, his speed stretched him out to a one and three quarter length win. It wasn't only Best's first Group

1 win. It was Quinn's as well. 'He's a proper horse,' the rider said in the winner's enclosure. 'He's built like an absolute tank. I looked at him in the paddock and I had to look again. He's an absolute machine.'

It was no fluke, either. Kingsgate Native has proved to be a pretty good horse. He followed up the next June with the Golden Jubilee Stakes at Royal Ascot at 33-1 and, after an aborted spell at stud, took victory in the King George Stakes at Goodwood in 2009 and the Temple Stakes at Haydock in May 2010.

***

THE fastest race of York's season, today the Nunthorpe Stakes regularly decides the accolade of Europe's leading sprinter. Worth a massive £240,000 in 2010 it formed the feature contest on Friday – the breathtaking final act in a four-day Ebor Festival already full of superlatives.

In the last 90 years, racing's quickest have burned their way into the history books over those five furlongs. The names of Tag End, Dayjur, Lochsong and Borderlescott will live on forever in their pages.

SEPTEMBER

THE ST LEGER AT YORK

UPHEAVAL brought the St Leger to York in both 1945 and 2006 – but the circumstances in which they arrived could not have been more different.

The end of the Second World War brought a wave of relief to Britain not experienced since. Rationing was still in place, buildings were bombed out, but the euphoria of having survived nearly six years of conflict outweighed the difficulties that remained – at least for now. It was in this atmosphere that an estimated 200,000 people crammed into Knavesmire, on September 5, 1945, to watch the world's oldest Classic horse race.

The Leger came to York with Doncaster, the race's traditional home, still coping with the legacies of wartime and in no fit state to host it. But they weren't the only ones struggling. York was as well. In February 1945, a local writer reported that while the track had not been ploughed up the 'greater part of the land in the horseshoe formed by the course has been put under the plough by order of the West Riding War Agricultural Committee, and crops of grain and potatoes have been grown.' That a strip around the inside of the horseshoe was to revert to grass was responsible for the 'wishful thinking of the racing fraternity', the writer scoffed. But racing did resume and, with a three-day meeting fast approaching, police marshalled prisoners of war – some of whom may even have been housed in huts on Knavesmire – to clear an area for a car park. Holding the St Leger certainly caused quite a stir.

'The air was a riot, with itinerant sellers, coloured tipsters with fantastic feathers and outsize trousers, palmists, fairs and the jingle of a dozen other attractions,' wrote Carlton for the *Daily Dispatch*. Hotels had been booked up for months, and not only in York, with racegoers also renting accommodation near the racecourse in a bid to find a room. Private houses were offered for £10 a night. The rings were packed with the free part of the Knavesmire transformed into a vast picnicking ground. But it was not all joy.

People turned out in such vast numbers that many actually missed the St Leger race while still trying to enter through the turnstiles. And if the council was unconfined in its pleasure at having racing return to the city, the Ministry of Fuel was not. They banned attempts to use the VJ Day celebration lights to illuminate York during race week and there were also concerns, in this period of austerity, as to whether there would be enough food and beer to go round. In the event, such fears were unfounded – whether those present could enjoy it was another question entirely.

'We queued, nay fought, our way, to approach the bookmakers and the Totalisers,' said a *Yorkshire Post* reporter. 'To thousands York's first, and probably last, St Leger will remain in memory as the Queue St Leger. We pushed and jostled, but we took it in good part.' The enthusiasm was obvious. It was a momentous sight as people continued to flood towards the course in their tens of thousands. 'By noon the rails on the popular 3s side were lined six and seven deep,' the *Post* continued. 'When racing started these people could not have left their place to make a bet, however much they wanted. By the time for the St Leger the ring was packed as tightly as it could be. 'Those who saw the race could not bet; those who had a bet could not see the race. It was the same in the other rings. Just after the second race there came an appeal on the loud-speakers for people still queuing for Tattersalls to go higher up the course, as the big ring was full. An attempt was made to rush the turnstiles, and the police had to fight their way through the crowd to bring order out of chaos.'

With faces everywhere, the sea of people stretched down the course for more than three furlongs. The caps of jockeys flashed back with punters none the wiser as to who had won a race, or who was even running. In the midst of all this humanity was the St Leger, the third race on the card. Ten lined up but there was disappointment that Dante, the Northern-trained colt who had swept to a Derby win at Newmarket, wasn't among them.

It had been assumed for most of the summer that Sir Eric Ohlson's colt, trained at Middleham by Matt Peacock, would make his way seamlessly from Derby to St Leger glory. He was a solid 4-6 favourite for the race as late as August 10 but at Middleham they already knew the worst. Dante was going blind. Fifteen days later, the horse was scratched and Yorkshire's hopes of a home-trained St Leger winner were at an end. In fact, the field did not contain any of that season's Classic winners and, with the local hero missing, attention turned to Rising Light – the son of Hyperion who was owned by King George VI. He was not the favourite. That honour fell to the Aga Khan's Naishapur, runner-up in the Oaks.

Also in the field was the 11-2 shot Chamossaire – the only blinkered horse among the runners. Trained by Dick Perryman at Newmarket, the colt had finished fourth in both the 2,000 Guineas and the Derby, where he'd had the better of Rising Light. So it was to prove again. Stirling Castle, ridden by Harry Wragg, took them away followed by Loretto, with Blue Smoke, Rising Light and Chamossaire closely behind. Wragg's mount still led into the straight but, a quarter of a mile from the finish, Chamossaire made his challenge. The *Daily Dispatch*'s Carlton noted: 'He finished with such resolution that at the post he had two lengths to spare over the King's Rising Light. The latter momentarily raised the hopes of the crowd when he came through halfway up the straight, but it was obvious that he would not catch the leader.' The vast crowd was stunned. Though Chamossaire, owned by the millionaire Squadron-Leader Stanhope Joel, and piloted by Tommy Lowrey, was a popular winner he was not what the audience had wanted – a success for His Majesty.

'What we all forgot was the Yorkshire Roar, the time honoured tribute to every St Leger winner,' reported the *Yorkshire Post*'s correspondent. 'Chamossaire won the St Leger almost in silence. Perhaps we should really have let ourselves go if it had been a Royal victory, as for one brief moment seemed likely when the King's Rising Light began his challenge. That started the first mutterings which precede a crescendo of cheers; but his challenge never became a real threat and the cheer died away. Chamossaire deserved better than that.'

The bookmakers weren't happy either with money going on both placed horses, Rising Light and Stirling Castle. 'York has had the seal on one of the blackest seasons we have experienced. So bad have been our losses that many of us have decided not to accept any place betting,' said one. And if poor little Chamossaire's reputation had not been disparaged enough, the racing experts took an unenthusiastic view of the contest. In that year's *Bloodstock Review*, the race was considered 'unspectacular' and a 'pattern of conventionality' though, they conceded, 'it was run in a very good time, to the great credit of the winner'.

The scenes at Knavesmire that day could hardly have been described as unspectacular. It would take the visit of Pope John Paul II – 37 years later – before crowds of that size were seen at York again. And things were to work out well for Chamossaire, named after a mountain in the Swiss Canton of Vaud. The Precipitation colt retired to stud in 1947, having won four races, and sired the 1956 St Leger winner Cambremer. Even at the year of his death, 1964, he was champion sire in Britain, after his son Santa Claus brought home presents of English and Irish Derby wins that summer.

***

SIXTY years later, it was announced the St Leger would return to Knavesmire. Not because of bullets and bombs, but bulldozers. They were cutting a new grandstand at Doncaster – leaving the Town Moor racecourse unable to host the 2006 renewal of the one mile, six furlong Group 1 contest.

Worth £10,120 in 1945, its value had increased a little by 2006. The victor would now scoop a princely £270,000. It was worth its weight in gold to York's economy as well – handing as much as a £1 million boost to the city's hotel, bar and restaurant industry. First, it had to be won. Doncaster put the fixture out to bidding and several high-profile racecourses, including a redeveloped and rejuvenated Ascot, were said to be in the frame.

York had held the Royal Meeting the previous year following Ascot's building work and seemed the odds-on favourite to land the fixture. But William Derby, York chief executive and clerk of the course, said Knavesmire was never the sure thing people thought. 'It didn't feel like that at the time when we were discussing it,' he said. 'Ascot had opened its redevelopment so there were options. It was a reasonably similar process to Royal Ascot in that we spoke to Arena Leisure, who run Doncaster, and they explained to us that they wanted to close down to do their redevelopment and we talked about the possibility of the St Leger coming to York.'

Months of negotiation ensued before, on December 13, 2005, the Mayor of Doncaster, Martin Winter, officially put the seal on York's bid. It was the incentive of keeping the race in Yorkshire that tipped the balance decisively in Knavesmire's favour. Derby was ecstatic. 'We're proud of our role in Yorkshire racing and understand the St Leger is a highlight of the season for fans in the county, so we're delighted the fixture is staying within its boundaries,' he said at the time. 'We're delighted and honoured by this decision, which promises another great racing summer for people in York and the surrounding region.'

But, compared with Royal Ascot at York, there were important practical differences. Then, Derby and his staff had been merely hosts. An Ascot team had controlled every facet of the five-day meeting. This time, it was York's show. Run by the racecourse as part of their regular programme. The traditional four-day St Leger festival was shrunk to two – comprising a programme which also contained six Group 2 races and a Group 3 race along with a collection of Listed contests. Derby explains: 'In terms of the constraints of our season, we wanted to condense it into a hugely high-quality two-day festival on September 8 and 9 and so we worked on that basis. We had a huge amount of support from Doncaster Racecourse and the town to achieve that and it was a wonderful meeting. We had fabulous crowds, especially on the St Leger Saturday, with a wonderful blue sky day.'

There was also wonderful racing, and not just in the St Leger. Sergeant Cecil wrote himself even further into Knavesmire folklore when he won the Doncaster Cup. Having claimed the Lonsdale Cup a couple of weeks earlier, and with the 2005 Ebor Handicap also in the trophy cabinet, Rod Millman's stayer was going for another top class victory on Knavesmire and Sergeant Cecil was at the top of his game in the Group 2 race on the first day of the festival.

The Sergeant was sent off the even-money favourite to beat his seven rivals but it was an eventful race for jockey Frankie Dettori, who was renewing his acquaintance with the gelding having also been on board for that Lonsdale triumph. Having settled him at the back of the field, Dettori led him up to the 11-year-old Alcazar around a furlong out. In the process, Alcazar caught an accidental swish of the Italian jockey's whip leading to a Stewards' inquiry when Sergeant Cecil flashed over the line a length clear. Dettori's accident hadn't affected the outcome of the race, which was soon confirmed as another brilliant Cecil performance.

For Millman, there was relief – at both the verdict and the gelding's stunning victory. 'There was pressure that day because he had won the Lonsdale quite well,' he says. 'I had a lot of confidence. I thought he should win and he did. I didn't think he would get beat and perhaps I put myself under a lot of pressure.' Dettori, on the other hand, was exultant. 'He's amazing. He had me a bit snookered as he wasn't really travelling and then he came back on the bridle,' he said following the race. 'He perhaps went a bit too soon but he had plenty in hand – what a star he is. He's never let anyone down and I'm now part of this dream of everybody.'

The 'dream' would get better for Dettori, who owned that meeting and Leger day in particular. He won the Park Stakes on Iffraaj and would also claim the Strensall Stakes on Echo Of Light. In between was the St Leger and Sixties Icon. The son of Galileo, the Epsom and Irish Derby double winner of 2001 was not your typical Leger runner. In a race more notable for requiring lung-busting fortitude, Sixties Icon had a deceptive turn of pace – speed as well as stamina. But he had been trained with the Leger in mind and, for trainer Jeremy Noseda, York was the perfect track.

'He was a talented horse and it had been his aim since he ran in the Derby (where he finished seventh) that year,' he reveals. 'It (York) wasn't quite as stiff a galloping mile and three quarters as Doncaster. It's an extended mile and three quarters at Doncaster. From a personal point of view, I like to be at York because I think it is near enough my favourite racetrack in England.'

With Dettori on board, it seemed most of Knavesmire was backing Sixties Icon for the Leger and the three-year-old went off the 11-8 favourite. That didn't worry Noseda. 'Those situations are why we do this business,' he says. 'To me, the pressure of racing is when you haven't got the horses who can compete in races like that. If you are lucky enough to have the horse that is running in these type of races, yes there is pressure, but that's the pressure you want. That's why you do it.'

Those who had put their hard earned down on Sixties Icon would find it was money well spent. Held up at the back early on, Sixties Icon was still on the bit when tracking the leaders two furlongs out. When Dettori told him to get a move on, he rocketed away – shaken up to lead inside the final furlong and cruising to a two and a half length victory over 50-1 shot The Last Drop, with Red Rocks a length further back in third – causing his Italian pilot to wag his finger in triumph at the finishing post. It was Dettori's fourth Leger win, his hundredth winner of that season and trainer Noseda's first British Classic victory. But he could not be there.

'The only sad thing was I was in Keeneland at the sales so I watched it on television,' he says. 'It was a little bit surreal to be honest. I was confident that he would win. Everything went right in the race. He travelled well and he never really looked like getting beaten. It was a surreal experience to be that far away. I knew I had to be in Keeneland because it's the sales and you are looking at the stock that's going to define your next couple of years. You have to do that but I sat there in the evening at Keeneland and had dinner and it felt rather strange. But it was a good day, it was an important day and I enjoyed it immensely.'

And did he find a superstar at those sales? 'I don't think we did,' he laughs. 'Not as yet. But there might be one who hasn't made his mark yet and might still do it.'

Dettori would later claim it was his easiest Classic win. Also delighted were the 31,046 who turned out to witness the moment – leaving York chief executive and clerk of the course William Derby thrilled the racecourse had been able to top their Royal Ascot exertions of the year before.

'It was a wonderful meeting,' he remembers. 'Sixties Icon was a hugely popular winning favourite. It was a real joy and one of those days when things came together and we really enjoyed it as a raceday and an occasion. Most people seemed to have backed Sixties Icon and it was another great chapter in York Racecourse's history.'

OCTOBER - EPILOGUE

WE started with Sea The Stars and it is with the wonder horse we end. While York Racecourse continues to attract the sort of horses we will be talking about for decades to come, just like the Juddmonte International and Arc legend, its races will always be great. The public certainly seem to agree.

While the leisure industry continued to be rocked by the turmoil of an economy in recession, record numbers of racegoers passed through the York turnstiles during 2010. They have been racing on Knavesmire since 1731, but this was the year attendances broke through the 350,000 mark for the first time. It was a season which also brought a record modern day crowd for a single meeting, when more than 42,000 attended Music Showcase Saturday in July – a fixture containing races which did not merit inclusion in this rundown of the greatest. A total of 358,035 went to the races in 2010. That was 36,279 more than the year before, and that had also been a record campaign.

'To set another record in a year when the economic climate remains so challenging for everyone is testimony to the support we have received from racegoers and gives us great delight,' said clerk of the course William Derby as the end of term figures were released. 'They have enjoyed some top drawer performances on the track.'

There, in a nutshell, is the key to why York continues to be regarded as one of the world's great Flat racing venues: top drawer performances. York has always been graced by the best horses – whether it be Sea The Stars, Reference Point, Brigadier Gerard or Brown Jack. It brings greatness for some and is a step on the journey to better things for others.

The York Race Committee are well aware of the delicate balance over which they hold sway. Only by attracting the best horses to the Minster city can they continue to pull in the punters and, consequently, continue to provide the kind of prize money that tempts the trainers of those thoroughbreds in the first place. It is one big circle.

Progress, meanwhile, keeps on coming at York. After extending the flagship Ebor Festival in August to four days in 2009, race chiefs took the decision to move the Ebor Handicap from its traditional Wednesday home to a Saturday. That change was due to begin with the 2011 campaign. The decision did not come without criticism. But keeping the balance between the new and old is a tightrope York Racecourse has been walking for more than two and a half centuries. Modern grandstands join hands with architecture from days gone by, new races continue to be weaved with those which have the longest of histories.

Let's go through it one more time. In May there is the Dante Stakes, the Musidora Stakes and the Yorkshire Cup – the leading Epsom Derby and Oaks trial and the first major stayers' event of the season. July sees the staging of the John Smith's Cup – a top class handicap with a prize fund to attract the very best in the class. In August, the Ebor Festival heralds the Juddmonte International, Ebor Handicap, Yorkshire Oaks and the Nunthorpe Stakes – York's most prestigious and richest race, Europe's richest handicap and Knavesmire's signature contest, one of the top fillies' events of the calendar and the richest sprint on the continent.

No other racecourse except its natural home of Ascot has ever hosted the Royal Meeting. No other racecourse has held a modern day St Leger. York did it twice. Then there are Voltigeurs, Gimcracks and Lonsdales; Galtres, Acombs and Lowthers. But don't just take my word for it.

'It is one of, if not the best track in Britain,' insists trainer Mark Johnston, a man whose opinion is respected throughout the sport. 'If I have got an owner coming, whether it's from Hong Kong, or Australia, or America – a foreigner coming to Britain to see racing – I would take them to York.' Need we say more?

BIBLIOGRAPHY

Abelson, Edward and John Tyrrel, *The Breedon Book of Horse Racing Records*, (Breedon Books, 1993)

Benson, George, *York Race Meetings*, (Unknown)

Dennis, Steve, *Sergeant Cecil – The Impossible Dream: From Rags to Riches* (Racing Post, 2007)

Dettori, Frankie, *Frankie: The Autobiography of Frankie Dettori* (Collins Willow, 2004)

Duffield, George and Michael Tanner, *Gentleman George: The contradictory life of George Duffield*, (Highdown, 2002)

Fairfax-Blakeborough, J, *Northern Turf History, Vol III* (J A Allen & Co, 1953)

Francis, Dick, *Lester: The Official Biography* (Michael Joseph, 1986)

Haigh, Paul, *The Racehorse Trainer*, (Partridge Press, 1990)

Haigh, Paul, *The World's Greatest Racehorses*, (Highdown, 2006)

Hislop, John, *The Brigadier: The story of Brigadier Gerard*, (Secker & Warburg, 1973)

Holt, Oliver, *If you're second you're nothing: Ferguson and Shankly*, (PAN, 2006)

Lambie, James, *The Story of Your Life: A history of the Sporting Life newspaper 1859-1998* (Troubador, 2010)

Magee, Sean, *Sea The Stars: The story of a perfect racehorse*, (Racing Post, 2009)

Piggott Lester, *Lester: The Autobiography of Lester Piggott*, (Partridge Press, 1995)

Scott, Brough, *The Best of the Racing Post*, (Wetherby, 1992)

Scott, Brough, *Of Horses and Heroes*, (Highdown, 2008)

Stevens, John, *Knavesmire: York's great racecourse and its stories*, (Pelham, 1984)

Timeform, *Racehorses of: 1955, 1958, 1960, 1966, 1968, 1970, 1971, 1972, 1973, 1975, 1976, 1978, 1979, 1980, 1981, 1982, 1983, 1984, 1986, 1987, 1988, 1989, 1990, 1992, 1993, 1994, 1996, 1999, 2002, 2005* (Timeform, Halifax).

Townsend, Nick, *Mark Johnston: The authorised biography*, (High down, 2006)

West, Julian, *Travelling the Turf*, (Kensington West, 2006)

Wilkerson, Peter, *The Great Match – The Flying Dutchman and Voltage*, (Hertford Offset Limited, 2003)

Wilkinson, David, *Early Horse Racing in Yorkshire and the origins of the thoroughbred*, (Old Bald Peg Publications, 2003)

Newspapers: *Yorkshire Evening Press, The Press, The Independent, Sporting Life, Racing Post, Northern Echo, Yorkshire Post, Daily Dispatch,* York Racecourse cards

For up-to-date news on our latest books visit
www.scratchingshedpublishing.co.uk